Intersectionality

Key Concepts

Barbara Adam, *Time*
Alan Aldridge, *Consumption*
Alan Aldridge, *The Market*
Jakob Arnoldi, *Risk*
Will Atkinson, *Class*
Colin Barnes and Geof Mercer, *Disability*
Darin Barney, *The Network Society*
Mildred Blaxter, *Health 2nd edition*
Harriet Bradley, *Gender 2nd edition*
Harry Brighouse, *Justice*
Mónica Brito Vieira and David Runciman, *Representation*
Steve Bruce, *Fundamentalism 2nd edition*
Joan Busfield, *Mental Illness*
Margaret Canovan, *The People*
Andrew Jason Cohen, *Toleration*
Alejandro Colás, *Empire*
Mary Daly, *Welfare*
Anthony Elliott, *Concepts of the Self 3rd edition*
Steve Fenton, *Ethnicity 2nd edition*
Katrin Flikschuh, *Freedom*
Michael Freeman, *Human Rights 2nd edition*
Russell Hardin, *Trust*
Geoffrey Ingham, *Capitalism*
Fred Inglis, *Culture*
Robert H. Jackson, *Sovereignty*
Jennifer Jackson Preece, *Minority Rights*
Gill Jones, *Youth*
Paul Kelly, *Liberalism*
Anne Mette Kjær, *Governance*
Ruth Lister, *Poverty*
Jon Mandle, *Global Justice*
Cillian McBride, *Recognition*
Anthony Payne and Nicola Phillips, *Development*
Judith Phillips, *Care*
Chris Phillipson, *Ageing*
Michael Saward, *Democracy*
John Scott, *Power*
Timothy J. Sinclair, *Global Governance*
Anthony D. Smith, *Nationalism 2nd edition*
Deborah Stevenson, *The City*
Leslie Paul Thiele, *Sustainability*
Steven Peter Vallas, *Work*
Stuart White, *Equality*
Michael Wyness, *Childhood*

Intersectionality

Patricia Hill Collins
Sirma Bilge

polity

First published in 2016 by Polity Press
Reprinted 2016 (six times), 2017 (twice), 2018, 2019

Polity Press
65 Bridge Street
Cambridge CB2 1UR, UK

Polity Press
350 Main Street
Malden, MA 02148, USA

ISBN-13: 978-0-7456-8448-2
ISBN-13: 978-0-7456-8449-9(pb)

A catalogue record for this book is available from the British Library.

Library of Congress Cataloging-in-Publication Data

Names: Collins, Patricia Hill, author. | Bilge, Sirma, author.
Title: Intersectionality / Patricia Hill Collins, Sirma Bilge.
Description: Cambridge, UK ; Malden, MA : Polity Press, 2016. | Series: Key concepts series | Includes bibliographical references and index.
Identifiers: LCCN 2015037051| ISBN 9780745684482 (hardback : alk. paper) | ISBN 9780745684499 (pbk. : alk. paper)
Subjects: LCSH: Critical theory. | Sociology. | Interdisciplinary research.
Classification: LCC HM480.H55 2016 | DDC 301–dc23 LC record available at http://lccn.loc.gov/2015037051

Typeset in 10.5 on 12 pt Sabon
by Toppan Best-set Premedia Limited
Printed and bound in the United States by LSC Communications

Contents

Preface

Because this book was born in conversation and has been written collaboratively, we thought we would share a bit about our process. We first met in 2006 in Durban, South Africa, at the 16th World Congress of Sociology, the first meeting of this international group of delegates from more than 150 countries to be held in continental Africa. Patricia was a keynote speaker early on in the week-long event, and Sirma, a new assistant professor, was a presenter in the intersectionality session organized by Nira Yuval-Davis. By a happy coincidence, we took the same bus on a field trip to the Kwa Muhle Apartheid Museum and to townships that were the legacy of apartheid. We had our first albeit all too brief conversation during that tour. Six years later, we met again at the 6th International Congress of French-Speaking Feminist Research (*Congrès international des recherches féministes francophones*) in Lausanne, Switzerland. Organized since the mid-1990s in different cities across the French-speaking world, from Paris to Dakar to Rabat to Ottawa, the Lausanne conference, with its theme "Interlocking power relations and the discriminations and privileges based on gender, race, class and sexuality," garnered some 610 delegates, feminist scholars, and activists from Europe (Switzerland, France, and Belgium), Africa (Morocco, Tunisia, Algeria, Burkina Faso, Senegal, Cameroon, Gabon), the Americas (Canada/Québec and Brazil), and the Middle East

(Turkey). This time, we were both on keynote panels. Afterwards, we struck up a conversation that we continued during a visit to the Musée de l'Art Brut, a small but striking museum that contained art by groups that had been considered outsiders, such as the art of psychiatric inmates. During this visit, we discovered that we shared similar perspectives not just on the conference and our sensibilities concerning intersectionality. We learned that Sirma is a painter, that Patricia is a dancer, and that the arts infuse our intersectional sensibilities. While we didn't know it then, our collaboration for this book had already begun.

Neither one of us could have written this book alone. We felt the need for a book that would introduce the complexities beyond the audiences that were comfortable to each of us. We started our conversation from our different locations within intersectionality and worked our way towards carving out points of connection. Sirma writes about intersectionality in French and English within a francophone academic context of the linguistically restless city of Montreal, on unceded Mohawk territory, where French and English compete. Acutely aware of the problems of translation across her three languages of Turkish, French, and English, Sirma brings a commitment to situating intersectionality within global frameworks and the geopolitics of knowledge. Always mindful of her roots in a working-class, African-American neighborhood in Philadelphia, Patricia writes to academic audiences and general readers in US and UK contexts. Her work is widely recognized, yet the demands of helping to institutionalize intersectionality in the academy has limited her involvement in activist settings. During two years of dialog and conversation, we hammered out the arguments that we felt would be most useful to our readers.

We could see how we complemented one another, and knew that the ideas that could travel across the kinds of differences that shaped our own lives were likely to be the strongest ideas for intersectionality. One core premise of intersectionality concerns the relationships between ideas, practices and, in this case, the practices of producing this book. This entailed working through and across many differences. Yet we quickly found out that dialog is hard work. In a sense, we lived our material via the process we chose in writing this book. Don't get us wrong! It is not as easy as it sounds, and there is nothing romantic about that! It is labor and it's tension, yet generative tension.

There were so many moving points to this kind of conversation and, by implication, to the kind of work that intersectionality must do. The process involved getting fluent in each other's language of intersectionality, in each other's ways of putting things together, perspective and perception. We also needed to speak several languages, for intersectionality is everywhere, and it is polyglot: it speaks the language of activism and community organizing as much as it speaks that of the academy, or of institutions. It speaks to young people through social media and popular culture and to established scholars through journals and conferences. These different fields of practice of intersectionality do not engage each other as much as they should, perhaps because they lack a common language. If such is the case, then our book needs to speak to these different constituencies in ways that are not mutually exclusive, in a language that is audible and makes sense for them.

Consider this book an invitation for entering the complexities of intersectionality. This book provides some navigational tools for moving through intersectionality's vast terrain. It is a roadmap for discovery and not a portrait of a finished product. We simply could not include everything in one book. You may find that some of your favorite authors are barely mentioned and that authors whom you have never heard of are discussed at length. We mention many areas of intersectionality but could not include an extensive discussion of public health, epistemology, environmental issues, art, reproductive justice, and many other areas where people have taken up the ideas of intersectionality. Just as we brought different areas of expertise and interest to the process of writing the book, yet learned to listen to one another and translate along the way, we encourage you to do the same as you pursue these areas.

Just as our collaboration was crucial for the book, we value the support of others who helped us along the way. We both thank the team at Polity Press for shepherding this project through unexpected delays. Thanks to Louise Knight, our editor, who brought the idea for this book to us and trusted our ability to get it done; to Clare Ansell, senior production editor at Polity; and Pascal Porcheron and Nekane Tanaka Galdos, editorial assistants on various aspects of the project. We also express our gratitude to Gail Ferguson, the heroic copyeditor on this project, who patiently waded through the fusion of references required for this book. We also appreciated the comments of the two anonymous reviewers whose critical eye greatly strengthened this text.

First and foremost, Sirma wishes to thank her partner Philippe Allard who always stood by her through the ups and downs of all her writing projects, and to her sister Gönenç Bilge-Sökmen and her mother Figen Bilge for their unfailing love and support despite the great physical distance that separates her from them. Sirma thanks graduate students of her past and present seminars at the Université de Montréal for being a constant reminder of the utter necessity of pursuing critical work, and for making her feel intellectually and emotionally less out of place. They are far too many to list here. Her appreciation also goes to colleagues in her department, Sociology, with special thanks to Anne Calvès and to Christopher McCall, the department's head, for their support. Sirma expresses heartfelt gratitude for the friendship and solidarity of some amazing feminists of color and allies, for many impassioned conversations: thanks especially to Sara Ahmed, Paola Bacchetta, Leila Bdeir, Karma Chávez, Alexa Conradi, João Gabriell, Eve Haque, Jin Haritaworn, Délice Mugabo, Jen Petzen, Julianne Pidduck, Malinda Smith, and Michèle Spieler. Arashi needs to be thanked for bringing feline grace and mandatory playtime to her life. Last but not least, Sirma wishes she could thank her father, Uğur Bilge, for his constant support, for never failing to ask "isn't it finished yet?" and to prompt her to translate it into Turkish. Uğur Bilge suddenly passed away in 2014; Sirma dedicates this book to his memory.

Patricia would like to thank graduate students, past and present, at the University of Maryland: Valerie Chepp, Margaret Austin Smith, Jillet Sam, Rachel Guo, Kendra Barber, Kathryn Buford, Kristi Tredway, Wendy Laybourn, Angel Miles, and Michelle Beadle. Patricia thanks Ana Claudia Perreira for the many wonderful conversations about intersectionality and Afro-Brazilian women, as well as for arranging an invitation to the Black Women's Festival that deepened her interest in Brazil. Special thanks go out to Roberto Patricio Korzeniewicz, whose strong leadership of the Department of Sociology provided a welcome home for this project. Finally, Patricia could not have finished this project without the support of her family: Roger Collins, Valerie Collins, Lauren Pruitt, and the inspiration provided by her amazing grandson Harrison who was born in 2013. Patricia dedicates this book to Harrison and his generation.

1
What is Intersectionality?

In the early twenty-first century, the term "intersectionality" has been widely taken up by scholars, policy advocates, practitioners, and activists in many places and locations. College students and faculty in interdisciplinary fields such as women's studies, ethnic studies, cultural studies, American studies, and media studies, as well as those within sociology, political science, and history and other traditional disciplines, encounter intersectionality in courses, books, and scholarly articles. Human rights activists and government officials have also made intersectionality part of ongoing global public policy discussions. Grassroots organizers look to varying dimensions of intersectionality to inform their work on reproductive rights, anti-violence initiatives, workers' rights, and similar social issues. Bloggers use digital and social media to debate hot topics. Teachers, social workers, high-school students, parents, university support staff, and school personnel have taken up the ideas of intersectionality with an eye toward transforming schools of all sorts. Across these different venues, people increasingly claim and use the term "intersectionality" for their diverse intellectual and political projects.

If we were to ask them, "What is intersectionality?" we would get varied and sometimes contradictory answers. Most, however, would probably accept the following general description:

Intersectionality is a way of understanding and analyzing the complexity in the world, in people, and in human experiences. The events and conditions of social and political life and the self can seldom be understood as shaped by one factor. They are generally shaped by many factors in diverse and mutually influencing ways. When it comes to social inequality, people's lives and the organization of power in a given society are better understood as being shaped not by a single axis of social division, be it race or gender or class, but by many axes that work together and influence each other. Intersectionality as an analytic tool gives people better access to the complexity of the world and of themselves.

We begin this book by recognizing the tremendous heterogeneity that currently characterizes how people understand and use intersectionality. Despite debates about the meaning of this term, or even whether it is the right term to use at all, intersectionality is the term that has stuck. It is the term that is increasingly used by stakeholders who put their understandings of intersectionality to a variety of uses. Despite these differences, this general description points toward a general consensus about how people understand intersectionality.

Using intersectionality as an analytic tool

People generally use intersectionality as an analytic tool to solve problems that they or others around them face. Most US colleges and universities, for example, face the challenge of building more inclusive and fair campus communities. The social divisions of class, race, gender, ethnicity, citizenship, sexuality, and ability are especially evident within higher education. Colleges and universities now include more college students who formerly had no way to pay for college (class), or students who historically faced discriminatory barriers to enrollment (race, gender, ethnicity or citizenship status, religion), or students who experience distinctive barriers and discrimination (sexuality and ability) on college campuses. Colleges and universities find themselves confronted with students who want fairness, yet who bring very different experiences and needs to campus. Initially, colleges recruited and served groups one at a time, offering, for example, special programs for African Americans, Latinos, women, gays and lesbians, veterans, returning students, and persons with disabilities. As the list grew, it became clearer that this one-at-a-time approach not only was slow, but that most students fit into more than one category. First-generation college students could include Latinos, women, poor whites, returning veterans, grandparents, and transgender individuals. In this context, intersectionality can be a useful analytic tool for thinking about and developing strategies to achieve campus equity.

Ordinary people can draw upon intersectionality as an analytic tool when they recognize that they need better frameworks to grapple with the complex discriminations that they face. In the 1960s and 1970s, African-American women activists confronted the puzzle of how their needs simply fell through the cracks of anti-racist social movements, feminism, and unions organizing for workers' rights. Each of these social movements elevated one category of analysis and action above others, for example, race within the civil rights movement, or gender within feminism or class within the union movement. Because African-American women were simultaneously black *and* female *and* workers, these single-focus lenses on social inequality left little space to address the complex social problems that they face. Black women's specific issues remained subordinated within each movement because no social movement by itself would, nor could, address the entirety of discriminations they faced. Black women's use of intersectionality as an analytic tool emerged in response to these challenges.

Intersectionality as an analytic tool is neither confined to nations of North America and Europe nor is it a new phenomenon. People in the Global South have used intersectionality as an analytic tool, often without naming it as such. Consider an unexpected example from nineteenth-century colonial India in the work of Savitribai Phule (1831–1897), regarded as an important first-generation modern Indian feminist. In an online article titled "Six Reasons Every Indian Feminist Must Remember Savitribai Phule," published in January 2015, Deepika Sarma suggests:

Here's why you should know more about her. *She got intersectionality*. Savitribai along with her husband Jyotirao was a staunch advocate of anti-caste ideology and women's rights. The Phules' vision of social equality included fighting against the subjugation of women, and they also stood for Adivasis and Muslims. She organized a barbers' strike against shaving the heads of Hindu widows, fought for widow remarriage and in 1853, started a shelter for pregnant widows. Other welfare programmes she was involved with alongside Jyotirao include opening schools for workers and rural people, and providing famine relief through 52 food centers that also operated as boarding schools. She also cared for those affected by famine and plague, and died in 1897 after contracting plague from her patients. (Sarma 2015)

Phule confronted several axes of social division, namely caste, gender, religion, and economic disadvantage or class. Her political activism encompassed intersecting categories of social division – she didn't just pick one.

These examples suggest that people use intersectionality as an analytic tool in many different ways to address a range of issues and social problems. They find intersectionality's core insight to be useful: namely, that major axes of social divisions in a given society at a given time, for example, race, class, gender, sexuality, dis/ability, and age operate not as discrete and mutually exclusive entities, but build on each other and work together. Many people typically use intersectionality as a *heuristic*, a problem-solving or analytic tool, much in the way that students on college campuses developed a shared interest in diversity, or African-American women used it to address their status within social movement politics, or Savitribai Phule advanced women's rights. Even though those who use intersectional frameworks all seem to be situated under the same big umbrella, using intersectionality as a heuristic device means that intersectionality can assume many different forms.

In this book, we examine the perspectives, definitions, and controversies that characterize intersectionality but, for now, we want to show three uses of intersectionality as an analytic tool. As Cho et al. point out (2013: 795), "what makes an analysis intersectional is not its use of the term 'intersectionality,' nor its being situated in a familiar genealogy, nor its drawing on lists of standard citations." Instead, they argue, "what intersectionality *does* rather than what intersectionality *is*" lies at the at the heart of intersectionality (ibid.; our italics). In the remainder of this section, we demonstrate three uses of intersectionality as an analytic tool that were inspired by important global events that took place in 2014.

Power plays: the FIFA World Cup

Brazil's international reputation as a football (soccer) powerhouse raised high hopes for its winning the 2014 FIFA World Cup. As one of the most successful national teams in the history of the World Cup, Brazil was the only country whose teams had qualified for and attended every World Cup tournament. Brazil had also produced some of the greatest players in the history of world football. The legendary Pelé remains Brazil's highest goal-scorer of all time. Italy, Germany, and Argentina are all football powerhouses, yet, in terms of star power and status, they were no match for Brazil.

Because the 2014 tournament was held in Brazil, the stakes were especially high. The potential payoff for a winning Brazilian team in Brazil could be huge. Hosting the FIFA World Cup would enable Brazil to shed vestiges of its troubled history of being ruled by a military dictatorship (1964–1985), as well as signal its arrival as a major economic player. Brazil's victory, both on the field and via its hosting, would attract global attention. The World Cup was the most widely watched and followed sporting event in the world, exceeding even the Olympic Games. From the perspective of Brazil's policy makers and financiers, the possibilities of reaching a massive global market were endless. For example, the cumulative audience for all matches during the 2006 World Cup was estimated to be 26.29 billion people, with an estimated 715.1 million people watching the final match in Berlin, an astonishing one-ninth of the entire population of the planet.

So how did the 2014 FIFA World Cup games go? The challenges associated with hosting the games began well before the athletes arrived on the playing fields. Brazil estimated a figure of US$11.3 billion in public works-spending for the event. The initial plan presented to the public

emphasized that the majority of the spending on infrastructure for the World Cup would highlight general transportation, security, and communications. Less than 25 percent of
total spending would go toward the twelve new or refurbished stadiums. Yet, as the games grew nearer, cost overruns
increased stadium costs by at least 75 percent, with public
resources reallocated from general infrastructure projects.
The FIFA cost overruns aggravated ongoing public demonstrations in several Brazilian cities against the increase in
public transportation fares and political corruption. For
example, on June 20, 2013, one and a half million people
demonstrated in São Paulo, Brazil's largest metropolitan area
with a population of 18 million people. In this context, the
exorbitant cost of stadiums, the displacement of urban dwell-
ers for construction, and the embezzlement of public funds
became a new theme at the forefront of public protests (Castells 2015: 232). As the countdown to the kickoff began,
Brazilians took to the streets with banners against the World
Cup. "FIFA go home!" and "We want hospitals up to FIFA's
standards!" were common slogans in protests throughout
more than a hundred cities. "The World Cup steals money
from healthcare, education and the poor. The homeless are
being forced from the streets. This is not for Brazil, it's for
the tourists," reported a *Guardian* article (Watts 2014).

The games began as this social unrest intensified. Of the
thirty-two teams that qualified for the World Cup, Brazil was
one of four that reached the semifinals, facing an undefeated
Germany. The match wasn't even close. Germany led 5–0 at
half time, scoring an unheard of four goals in a span of six
minutes, and went on to win the World Cup. For its stunned
fans in the stadium, as well as for the massive global audience, Brazil's loss was shocking. The media depicted the
match as a national disgrace, with Brazilian newspapers carrying headlines such as "The Biggest Shame in History," "A
Historical Humiliation!," and "Brazil is Slain." Global media
joined in with headlines that described the defeat as the "ulti-
mate embarrassment" and the "most humiliating World Cup
host nation defeat of all time."

On the surface, intersectionality seems far removed from
Brazil's 2014 FIFA World Cup experience. Because many
people enjoy sporting events or play sports themselves, sports

seem distant from intersectionality's concern with social inequality. Yet using intersectionality as an analytic tool to examine the FIFA World Cup sheds light on the organization of power. Intersectionality as an analytic tool examines how power relations are intertwined and mutually constructing. Race, class, gender, sexuality, dis/ability, ethnicity, nation, religion, and age are categories of analysis, terms that reference important social divisions. But they are also categories that gain meaning from power relations of racism, sexism, heterosexism, and class exploitation.

One way of describing the organization of power identifies four distinctive yet interconnected domains of power: interpersonal, disciplinary, cultural, and structural. These four dimensions of the organization of power provide opportunities for using intersectionality as an analytic tool to better understand the 2014 FIFA World Cup.

The interpersonal domain of power First, power relations are about people's lives, how people relate to one another, and who is advantaged or disadvantaged within social interactions. Without the athletes, there would be no World Cup. The athletes are individuals and, whether famous or not, their actions shape power relations just as much as the policy makers who bid on the games, the media that covered the Brazilian national team's defeat, or the activists who took to the street to protest cost overruns.

As a people's sport, football can be played almost anywhere by almost anyone. Each team is composed of a constellation of individuals who, on some level, love football and have chosen to play. One does not need expensive lessons, or a carefully manicured playing field, or even shoes. It requires no special equipment or training, only a ball and enough players to field two teams. Compared with ice skating, tennis, skiing, or American football, soccer has far fewer barriers between athletic talent and the means to develop that talent. Across the globe, there is no way of knowing exactly how many people play football. Yet FIFA's surveys provide a good guess: an estimated 270 million people are involved in football as professional soccer players, recreational players, registered players both over and under age 18, futsal and beach football players, referees, and officials. This is a vast pool of potential elite athletes and a massive audience reaching across categories of social class, age, gender, ethnicity, and nation. When one adds the children and youth who play football but who are not involved in any kind of organized activity detectable by FIFA, the number swells greatly.

The fanfare granted to the World Cup is a small tip of the iceberg of the everyday social interactions that shape people's relationships with one another in regard to football. From elite athletes to poor kids, football players want to play on a fair playing field. It doesn't matter how you got to the field: all that matters once you are on the field is what you do on the field. The sports metaphor of a *level playing field* speaks to the desire for fairness. Whether winners or losers, this team sport rewards individual talent yet also highlights the collective team nature of achievement. When played well and unimpeded by suspect officiating, football rewards individual talent. In a world that is characterized by so much unfairness, competitive sports such as football become important venues for seeing how things should be. The backgrounds of the players should not matter when they hit the playing field. What matters is how well they play. The cries of anguish from the losing 2014 Brazil team may have made the news, but few people questioned the outcome of the game. Fair play ruled.

Football is a people's sport, but not all people get to play. One important rule of football, and of most sports for that matter, is that men and women do not compete directly against one another. The rules of fair play may apply *within* gender categories, yet how fair are those categories? Sports generally, and professional sports in particular, routinely provide opportunities for men that are denied to women. By this rule of gender segregation, the 2014 World Cup showed that the kind of football that counts for FIFA and fans alike is played by men.

Using intersectionality as an analytic lens highlights the multiple nature of individual identities and how varying combinations of class, gender, race, sexuality, and citizenship categories differentially position each individual. Regardless of the love of soccer, these axes of social division work together and influence one another to shape each individual biography.

The disciplinary domain of power   When it comes to the organization of power, different people find themselves encountering different treatment regarding which rules apply to them and how those rules will be implemented. Within football's disciplinary domain, some people are told they lack talent and are discouraged from playing, whereas others may receive extra coaching to cultivate the talent they have. Many are simply told that they are out of luck because they are the wrong gender or age to play at all. In essence, power operates by disciplining people in ways that put people's lives on paths that make some options seem viable and others out of reach.

For example, South Africa's 2010 hosting of the World Cup helped highlight the disciplinary practices that African boys faced who wanted to play football in Europe. European football clubs offer salaries on a par with those offered within US professional football, basketball, and baseball to play for teams in the United Kingdom, France, Italy, and Spain. The surge in the number of Africans playing at big European clubs reflects the dreams of young African football players to make it big. Yet these practices also makes them vulnerable to exploitation by unscrupulous recruiters. Filmmaker Mariana van Zeller's 2010 documentary *Football's Lost Boys* details how thousands of young players are lured away from their homelands, with their families giving up their savings to predatory agents, and how they are often left abandoned, broke, and alone. Some refer to the treatment of young African players as human trafficking.

The increasing racial/ethnic diversity on elite European teams who recruit African players, other players of color from poorer nations, and racialized immigrant minorities may help teams to win. But this racial/ethnic/national diversity of elite football teams has also highlighted the problem of racism in European football. The visible diversity among team players upends long-standing assumptions about race, ethnicity, and national identity. When the national team of France won the 1998 World Cup, defeating Brazil 3–0, some fans saw the team as non-representative of France because most of the players weren't white. Moreover, white European fans may love their teams, yet many feel free to engage in racist behavior, such as calling African players monkeys, chanting racial slurs, and carrying signs with racially derogatory language. In one case, Polish fans threw bananas at a Nigerian football player. The fans aren't the only problem – racial slurs among players are also an issue. For example, at the 2006 World Cup, France's Zinedine Zidane, a three-time winner of FIFA's world player of the year violated a rule of fair play by headbutting Italy's Marco Materazzi in the chest. Zidane, the son of Algerian immigrants, said he was goaded by Materazzi's racist and sexist slurs against his mother and sister. Materazzi was kept in play while Zidane was ejected from what was to be his last ever World Cup match.

The cultural domain of power   When it comes to the organization of power, ideas matter in providing explanations for social inequality and fair play. Televised across the globe, the World Cup sends out important ideas about competition and fair play. Sports contests send an influential message: not everyone can win. On the surface, this makes sense. But why do some people win and other people lose? More importantly, why do some people consistently win and others consistently lose? FIFA football has ready-made answers. Winners have talent, discipline, and luck, and losers suffer from lack of talent, inferior self-discipline, and/or bad luck. This view suggests that fair competition produces just results. Armed with this worldview concerning winners and losers, it's a small step to using this frame to explain social inequality itself.

What conditions are needed for this frame to remain plausible? This is where the idea of a level or flat playing field becomes crucial. Imagine a tilted football field that was installed on the side of a gently sloped hill with the red team's goal on top of the hill and the blue team's goal in the valley. The red team has a clear advantage: when they try to score, gravity propels the ball toward their opponent's goal. No matter how gifted, their team players need not work as hard to score. In contrast, the blue team has an uphill battle to score a goal. The blue team members may need to be especially gifted to continue playing the game. They may have talent and self-discipline but they have the bad luck of playing on a tilted playing field.

Football fans would be outraged if the actual playing field were tilted in this way. Yet this is what social divisions of class, gender, and race do – we all think we are playing on a level playing field when we are not. The cultural domain of power helps manufacture messages that playing fields are level, that all competitions are fair, and that any resulting patterns of winners and losers have been fairly accomplished.

With the advent of new communications technologies, mass media has increased in significance for the cultural domain of power. Via contests between nations, cities, regions, and all sorts of things, mass media stages entertainment that reinforces the myth of a level playing field where one doesn't actually exist. For FIFA, 195 or so nation-states theoretically can compete in the World Cup as long as they play by the rules and their teams are good enough. This is the myth of equal opportunity to compete. When national teams compete, nations themselves compete. Yet because rich nations have far more resources than poor ones, few nation-states can field teams.

The message of mass-media spectacles goes beyond any one event. The competitive and repetitive nature of contests – such as the World Cup and the Olympics – reflects intersecting power relations of capitalism and nationalism. Competing mass-media spectacles reiterate the belief that unequal outcomes of winners and losers are normal outcomes of marketplace competition. In other words, social inequalities that are fairly produced are socially just. The repetitive nature of sporting events, beauty pageants, reality television, and the like provide a useful interpretive context for viewing the marketplace relations of capitalism as being similarly organized. These mass media spectacles and associated events also present important scripts of gender, race, and nation that work together and influence one another. The bravery of male athletes on national teams makes them akin to war heroes on battlefields, while the beauty, grace, and virtue of national beauty pageants are thought to represent the beauty, grace, and virtue of the nation. Mass-media spectacles may appear to be mere entertainment, yet they serve political ends.

The structural domain of power Fair play on a level playing field may be the ethos of football, yet how much of this fair play characterizes the organization of FIFA football itself? The structural domain of power here refers to how

FIFA itself is organized or structured. Because intersectionality embraces complexity, it questions how intersecting power relations of class, gender, race, and nation shape the institutionalization and organization of the World Cup. As a global industry, FIFA has organized the populist sensibility of football into a highly profitable global network. With an executive committee of 25 businessmen, FIFA's headquarters are located in Switzerland, where the government provides it legal protection as an international NGO. Its legal status has allowed FIFA to control billions of euros without substantial government oversight. As big business, FIFA has managed to organize football into a global industry with tremendous reach and considerable influence with governments. For example, in 2012 FIFA succeeded in having the Brazilian parliament adopt a General World Cup Law that imposed bank holidays on host cities on the days of the Brazilian team's matches, cut the number of places in the stadiums, and increased prices for ordinary spectators. The law also allowed alcoholic drinks to be taken into the stadiums, a change in the law which was of special benefit to Anheuser-Busch, the makers of Budweiser beer and one of FIFA's main sponsors. The bill also exempted companies working for FIFA from taxes and fiscal charges, banned the sale of any goods in official competition spaces, their immediate surroundings and their principal access routes, and penalized bars who tried to schedule showings of the matches or promote certain brands. Finally, the bill defined any attack on the image of FIFA or its sponsors as a federal crime.

Given FIFA's global reach and largely unchecked powers, it should come as no surprise that, because FIFA is unregulated, it has for years come under suspicion of corruption. In June 2015, the US Department of Justice issued indictments against top FIFA officials and others involved in FIFA, bringing FIFA's corruption allegations into public purview. At the request of the United States, Interpol issued six alerts for two former senior FIFA officials and four corporate executives. They were a former FIFA vice-president from Trinidad and Tobago who was accused of accepting bribes in connection with the awarding of the 2010 World Cup to South Africa; a Paraguayan citizen and former FIFA executive committee member; three business persons who control two sports-marketing business based in Argentina; and a Brazilian citizen who owns broadcasting businesses. Accused of rigging the bidding process for awarding the games, the indictments traced financial payoffs to key FIFA figures in exchange for FIFA's endorsements. At the heart of the corruption were charges of "pay to play," rather than fair play.[1]

Social inequality: a new global crisis?

Drawing more than 6,000 participants from all over the world, the Eighteenth International Sociological Association (ISA) World Congress of Sociology convened in Yokohama, Japan on July 13–19, 2014. In his presidential address, Michael Burawoy, a distinguished Marxist scholar, argued that inequality was the most pressing issue of our time. Burawoy suggested that growing global inequality had spurred new thinking not only in sociology but also in economics and related social sciences. Burawoy had long been a proponent of public sociology, the perspective that the tools of sociology should be brought to bear on social issues of great significance to the public (Burawoy 2005). Interestingly, Burawoy also stressed the significance of the 2013 election of Pope Francis. As the first pope from the Global South, Pope Francis is unusually committed to tackling the questions of social inequality, poverty, and environmental justice: he did not hesitate to describe economic inequality as "the root of social evil." It is not every day that a Marxist scholar quotes the Pope before an international gathering of social scientists.

That same year, more than 220 business leaders and investors from 27 countries assembled in London at the May 2014 Conference on Inclusive Capitalism. As Nafeez Ahmed reported in a May 28, 2014 article in the *Guardian*, the attendees gathered to discuss "the need for a more socially responsible form of capitalism that benefits everyone, not just a wealthy minority." Representing the most powerful financial and business elites who control approximately US$30 trillion worth of liquid assets, or one-third of the global total, this group was concerned about, as the CEO of Unilever put it, "the capitalist threat to capitalism." The stellar guest list for the conference included Prince Charles, Bill Clinton, a

Bank of England governor, the executive chairman of Google, the co-founder and CEO of Blackstone, and the CEOs of UBS, GlaxoSmithKline, Dow Chemical, and Honeywell. Most attendees were handpicked by wealthy philanthropist Lady de Rothschild, reports the *Telegraph*'s Brooks-Pollock (July 24, 2014), to discuss one of the "fashionable issues of the day – rising inequality in capitalist societies and how to make the system work for everyone." Among the guests, Christine Lagarde, the head of the International Monetary Fund (IMF), invoked in her keynote speech the same reference to Pope Francis's description of increasing inequality as "the root of social evil," as well as Marx's insight that capitalism "carried the seeds of its own destruction." Something needed to be done, argued Lagarde. Here again, it is not every day that the head of the International Monetary Fund quotes both the Pope and Marx before the global financial elite.

The fact that a Marxist sociologist like Burawoy referenced the Pope, and that the IMF head cited both the Pope and Marx suggests the state of global inequality is serious enough to make people who are typically on opposite sides of many issues take notice. The International Monetary Fund offers a mainstream view of the causes and solutions to social inequality, one that resembles the winners and losers in FIFA's analysis of fair play. Many sociologists have long offered a critical assessment of this mainstream view, pointing instead to structural power relations. Yet growing global social inequality is so significant that both mainstream and critical groups are taking notice. What is happening?

Over the last thirty years, inequality in income and wealth has grown exponentially, both within individual nation-states and across an overwhelming majority of countries. Seventy percent of the world's population lives in countries where economic inequality has increased in the last three decades. Nearly half of the world's wealth, some US$110 trillion, is owned by only 1 percent of the world's population. If trends continue, by 2016, 1 percent is expected to own more than the other 99 percent together (Oxfam 2015). Despite the 2008 global financial crisis, the richest 1 percent constantly increased its share of the world's wealth between 1980 and 2014 – from 44 percent in 2009 to 48 percent in 2014.[2] The combined wealth of the world's richest 85 people equals the total wealth of the poorest half of the world's population, which accounts for 3.5 billion people (Oxfam 2014).

Using intersectionality as an analytic tool can foster a better understanding of growing global inequality. First, economic inequality does not fall equally on everyone. Rather than seeing people as a homogeneous, undifferentiated mass, intersectionality provides a framework for explaining how social divisions of race, gender, age, and citizenship status, among others, positions people differently in the world, especially in relation to global social inequality.

Some people are far more vulnerable to changes in the global economy, whereas others benefit disproportionately from them. For example, income differences that accompany labor market practices of hiring, job security, retirement benefits, health benefits, and pay scales do not fall equally on everyone. Labor market discrimination that pushes some people into part-time jobs with low pay, irregular hours, and no benefits, or that renders them structurally unemployed, does not fall equally across social groups. Similarly, intersectionality also fosters a rethinking of the concept of the wealth gap. Rather than seeing the wealth gap as unconnected to categories such as race, gender, age, and citizenship, differences in wealth reflect structures intersecting power relations. The racialized structure of the wealth gap has been well documented in the United States where disparities between whites, blacks, and Latinos have reached record highs (Chang 2010; Pew Research Center 2011).[3] Yet the wealth gap is not only racialized but also simultaneously gendered. The wealth gap is generally analyzed through an *either/or* lens, race or gender, but with noteworthy exceptions (see, e.g., Oliver and Shapiro 1995), less often through an intersectional *both/and* lens. Measuring economic inequality through data on households, rather than on individuals, helps document the wealth gap between racially differentiated households and sheds light on the situation of households headed by single women across races. Intersectional analyses demonstrate how the structure of the inequality gap is simultaneously racialized *and* gendered for women of color.[4]

Second, using intersectionality as an analytic tool complicates class-only explanations for global economic inequality. Intersectionality proposes a more sophisticated map of social inequality that goes beyond class-only accounts. Both the neoclassical economics accepted in US venues and Marxist social thought more often found in European settings foreground class. Both of these class-only explanations for social inequality treat race, gender, sexuality, and ethnicity as add-ons. Yet intersectional frameworks suggest that economic inequality can neither be assessed nor effectively addressed through class alone. As Zillah Eisentein argues in a *Feminist Wire* article:

> When civil rights activists speak about race they are told they need to think about class as well. When anti-racist feminists focus on the problems of gendered racism they are also told to include class. So [...] when formulating class inequality one should have race and gender in view as well. *Capital is intersectional.* It always intersects with the bodies that produce the labor. Therefore, the accumulation of wealth is embedded in the racialized and engendered structures that enhance it. (Eisentein 2014: our italics)

Positing that contemporary configurations of global capital that fuel and sustain growing social inequalities are about class exploitation, racism, sexism, and other systems of power fosters a rethinking of the categories used to understand economic inequality. Intersectional frameworks reveal how race, gender, sexuality, age, ability, and citizenship relate in complex and intersecting ways to produce economic inequality.

Third, using intersectionality as an analytic tool highlights the significance of social institutions in shaping and solving social problems. Many factors contribute to this widening economic gap, but one seems paramount: the rise in economic inequality grew during the same forty-year period that nation-state policies shifted from governmental philosophies of social welfare to neoliberalism.

Drawing on philosophies of representative and participatory democracy, social welfare states had long concerned themselves with protecting the interests of the public, grounded in a belief that democratic institutions could flourish only with a strong citizenry. Unemployment, poverty, racial and gender discrimination, homelessness, illiteracy, poor health, and similar social problems within a nation-state constituted threats to the public good that were just as prominent as external enemies beyond its national borders. To confront these domestic challenges, social welfare states aimed to promote public well-being via various combinations of establishing regulatory agencies for electricity, water, and similar entities, investments in public infrastructure and basic services, and providing direct state services. For example, in the United States, environmental safety and food security have long been the purview of the federal government in the belief that, in order to protect everyone, industrial polluters of water and air, as well as the meat-packing industry, require a fair yet vigilant regulatory climate. Social welfare policies provide for a range of projects, including highway funding, school funding, and public transportation, as well as programs that care for the elderly, children, poor people, the disabled, the unemployed, and other people who need assistance. Overall, the basic idea was that, by protecting its citizens and acting on behalf of the public good, social welfare states could maintain strong democratic institutions.

In contrast, as a philosophy, neoliberalism is grounded in the belief that markets, in and of themselves, are better able than governments to produce economic outcomes that are fair, sensible, and good for all. The state practices associated with neoliberalism differ dramatically from those of social welfare states. First, neoliberalism fosters the increased privatization of government programs and institutions like public schools, prisons, health care, transportation, and the military. Under the logic of neoliberalism, private firms that are accountable to market forces rather than democratic oversight of citizens can potentially provide less costly and more efficient services than government workers. Second, the logic of neoliberalism argues for the scaling back, and in some cases elimination of, the social welfare state. The safety net of government assistance to the poor, the unemployed, the disabled, the elderly, and the young is recast as wasteful spending characteristic of irresponsible government. Third, neoliberal logic claims that fewer economic regulations and more trade that is free of government constraints protects jobs. This freedom from environmental regulation and entities such as unions should produce greater profitability for some companies which should lead to more jobs. Finally, neoliberalism posits a form of individualism that rejects the notion of the public good. By neoliberal logic, people have only themselves to blame for their problems: solving social problems comes down to the self-reliance of individuals (Cohen 2010; Harvey 2005).

Citizens within democratic nation-states with strong social welfare traditions find themselves facing a dilemma: in what ways will their respective nation-states continue to endorse social welfare policies and in what ways will they embrace social policies informed by neoliberalism? On the one hand, refusing to implement policies that are informed by neoliberalism can make a state less competitive in the global marketplace. Making industries more competitive in the global marketplace via automation, deskilling, and job export increases the profitability of companies. Yet, on the other hand, neoliberalism can foster social unrest. Those same strategies eliminate jobs and suppress wages, leaving closed factories, unemployed workers, and the potential for social unrest in their wake. Brazil's experience with FIFA captures the tensions that distinguish a nation-state that aimed for a balance between social welfare policies and neoliberal aspirations. The money spent on FIFA may have raised Brazil's profile in the global arena, yet it simultaneously sparked massive social protest about cost overruns and corruption.

Intersectionality certainly has many conceptual tools to analyze state power and how it articulates with global capitalism. Yet intersectionality's focus on people's lives provides space for alternative analyses of these same phenomena. As opposed to their leaders, the people who bear the brunt of neoliberalism may be more hopeful about reclaiming participatory democracy. Without hope of change, there would be no social protest. Drawing inspiration from Pope Francis, they may also view growing economic inequality, as well as the social forces that cause it, as "the root of social evil," yet refuse to sit passively watching it destroy their lives.

Latinidades: the black women's movement in Brazil

Two weeks after the raucous fans departed from Brazil's 2014 World Cup spectacle, more than a thousand women of African descent, their friends, family members, colleagues, and allies travelled to Brasilia, the national capital. They arrived at the iconic National Museum of the Republic, several blocks away from the refurbished but now empty World Cup stadium, to attend the seventh meeting of Latinidades, the Afro-Latin and Afro-Caribbean women's festival. As the largest festival for black women in Latin America, the event was scheduled to coincide with the annual International Day of Black Latin American and Caribbean Women. Latinidades's seasoned event organizers had recruited an impressive list of main sponsors: the State Secretary of Culture, the Office of Racial Equality, the Funarte Palmares Cultural Foundation and Petrobras, Brazil's multinational energy corporation. Unlike the goals of FIFA, Latinidades's success would not be judged by corporate profits or the success of mass-media spectacle. Unlike the hefty ticket prices for the World Cup, the six-day Latinidades festival was free and housed in public space.

Latinidades was no ordinary festival: its expressed purpose lay in promoting "racial equality and tackling racism and sexism." The festival drew mostly women of African descent but also many men and members of diverse racial/ethnic groups from all areas of Brazil's states and regions, as well as from Costa Rica, Ecuador, and other Latin American and Caribbean nations. This geographic heterogeneity reflected the many different ways participants were connected to promoting racial equality and tackling how racism and sexism affected Afro-Latin women. Community organizers, professors, graduate students, parents, artists, schoolteachers, high-school students, representatives of samba schools, government officials, and music lovers, among others, made the journey to Brasilia to attend Latinidades.

The festival's programming was inclusive, with something for all attendees, even the youngest ones. Latinidades had elements of an academic symposium, a political organizing event, an African cultural heritage event, and a mass-music festival rolled into one. Latinidades's academic component resembled a standard academic conference, complete with plenary sessions and an array of panels on issues as varied as health, psychology, literature from the African diaspora, and a session devoted to new books by and about black women. Important Afro-Brazilian feminist intellectuals attended. Some sessions examined community-organizing initiatives in favelas (low-income urban communities), as well as forms of wisdom associated with land, sustainability, and the environment.

The festival's strong activist orientation permeated both its sessions and its special events. For example, Angela Davis's keynote address got the audience on its feet, many with fists raised in the Black Power salute. The festival also set aside time for a planning meeting to educate attendees about the upcoming Black Women's March for a National Day of Denouncing Racism. Community organizers rubbed shoulders with academics, as did young people with revered elders.

Another programming strand throughout the festival's many activities emphasized the significance of African diasporic cultural traditions, especially in Brazil. Writers and artists were well represented. Conceição Evaristo, Afro-Brazilian author and professor of Brazilian literature, attended the festival. Her novel *Ponciá Vicencio*, a story of a young Afro-Brazilian woman's journey from the land of her enslaved ancestors to the emptiness of urban life, was a landmark in black Brazilian women's literature (Evaristo 2007). From the content of sessions, to a workshop for girls on black aesthetics and beauty, a session on the art of turbans and their connections to black beauty, a capoeira workshop, and a tree-planting ceremony of the seedlings of sacred baobab trees, Latinidades saw culture as an important dimension of Afro-Latin and Afro-Caribbean women's lives. After two days of intensive workshops, talks, and films, festival participants spilled outside the museum into its expansive plaza to enjoy two nights of music concerts. Latinidades was a festival where serious work and play coincided.

Not only was Latinidades a success, its very existence constituted one highly visible moment of an Afro-Brazilian women's movement that took several decades to build. Holding a festival that was devoted to the issues and needs of black women in Brazil specifically, as well as Afro-Latin and Afro-Caribbean women more generally, would have been impossible several decades earlier. Since the 1930s, when Brazil adopted an ideology of racial democracy, Brazil officially claimed not to have "races." The Brazilian government collected no racial statistics and, without racial categories, Brazil officially had neither race nor black people. Within this

social context, women of African descent may have constituted a visible and sizable segment of Brazilian society, yet in
a Brazil that ostensibly lacked race, the category of black
women did not exist as an officially recognized population.

How might using intersectionality as an analytic tool shed
light on Latinidades's commitment to challenging racism and
sexism against a group that officially did not exist? For one,
black women challenged Brazil's national identity narrative
concerning racial democracy. They saw the historical interconnections between ideas about race and Brazil's nation-
building project as setting the stage for the erasure of
Afro-Brazilian women. Brazil's cultivated image of national
identity posited that racism did not exist and that color lacks
meaning, other than celebrating it as a dimension of national
pride. This national identity neither came about by accident
nor meant that people of African descent believed it. By
erasing the political category of race, Brazil's national discourse of racial democracy effectively eliminated language
that might describe the racial inequalities that affected black
Brazilian people's lives. This erasure of "blackness" as a
political category allowed discriminatory practices to occur
against people of visible African descent in education and
employment because there were neither officially recognized
terms for describing racial discrimination nor official remedies for it (Twine 1998). Brazil's military government
(1964–1985) upheld this national ideology of racial democracy and also suppressed social protest in general. The end
of the dictatorship in 1985 created new opportunities for
seeing the connections between racism and Brazilian nationalism, as well as for social movements.

Second, using intersectionality as an analytic tool also
sheds light on how women of African descent or Afro-
Brazilian women are situated within gendered and sexualized
understandings of Brazilian history and national identity.
Brazil's specific history of slavery, colonialism, pre-dictatorship
democracy, dictatorship and post-dictatorship democracy
framed distinctive patterns of intersecting power relations of
gender and sexuality. Sexual engagements, both consensual
and forced, among African-, indigenous- and European-
descended populations created a Brazilian population with
varying hair textures, skin colors, body shapes, and eye

colors, as well as a complex and historically shifting series of terms to describe them. Claims of Brazil's racial democracy notwithstanding, Brazil, like other Latin American countries, developed a carefully calibrated lexicon of ethnoracial classification. Skin color, hair texture, facial features, and other aspects of appearance became de facto racial markers for distributing education, jobs, and other social goods. As Caldwell points out, "popular images of Brazil as a carnivalesque, tropical paradise have played a central role in contemporary constructions of mulata women's social identities. Brazil's international reputation as a racial democracy is closely tied to the sexual objectification of women of mixed racial ancestry as the essence of Brazilianness" (Caldwell 2007: 58). For Afro-Brazilian women, those of mixed ancestry or with more European physical features are typically considered to be more attractive. Moreover, women of visible African ancestry are typically constructed as non-sexualized, and often as asexual laborers or conversely as prostitutes (Caldwell 2007: 51). Appearance not only carries differential weight for women and men, but different stereotypes of black women rest on beliefs about their sexuality. These ideas feed back into notions of national identity, using race, gender, sexuality, and color as intersecting phenomena.

A third dimension of using intersectionality as an analytic tool concerns how intersectionality's framework of mutually constructing identity categories enabled Afro-Brazilian women to develop a collective identity politics. In this case, they cultivated a political black feminist identity at the intersections of racism, sexism, class exploitation, national history, and sexuality. The political space created by reinstalling democracy in the late 1980s benefited both women and blacks. Yet there was one significant difference between the two groups. In a climate where women's rights encompassed only the needs of white women and where blacks were not politically recognized, Afro-Brazilian women were differentially treated within both the feminist movement and the Black Movement. Clearly, women and men had different experiences within Brazilian society – there was no need to advocate for the integrity of the categories themselves. Yet the framing of the women's movement, even around such a firm subject as "woman," was inflected through other categories. Because upper-class and middle-class women were central to the movement, their status as marked by class yet unmarked by race (most were white) shaped political demands. Brazil's success in electing women to political office reflected alliances among women across categories of social class. With the noteworthy exception of Benedita da Silva, the first black woman to serve in the Brazilian Congress in 1986 and the Senate in 1994, feminism raised issues of gender and sexuality, but did so in ways that did not engage issues of anti-black racism that were so important to Afro-Brazilian women.

Unlike white Brazilian women, black Brazilians of all sexes and genders had to create the collective political identity of "black" in order to build an anti-racist social movement that highlighted the effects of anti-black racism. Brazil's history with transatlantic slavery left it with a large population of African descent – by some estimates, 50 percent of the Brazilian population. Claiming an identity as "black" seemed to contradict the national identity of racial democracy, and thus ran the risk of being accused of disloyalty and not being fully Brazilian. In this sense, the Black Movement that emerged in the 1990s did not call for equal treatment within the democratic state for an already recognized group. Rather, recognition meant both naming a sizable segment of the population and acknowledging that it experienced anti-black racial discrimination (Hanchard 1994).

Neither Brazilian feminism led by women who were primarily well off and white, nor a Black Movement that was actively engaged in claiming a collective black identity that identified racism as a social force could by itself adequately address Afro-Brazilian women's issues. Black women who participated in the Black Movement found willing allies when it came to anti-racist black activism but much less understanding of how the issues faced by black people took gender-specific forms. Indeed, they found little recognition of the special issues of living lives as black women in Brazil at the intersections of areas of racism, sexism, class exploitation, second-class citizenship, and heterosexism. Brazil's history of class analysis that saw capitalism and workers' rights as major forces in shaping inequality made space for exceptional individuals such as Benedita da Silva. Yet when it came to race, class politics asked them to see both gender and race as secondary. Black women faced similar pressures to subordinate their special concerns under the banner of class solidarity. These separate social movements of feminism, anti-racism, and workers' movements were important, and many black women continued to participate in them. Yet because no one social movement alone could adequately address Afro-Brazilian women's issues, they formed their own.

Taking a step back to view the issues that shaped the lived experiences of black Brazilian women illustrates how a collective identity politics emerged around a politicized understanding of a collective black women's identity based on common experiences of domination, exploitation, and marginalization (Caldwell 2007). For example, when black domestic workers organized, it was clear that women of African descent were disproportionately represented in this occupational category. Not all domestic workers were "black" but the job category was certainly closely associated with black women. Afro-Brazilian women were more vulnerable to violence, especially those living in favelas and who did domestic work. Drawing on cultural ties to the African diaspora, black women activists also saw their roles as mothers and othermothers as important for political action.

In brief, Latinidades thus marked the celebration of a long struggle to build a complex social movement that acknowledged race, gender, class, nation and sexuality as mutually constructing and multidimensional aspects of Afro-Brazilian women's lives. Women of African descent in Brazil knew on one level, through personal experience, that they were part of a group that shared certain collective experiences. They were disproportionately found in domestic work. Their images were maligned in popular culture. They were disproportionately targets of violence against women. They were mothers who lacked the means to care for their children as they would have liked, but had ties to the value placed on mothering across the African diaspora. Yet because they lacked a political identity and accompanying analysis to attach to these experiences, they couldn't articulate a collective identity politics to raise their concerns. None of their closest allies – black men in the Black Movement, or white women in the feminist movement, or socialists in organizations that advocated for workers' rights – would have their own best interests at heart as fervently as they did. Lacking a language that spoke directly to their experiences, black women such as Léila Gonzalez, Sueli Carneiro and a long list of activist/scholars painstakingly organized the various constituencies of black women that were needed to address black women's concerns (Carneiro 1995, 2014).

Core ideas of intersectional frameworks

Intersectionality is a way of understanding and analyzing the complexity in the world, in people, and in human experience. The previous section showed three different uses of intersectionality as an analytic tool that sheds light on the complexity of people's lives within an equally complex social context. Each case illustrates how the events and conditions of social and political life at play were not shaped by any one factor. Rather, the dynamics in each case reflected many factors that worked together in diverse and mutually influencing ways.

The FIFA World Cup, the global social inequality social problem, and the black Brazilian feminist social movement also help clarify six core ideas that appear and reappear when people use intersectionality as an analytic tool: inequality, relationality, power, social context, complexity, and social justice. These ideas are neither always present in a particular project, nor do they appear in projects in the same way. Instead, they provide guideposts for thinking through intersectionality. Just as these themes reappear, albeit in different forms, within intersectionality itself, they show up in different ways throughout the book. We briefly introduce them here, develop them throughout this text, and return to them in chapter 8.

1. *Social inequality*: All three cases grapple with social inequality, albeit from very different vantage points. The case of social inequality within World Cup football juxtaposes the search for fairness on the playing field with the unfairness of FIFA's global organization. The case of how growing global social inequality came to the attention of ISA and

the Conference on Inclusive Capitalism emphasizes different perspectives on social inequality that flow from intersectional analyses of capitalism and neoliberalism. Latinidades illustrates how the Afro-Brazilian women's movement responded intellectually and politically to historical and contemporary forms of social inequality, especially the intersections of racism and sexism, in shaping social class differences within the particular history of the Brazilian nation-state.

Many contemporary definitions of intersectionality emphasize social inequality, but not all do. Intersectionality exists because many people were deeply concerned by the forms of social inequality they either experienced themselves or saw around them. Intersectionality adds additional layers of complexity to understandings of social inequality, recognizing that social inequality is rarely caused by a single factor. Using intersectionality as an analytic tool encourages us to move beyond seeing social inequality through race-only or class-only lenses. Instead, intersectionality encourages understandings of social inequality based on interactions among various categories.

2. *Power*: All three cases highlight different dimensions of the organization of power relations. The case study of the World Cup examines the multi-faceted power relations of FIFA World Cup football. The case of global social inequality shows how intersectional frameworks that take power relations into account, especially those that emphasize intersections of neoliberalism, nationalism, and capitalism, provide more robust interpretations of global social inequality. In contrast, the Latinidades case shows how power relations operate within political projects and social movements. By examining how black women in Brazil organized to resist multiple forms of social inequality, the Latininades case illustrates political activism not only from top-down policy endeavors or global social movements, but rather from the space of community organizing and grassroots coalition politics.

These cases raise two important points about power relations. First, intersectional frameworks understand power relations through a lens of mutual construction. In other words, people's lives and identities are generally shaped by many factors in diverse and mutually influencing ways. Moreover, race, class, gender, sexuality, age, disability, ethnicity, nation, and religion, among others, constitute interlocking, mutually constructing or intersecting systems of power. Within intersectional frameworks, there is no pure racism or sexism. Rather, power relations of racism and sexism gain meaning in relation to one another.

Second, power relations are to be analyzed both *via their intersections*, for example, of racism and sexism, as well as *across domains of power*, namely structural, disciplinary, cultural, and interpersonal. The framework of domains of power provides a heuristic device or thinking tool for examining power relations. The World Cup case introduced this heuristic by analyzing each domain of power separately. It broke them down into the kinds of power relations that are solidified in social structures (e.g., organizations like FIFA and institutions like national governments) that are shared through ideas and media, or culture broadly speaking, that appear over and over again in the ways that informal social rewards and punishments get distributed in everyday interactions, and that play out in everyday interactions among people. These are the structural, cultural, disciplinary, and interpersonal domains of power, respectively. Looking at how power works in *each* domain can shed light on the dynamics of a larger social phenomenon, like the social unrest around the 2014 World Cup. Yet, in actual social practice, the domains overlap, and no one domain is any more important than another.

3. *Relationality*: The Latinidades case of the Afro-Brazilian women's movement illustrates a historical and contemporary commitment to develop coalitions or relationships across social divisions. Whether the relationality of multiple identities within the interpersonal domain of power or the relationality of analysis required to understand how class, race, and gender collectively shape global social inequality, this idea of connectedness or relationality is important.

Relational thinking rejects *either/or* binary thinking, for example, opposing theory to practice, scholarship to activism, or blacks to whites. Instead, relationality embraces a *both/and* frame. The focus of relationality shifts from analyzing what distinguishes entities, for example, the differences between race and gender, to examining their interconnections. This shift in perspective opens up intellectual and political possibilities. The global inequality case illustrates how class-only arguments may be insufficient to explain global social inequality, and that intersectional arguments that examine the relationships between class, race, gender, and age might be more valuable. Relationality takes various forms within intersectionality and is found in terms such as "coalition," "dialog," "conversation," "interaction," and "transaction." Because this core idea of relationality traverses much intersectional inquiry and practice, it is also central to this book. Power is better conceptualized as a relationship, as in *power relations*, than as a static entity. Power is not a thing to be gained or lost as in the zero-sum conceptions of winners and losers on the football playing field. Rather, power constitutes a relationship.

4. *Social context*: All three cases also provide opportunities for examining intersecting power relations *in context*. While both the World Cup and the black women's movement involve Brazil, the latter case highlights the significance of specific historical contexts in the production of intersectional knowledge and action, even in the absence of the term itself. The case of the black women's movement in Brazil shows how intellectual and political activism work by growing from a specific set of concerns in a specific social location, in this case the identity politics of Afro-Brazilian women.

The term "contextualize" comes from this impetus to think about social inequality, relationality, and power relations in a social context. Using intersectionality as an analytic tool means contextualizing one's arguments, primarily by being aware that particular historical, intellectual, and political contexts shape what we think and do. The cases of FIFA and Latinidades contextualize the main arguments in a Brazilian context. Moreover, presenting two different views of Brazil shows how different people can be in the same general social context yet hold different interpretations of it. This theme of different perspectives that can arise in different social contexts is important for understanding differences within intersectionality itself. Contextualization is especially important for intersectional projects produced in the Global South because scholars and activists working in Brazil, South Africa, Trinidad, Bangladesh, India, Nigeria, and other nation-states of the Global South face specific sets of difficulties in reaching wider audiences.

To understand increasing global social inequalities, relationality sheds light on how intersections of racism, class exploitation, sexism, nationalism, and heterosexism work together to shape social inequality. These systems operate relationally across structural, cultural, disciplinary, and interpersonal domains. Attending to social context grounds intersectional analysis.

5. *Complexity*: These core themes of social inequality, power, relationality, and social context are intertwined, introducing an element of complexity into intersectional analysis. Intersectionality itself is a way of understanding and analyzing the complexity in the world. Using intersectionality as an analytic tool is difficult, precisely because intersectionality itself is complex. This level of complexity is not easy for anyone to handle. It complicates things and can be a source of frustration for scholars, practitioners, and activists alike, who are looking for a neat tool to apply: a tidy methodology for intersectional research (the dream of some students perhaps); or a crisp instruction manual for applying intersectionality to various fields of practice (how to make an intersectional social work intervention; how to make intersectional policy analysis; how to use intersectionality for fostering coalitions in social movement politics). These are perfectly legitimate and undoubtedly useful expectations that scholars, practitioners, and activists engaged in intersectionality all have to address seriously and collaboratively.

6. *Social justice*: These cases engage varying angles of vision on social justice. The World Cup case suggests that competition is not inherently bad. People accept the concept of winners and losers if the game itself is fair. Yet fairness is elusive in unequal societies where the rules may seem fair, yet differentially enforced through discriminatory practices. Fairness is also elusive where the rules themselves may appear to be equally applied to everyone yet still produce unequal and unfair outcomes: in democratic societies, everyone has the "right" to vote, but not everyone has equal access to do so.

The case of global social inequality illustrates how complex the solutions to global economic inequality need to be in order to foster social justice. For one, the legitimacy of pursuing a social justice agenda is not self-evident. Many people believe that social ideals, such as the belief in meritocracy, fairness, and the reality of democracy, have already been achieved. For them, there is no global crisis of legitimacy: global social inequality is the outcome of fair competition, and democratic institutions work just fine. Yet by challenging myths that racial democracy had been achieved, or that the Black Movement could handle the gendered concerns of women, or that Brazilian feminism was adequate for all women, the social justice activism of the black women's movement in Brazil provides a different angle of vision on social justice.

Social justice may be intersectionality's most contentious core idea, but it is one that expands the circle of intersectionality to include people who use intersectionality as an analytic tool for social justice. Working for social justice is not a requirement for intersectionality. Yet people who are engaged in using intersectionality as an analytic tool and people who see social justice as central rather than as peripheral to their lives are often one and the same. These people are typically critical of, rather than accepting of, the status quo.

Our goal in this book is to democratize the rich and growing literature of intersectionality – not to assume that only African-American students will be interested in black history, or that LGBTQ youth will be the only ones interested in queer studies, or that intersectionality is for any one segment of the population. Rather, the task is to use intersectionality as an analytic tool to examine a range of topics such as those introduced here. In the following chapters, we explore various dimensions of intersectionality, especially the use of intersectionality as an analytic tool, as well as the varying forms that its core themes of social inequality, relationality, power, social context, complexity, and social justice assume.

2
Intersectionality as Critical Inquiry and Praxis

Far too much intersectional scholarship starts with the assumption that intersectionality is a finished framework that can simply be applied to a given research project or political program. Yet, as the cases of the FIFA World Cup, the ISA/World Conference on Inclusive Capitalism, and Latinidades suggest, the use of intersectionality can take many forms. Generalizing about intersectionality based on a particular case or one group's experiences in a particular social context risks missing the process of discovery that underlies how people actually use intersectional frameworks. Intersectionality itself is constantly under construction and these cases illustrate different ways of using intersectionality as an analytic tool. Yet how is intersectionality as a form of critical inquiry and praxis organized to do this analytic work? This chapter investigates intersectionality's two organizational focal points, namely, *critical inquiry* and *critical praxis*.

Intersectionality as a form of critical inquiry gained visibility in the academy when the term "intersectionality" seemed to be a good fit for scholarship and teaching that were already underway. In the 1990s, the term "intersectionality" came into use both inside and outside traditional disciplines, as well as inside and outside the academy. Initially, intersectional inquiry was inherently critical because it criticized existing bodies of knowledge, theories, methodologies, and classroom practices, especially in relation to social inequality. While intersectionality as a form of critical inquiry can occur any-where, colleges and universities became important venues for disseminating intersectionality through scholarship, teaching, conferences, grant proposals, policy reports, and literary and creative works.

Intersectionality as a form of critical praxis refers to the ways in which people, either as individuals or as part of groups, produce, draw upon, or use intersectional frame-works in their daily lives – as everyday citizens with jobs and families, as well as institutional actors within public schools, colleges and universities, religious organizations, and similar venues. Intersectionality's critical praxis can occur anywhere, both inside and outside the academy. This book pays special attention to intersectionality as critical praxis because popular understandings of intersectionality underemphasize the prac-tices that make intersectional knowledge possible, especially practices that involve criticizing, rejecting, and/or trying to fix the social problems that come with complex social ine-qualities. Critical praxis also constitutes an important feature of intersectional inquiry – one that is both attentive to intersecting power relations and essentially vital for resisting social inequality.

Within intersectionality as critical inquiry, faculty and stu-dents routinely overlook the power relations that make their scholarship and classroom practices possible and legitimate. If they consider the theme of political praxis at all, they treat politics as a topic of discussion, or as a silent background variable that has little influence on research design or on classroom practices. These assumptions relegate politics to areas outside the academy and contribute to the fiction that higher education is an ivory tower. Within intersectionality as critical praxis, most activists do consider power relations and social inequalities as central to their work, yet they may feel that ideas themselves, especially theoretical reflections on intersectionality, are luxuries they cannot afford. Some activ-ists even reject social theory, failing to see how ideas them-selves can move people to action.

Rejecting this scholar–activist divide suggests that intersec-tionality as a form of critical inquiry and praxis can occur anywhere. Critical thinking is certainly not confined to the academy, nor is political engagement found solely in social movements or community organizing. In lived experience, critical inquiry and praxis as organizational principles are rarely distinguished as sharply as presented here. Nonetheless, making this analytical distinction illuminates a core tension that lies within intersectionality: namely, when people imagine intersectionality, they tend to imagine one or the other, inquiry or praxis, rather than seeing the interconnections between the two.

Bringing these two organizational principles of intersectionality into closer alignment reveals the synergy between them. A synergistic relationship is a special kind of relationality, one where the interaction or cooperation of two or more entities produce a combined effect that is greater than the sum of their separate parts. In the case of intersectionality, the synergy between inquiry and praxis can produce important new knowledge and/or practices. Inquiry and praxis can each be effective without explicitly taking the other into account. Yet bringing them together can generate benefits that are greater than each alone. In future chapters, we use the term "intersectionality" as shorthand to reference this synergy between intersectionality as a form of critical inquiry and practice. In this chapter, we highlight the distinction between these two organizational principles so that we can explore how they do and might work together in using intersectionality as an analytic tool. Our sense of intersectionality aims to sustain a focus on the synergy linking ideas and actions, on the interrelatedness of inquiry and praxis.

Intersectionality as critical inquiry

Intersectionality as a form of critical inquiry invokes a broad sense of using intersectional frameworks to study a range of social phenomena, e.g., the organizational structure of football, the beliefs of bankers, and the actions of Afro-Brazilian women, across different social contexts, e.g., local, regional, national, and global. Intersectionality as critical praxis does the same, but in ways that explicitly challenge the status quo and aim to transform power relations.

Because intersectionality's growth and institutionalization over the past several decades has largely occurred within colleges and universities, this section focuses on intersectionality as a form of critical inquiry within academia as a way to ground the discussion. Students, teachers, scholars, and administrators often use the terminology of "study" to describe intersectionality, a term that conjures up images of scholars doing research within traditional disciplines and interdisciplinary fields. Yet this understanding may be too narrow for intersectionality's actual organization. The important idea here is not to equate intersectionality with a traditional field of study, for example, an academic discipline or an interdisciplinary program. People take actions that are far broader than passively receiving knowledge or contemplating or even criticizing the world around them. Many supplement or work exclusively as independent scholars in new media such as film, music, and digital media, another increasingly important site of intersectionality's critical inquiry.

One way to get a sense of intersectionality within academia is to examine the actions and ideas of scholars/activists who were involved in bringing race/class/gender studies into the academy.[1] In 2001, sociologist Bonnie Thornton Dill interviewed 70 faculty members from seventeen colleges and universities in the United States, many of whom had helped launch interdisciplinary programs on race, class, and gender studies, about their perceptions of the core features and status of this emerging area of inquiry (Dill 2002, 2009). The conversations had two major focal points: defining, describing, and characterizing intersectional work, or what it means to work at the intersections; and exploring the organizational and leadership structures through which the work is done. Dill's subjects identify building institutional capacity as an important dimension of race/class/gender. Or, as Dill succinctly states, "intersectionality is the intellectual core of diversity work" (Dill 2009: 229).

Bonnie Thornton Dill's own career trajectory reflects the synergy of critical inquiry and praxis. In her scholarship on women of color and their families, Dill helped promote intersectional scholarship within family studies (Dill 1988). Working with Lynn Weber and Elizabeth Higginbotham, Dill's leadership at the University of Memphis's Center for

Research on Women of Color and of the South provided an important institutional home for race/class/gender studies in the 1980s (Collins 2007: 588–92). Dill has also served in various organizational capacities which helped establish the institutional infrastructure of intersectionality, for example, helping to build both Women's Studies and the Consortium of Race, Gender, and Ethnicity at the University of Maryland, and serving as president of the National Women's Studies Association. Given Dill's social location of actually working at the synergy of critical inquiry and praxis, her 2001 study provides an important starting point for tracing theoretical, epistemological, and political developments within race, class, and gender studies, a precursor of intersectionality in the academy. This important project also sheds light on the meaning of "working at the intersections" for practitioners who spanned this period when social justice projects travelled into the academy.

Dill's respondents remind us both how hard it was to bring race, class, and gender scholarship to the forefront of academic life, as well as how intersectionality as a form of critical inquiry is indebted to this group of social actors:

> Over the last thirty years, the scholarship that laid the ground-work for what has come to be known as intersectional analysis has been pioneering work. It has been done in the face of indifference and hostility. Scholars engaged in building programs in women's studies, ethnic studies, and in lesbian, gay, bisexual, and transgender studies have had their intellect, their scholarship, their professionalism, and even their sanity questioned. In more recent years, they have been attacked by agents in the destabilization of a perceived collegial university based on unitary principles of US cultural literacy. (Dill 2009: 229)

Dill's study examines the collective standpoint or point of view of social actors who were also involved in crafting a synergy between critical inquiry and praxis in the academy.

The views of these practitioners who carried race/class/gender studies into the academy provide an important window for tracking the entry and subsequent treatment of core themes within intersectionality as a form of critical inquiry. In her preliminary report of her interview findings, Dill concludes, "what I take from these interviews is that work 'at the intersections' is an analytical strategy, an approach to understanding human life and behavior rooted in the experiences and struggles of disenfranchised people. It is also an important tool linking theory with practice that can aid in the empowerment of communities and individuals" (Dill 2002: 6).[2]

Two themes encapsulate how scholars/activists in race/class/gender studies laid a foundation for intersectionality as a form of critical inquiry. Drawing from ties to social movement politics before moving into positions within higher education, they identified two facets of "working at the intersections," or, using the language presented in this book, adopting intersectionality as an analytic tool: (1) an approach to understanding human life and behavior rooted in the experiences and struggles of disenfranchised people; and (2) an important tool linking theory with practice that can aid in the empowerment of communities and individuals.

The first theme of working at the intersections consists of using the experiences and struggles of disenfranchised groups to broaden and deepen understandings of human life and behavior. Working at the intersections had many noteworthy effects on scholarship. For one, intersectionality catalyzed new interpretations of work (Browne and Misra 2003), family (Dill 1988; Naples 1996; Zinn 2010), reproduction, and similar core social constructs and, in the process, criticized and/or revitalized entire areas of study (see, e.g., Dill and Zambrana 2009). For another, intersectional knowledge projects fostered new questions and areas of investigation within existing academic disciplines, especially in those fields that focus on the interconnectedness of the academy and some aspect of the general public. Tracing the patterns of incorporation of race, class, and gender studies generally, and intersectionality in particular, within the discipline of sociology illustrates this tendency (Collins 2007).

Several defining texts in the field of race/class/gender studies helped develop and/or use intersectional frameworks (e.g., Anthias and Yuval-Davis 1992; Sandoval 2000). Such texts make the case for intersectionality as an analytical strategy by showing the inadequacies of failing to consider race, gender, ethnicity, or other categories of analysis that are now routinely considered within intersectional scholarship. Feminist scholars in postcolonial studies found important theoretical insights in intersectionality that enabled them to assess the influence of continental post-structuralist philosophy on the field and use intersectional frameworks in ways that reflect colonial and postcolonial realities (e.g., Alexander and Mohanty 1997; McClintock 1995; Stoler 1995). More importantly, they did so by highlighting the experiences of blacks, women, Latinas, poor people, and other groups who had been neglected and marginalized within existing scholarship.

Second, Dill's respondents identify working at the intersections as "an important tool linking theory with practice that can aid in the empowerment of communities and individuals." This theme resembles this book's focus on intersectionality as a form of critical inquiry and praxis. Intersectionality is not simply a method for doing research but is also a tool for empowering people. In the academy, academic disciplines that have been oriented to public engagement have shown a special affinity with intersectionality. To varying degrees, scholars and practitioners in social work, criminology, public health, law, and education recognize that knowledge production in their respective fields cannot be separated from professional practices. Typically, this means reflecting on how research practices and professional practices mutually inform each other – the contours of the field's practices shape the themes, questions, and concerns of researchers and vice versa. Because they straddle scholarship and practice, academic disciplines with a strong clinical or applied focus have been especially receptive to intersectional frameworks.

Intersectionality often finds a welcome home in fields that already see theory and practice as interconnected. For example, as a profession, social work has a history not just of clinical practice but also of critical praxis (see., e.g., Addams 1994). Social work as a field of study has embraced intersectionality. Edited volumes within the field constitute an important starting point for developing those intersectional analyses (e.g., Lockhart and Danis 2010; Murphy et al. 2009; Sokoloff and Pratt 2005). The journal *Intersectionalities: A Global Journal of Social Work Analysis, Research, Polity, and Practice* describes its purpose as: "to share knowledge and facilitate collaborative discourse amongst social work theorists, practitioners, educators, activists, researchers, and the community members they serve within local, regional and global contexts. The journal seeks to promote social justice by providing a forum for addressing issues of social difference and power in relation to progressive practice, education, scholarly inquiry, and social policy." The expressed focus is to link intersectional analysis to the field of social work: "The journal aims to underscore issues relating to oppression, privilege and resistance in society and social work. Of critical consideration are the ways in which intersections of age, disability, class, poverty, gender and sexual identity, madness, spirituality, geographical (dis)location, rurality, colonialism/ imperialism, indigeneity, racialization, ethnicity, citizenship and the environment are enmeshed in processes of social justice and injustice."

Legal scholarship and practice enjoy a special rapport with intersectionality. Intersectionality's close affinity with critical race theory and LatCrit theory highlights the ways in which scholars in policy-oriented fields have aimed to use intersectionality to shape public practice (Matua 2010). Critical race and LatCrit scholars include Kimberlé Crenshaw, Mari Matsuda, Richard Delgado, Patricia J. Williams, Charles Lawrence, and Regina Austin. The praxis orientation was and still is central to Crenshaw's work and reflects how a broader group of legal scholars and practitioners share social justice sensibilities (Crenshaw, Gotanda, Peller, and Thomas 1995).

The field of criminal justice also incorporates a practice component. As a field that studies the penal system and trains people to work in it, criminal justice holds a complicated and contradictory relationship with its many stakeholders. Criminal justice trains the large numbers of people who manage the penal institutions of a rapidly growing prison industry. For those working in criminal justice, these jobs may be the best jobs available. The criminal justice system also administers the punitive policies that have accompanied the shift away from social-welfare state focus on rehabilitation, a philosophy that offers education, counselling, and the hope that prison may help offenders, to a more punitive neoliberal philosophy that punishes people because they are assumed to be inherently deviant (McCorkel 2013). Criminal justice, through its policies, its scholarship, and its funding ties to nation-states themselves, is one very important site where the effects of neoliberal policies on oppressed groups is most palpable. Given the increasing overrepresentation of racial-ized people within prisons in many countries with multi-ethnic and multiracial demographics, criminologists have looked to intersectionality's analytical frameworks for inter-sectional critiques of mass incarceration.

Education constitutes another so-called applied field – a field grounded in a history of praxis – that has proved highly receptive to intersectionality. Researchers in education tackle questions of how interactions between social inequalities such as race, class, gender, sexuality, and ability shape educational experiences and outcomes of disenfranchised populations. The synergy linking scholarship and practice affects not just teacher training, curriculum design and research on pedagogy for schools, but it also shapes the many sub-specialities within education scholarship.

Public health is another applied field characterized by a growing interest in how intersectionality's focus on complex social inequalities might shed light on health and illness (Schulz and Mullings 2006; Weber and Fore 2007). Because public health remains committed to improving the practices of health care, the challenge for this field lies in integrating intersectional frameworks into clinical practice as well as public policy. Simon Fraser University's Intersectionality-Based Policy Analysis (IBPA) initiative, housed at the Institute for Intersectionality Research and Policy, provides a signifi-cant example of these kinds of initiatives in health. The Institute aims to generate research with direct applicability to Canadian health policy (Hankivsky 2012).

Thus far, this chapter has identified being critical as some-thing that is important to intersectionality. But what does it mean to be *critical*? The qualifier "critical" is important to the ways in which we understand intersectionality as a form of critical inquiry. Dill's study not only contextualizes inter-sectionality's origins in the academy, it also sheds light on the meaning of "critical." As used in this book, the term "criti-cal" means criticizing, rejecting, and/or trying to fix the social problems that emerge in situations of social injustice. Global economic inequality and social inequalities fall more broadly under this umbrella. This concept of critical is drawn from twentieth-century social movements for equity, freedom, and social justice. People who were involved in social movements for anti-colonial liberation struggles, women's rights, racial desegregation, and sexual freedom knew that their ideas and actions mattered. Within the specific historical setting of a desegregating and decolonizing world, being critical required a self-reflexivity of thought, feeling, and action about one's own practice, as well as openness to similar projects. Contemporary scholars and practitioners who are drawn to intersectionality often express similar sensibilities toward social inequality. They seek analyses of social issues that do not merely describe the world but that take a stand. Such projects would criticize social injustices that characterize complex social inequalities, imagine alternatives, and/or propose viable action strategies for change. The scholars who were involved in bringing race/class/gender studies into the academy illustrate this critical sensibility.

Although this book understands intersectionality as a critical endeavor, it is not universally understood and practiced in this way. When it comes to intersectionality, it is especially important to remain mindful of how thinkers and practitioners are being critical. Surprisingly, some projects invoke intersectional rhetoric in defense of an unjust status quo, using intersectional frameworks to criticize democratic inclusion. They can use intersectionality as an analytic tool to *justify* social inequality. For instance, Jessie Daniels's study of white supremacist literature shows how this literature identifies the connections among women, blacks, Jews, "mud people," lesbians, and various forms of mixing as the root cause of the declining fortunes of white men (Daniels 1997). Within this discourse, black men purportedly lead good white women astray, often through sexual seduction. This interracial sexual contact effectively ruins white women yet enhances the status of black men. The "mud people," or mixed-race individuals who result from these unions, present a tangible reminder of the blurring of taboo racial boundaries. Lesbians, who are assumed to be Jewish, push their feminist values on white women. As a result, as depicted in white supremacist literature, the mixing of races, genders, sexualities, and religions contributes to the fall of white men from places of economic and political superiority (Daniels 1997; Ferber 1998). Ironically, intersectionality as an analytic tool is deployed not as a tool for democratic inclusion, but rather to justify racial, ethnic, gender, and sexual segregation and subsequent social hierarchy. The example suggests that if white supremacist discourse can find a way to deploy intersectional arguments, so too can other less contentious projects.

Using the term "critical" is also not necessarily the same as being progressive. These terms are often conflated, leaving the impression that we already know what critical means before we use it. Being progressive (or conservative for that matter) does not mean carrying a toolkit of predetermined "critical" beliefs from one setting to another and thoughtlessly applying them. This can foster a dogmatic form of being critical that borders on policing ideas. Instead, whether specific social actions are in fact critical is measured not through abstract formulas but rather in light of their historical and social context. In 1968, African-American activist Fannie Lou Hamer criticized the racial politics of Mississippi by demanding her right to vote; she paid dearly for her progressive actions. By standing up to racial injustice, she lost her home, was beaten, and jailed. We forget that in 1968 Mississippi, African Americans who tried to exercise their citizenship rights to vote were taking not just progressive but radical action. Their actions did not need an ideological academic stamp of approval. Scholarship and practice that claim terms such as "critical," "progressive," "intersectional," and even "radical" are not necessarily oriented toward social justice.

Although social work, law, criminology, education, and health may be predisposed toward praxis, the practices within a given field may express varying levels of commitment to social justice. Moreover, as the example of the use of intersectionality within white-supremacist literature suggests, intersectionality itself need not embrace a progressive perspective. Some practitioners take up intersectionality to humanize practices in their fields, while leaving more controversial dimensions of intersectionality behind. For example, these fields are all expected to implement social policies influenced by variations of neoliberalism, namely, privatization, shrinking the government sector, deregulation, and holding individuals personally responsible for their own social problems. Working within institutional structures that embrace these ideas makes it difficult to challenge them. At the same time, these fields have varying historical relationships to social justice initiatives that in some places have strong ties to participatory democracy and in other cases reject it. Stated differently, applied fields are not inherently inclined to intersectionality as a form of critical inquiry and practice. Because these fields all have distinctive institutional histories and work in specific social contexts, they also have varying ties to social justice initiatives.

Intersectionality as critical praxis

Practitioners and activists are often frontline actors for solving social problems that come with complex social inequalities, a social location that predisposes them to engage intersectionality as critical praxis. Teachers, social workers, parents, policy advocates, university support staff, community organizers, clergy, lawyers, graduate students, and nurses often have an up-close and personal relationship with violence, homelessness, hunger, illiteracy, poverty, sexual assault, and similar social problems. For practitioners and activists, intersectionality is not simply a heuristic for intellectual inquiry but is also an important analytical strategy for *doing* social justice work.

A praxis perspective does not merely apply scholarly knowledge to a social problem or set of experiences but rather uses the knowledge learned within everyday life to reflect on those experiences as well as on scholarly knowledge. This *praxis* perspective does not separate scholarship from practice, with scholarship providing theories and frameworks, and practice relegated to people who apply those ideas in real-life settings or to real-life problems. Instead, this set of concerns sees *both* scholarship *and* practice as intimately linked and mutually informing each other, rejecting views that see theory as superior to practice.

Groups that are local, grassroots, and/or small-scale may draw upon intersectionality to guide their critical praxis, yet their intersectional praxis can remain understudied. Yet recent scholarship, especially that drawing upon intersectionality, has pointed out the importance of intersectionality within grassroots organizations' political praxis. Several studies have examined various dimensions of coalitions. Take, for example, the work of the Asian Immigrant Women Advocates (AIWA), a progressive community organization in Oakland and San Jose, California. In their historical account of AIWA, Chun, Lipsitz, and Shin provide a vibrant illustration of how women in this social movement use intersectional frameworks to grapple with interlocking forms of oppression (2013: 917). Organized to defend the interests of limited-English-speaking, low-wage immigrant women workers, AIWA avoids political organizing that is structured along discrete ethnic origins and nationalities such as Chinese, Korean, or Vietnamese. They use intersectionality as a tool that allows members various entry points and ways of engagement. In doing so, AIWA promotes an understanding of identities as instruments to be forged and used strategically in complex and flexible ways (918). Their in-depth ethnographic and archival research reveals that the organization uses intersectionality principally in three ways: as an analytic framework to tackle the interlocking arenas of gender, family, work, and nation; as a reflexive approach for linking social movement theory and practice; and as a guiding structure for promoting new identities and new forms of democratic activity among immigrant women workers (2013: 920).

Other community-based organizations form networks or coalitions of like-minded groups, drawing upon intersectionality to shape the logistics of how they organize as well as the political agendas that they pursue. In *Dry Bones Rattling: Community Building to Revitalize American Democracy*, activist sociologist Mark Warren sets out to challenge conventional assumptions that religious intervention in politics can only mean efforts to impose a group's moral teachings on society (Warren 2001). Warren follows the work of the Texas Industrial Areas Foundation (IAF), an interfaith and multiracial network of community organizers. Over two decades, the IAF worked to rebuild some of the most devastated communities. As Warren points out, "If these groups were simply religious advocates for the poor, they would not be very remarkable: America is full of advocacy groups, secular and religious. We lack not advocacy groups, but organizations in which people themselves participate actively in democracy" (Warren 2001: 4). This important network of citizens working within civil society expressed an intersectional analytic sensibility long before the term became fashionable. Also, the IAF network figured out a way to combine faith-based community building with non-partisan political action, a combination that has made the network a premier experiment in reviving democracy.

Generations Ahead, a social justice organization dedicated to expanding the public debate on genetic technologies, also sheds light on the coalitional work that can be part of intersectional praxis. From its inception in 2008 to its closing in 2012, Generations Ahead deployed an intersectional approach to political organizing to address the social and ethical implications of genetic technologies and reproductive genetics. It was one of the few organizations in the United States that worked with a diverse spectrum of social justice stakeholders, namely, reproductive health, rights and justice, racial justice, LGBTQ, and disability and human rights organizations. Organizing based on an intersectional analysis can help forge alliances between reproductive justice, racial justice, women's rights, and disability rights' activists to develop strategies to address reproductive genetic technologies (Roberts and Jesudason 2013: 313–14).

Groups such as the Asian Immigrant Women Advocates, the Texas Industrial Areas Foundation and Generations Ahead illustrate how grassroots and community organizations draw upon intersectional frameworks as part of their critical praxis. These examples show different dimensions of how groups recognize the significance of coalitions and alliances, both within their own organization and across organizations. Well aware of the damage caused by single-issue politics on multiply oppressed populations or, conversely, the effects of a single issue on segments within a given community, intersectionality activists/scholars place difference and multiplicity at the core of their social justice praxis. Groups like AIWA draw upon intersectionality's theme of relationality to shape their internal politics. In contrast, groups such as TIAF recognize that they need to generate new ways of engaging in multi-issue activism and coalitional work. Neither group simply emphasizes difference, but rather redefines it in relation to their praxis. Collectively, these examples illustrate how intersectionality has been important both for grassroots political mobilization as well as for broader social movements.

In other cases, people who are within social institutions work to make intersectionality as critical praxis central to their organization. Intersectional scholars and practitioners have taken aim at government agencies with an eye toward changing the terms of public policy itself (Manuel 2006). The Intersectionality-Based Policy Analysis (IBPA) initiative, developed by the Institute for Intersectionality Research and Policy at Simon Fraser University, is a persuasive example of this kind of enterprise in health research and policy. Seeking to produce research with direct applicability to Canadian health policy, the IBPA aims to make its materials accessible and relevant to stakeholders in health policy arenas. This entails the important work of translating ideas and facilitating collaboration among stakeholders. The IBPA developed a participatory process involving researchers, practitioners, and users of health services. Their mission statement illustrates the aspirations of social actors to bring intersectionality into the public policy arena: "IBPA provides a new and effective method for understanding the varied equity-relevant implications of policy and for promoting equity-based improvements and social justice within an increasingly diverse and complex population base" (Hankivsky 2012).

Human rights constitutes another vitally important arena for intersectionality as critical praxis. The ideas expressed in the 1948 Universal Declaration of Human Rights invoke understandings of intersectionality that promote social justice initiatives. Article 1 affirms that all human beings "are born free and equal in dignity and rights"; and Article 2 states that everyone "is entitled to all the rights and freedoms set forth in this Declaration without distinction of any kind, such as race, colour, sex, language, religion, political or other opinion, national or social origin, property, birth or other status" (Freeman 2011: 5). Yet, because the protected categories gain meaning only in relation to one another, actualizing human rights means transcending the limitations of a strictly legal statement of human rights. With its focus on analysis and action, intersectionality potentially provides an important and critical lens for human rights (Blackwell and Naber 2002; Crenshaw 2000).

Colleges and universities constitute crucial, though often overlooked, sites where intersectionality as critical praxis occurs. Within higher education, rigid distinctions among administrators, faculty, and staff too often make it difficult for these multiple groups to collaborate to create the conditions that make intersectionality as a form of critical inquiry and praxis possible. With much attention paid to the scholarship or research within intersectionality, one can overlook the importance of pedagogy as an important site of intersectionality's critical praxis. Sociologist Nancy Naples's article "Teaching Intersectionality Intersectionally" provides a significant analysis of the pedagogical implications of intersectionality (Naples 2009). In response to the challenges of doing intersectional research, Naples designed a course that not only would introduce her students to the complexities of intersectional scholarship, but would also aim to do so by using an intersectional pedagogy. Naples's extensive experience with ethnographic research made her especially attentive to the process of planning her course and evaluating its trajectory. As Naples points out, "few scholars discuss how to place different intersectional approaches in dialogue with one another. In fact, I wish more scholars who assert an intersectional analysis for their work would make their methodology explicit" (Naples 2009: 573).

Naples also provides an important analysis of the links between methodology and praxis. She identifies feminist sociologist Dorothy Smith's emphasis on reflection, action, and accountability as offering one of the most powerful methodological insights for intersectional research. Naples sees in Smith's work an "intersectional feminist praxis" that foregrounds the ways in which activism or experience shape knowledge, an insight that is often lost when theoretical approaches are institutionalized in the academy. It also reflects the feminist praxis that gave rise to the concept and acknowledges how theory develops in dialog with practice (Naples 2009: 574).

College classrooms may be the place where students first learn about intersectionality, yet their experiences in dormitories, dining halls, libraries, sporting events, and, for those who must work to pay for their education, their jobs become the places where intersectionality is lived. If the ideas of intersectionality hold little meaning for the practice of intersectionality in students' everyday lives, the legion of support staff within colleges and universities who take the form of chief diversity officers down to resident assistants in dormitories have missed an important opportunity for intersectional praxis. College administrators and support staff who implement policies for students or who work directly with students are teachers. College faculty who teach students are also frontline practitioners for intersectionality as critical praxis. Their practices entail multiple courses of action in different but interrelated areas of pedagogy, epistemology, theory, and methodology. They raise important questions about and negotiate tensions between disciplinary knowledge practices (be they pedagogical, epistemological, theoretical, or methodological) and what a critical praxis of intersectionality might need to keep its transformative potential. Collectively, they can engage in intersectionality as critical praxis.

The distinctions between critical inquiry and critical praxis as presented here are rarely as clear cut as people imagine them to be. When it comes to intersectionality, intellectual inquiry itself can constitute a site of praxis (Collins 2012a). Research and scholarship are vital, yet the real work of advancing intersectionality as a form of critical inquiry lies in building a base of undergraduate and graduate students. In this regard, edited volumes, especially readers, are important because they "bundle" readings for students in ways that provide a road map for thinking about a field of study (e.g., Andersen and Collins 2013). As a parallel development, edited volumes draw upon variations of the term "intersectionality" and incorporate selected key articles to help shape this field of inquiry (e.g., Berger and Guidroz 2009). Core texts that explain the main concepts to undergraduates also make important contributions (e.g., Weber 1998). Patrick Grzanka's edited volume not only surveys intersectional scholarship, it also provides a framework that suggests a significant shift in intersectional projects that are honed within the kind of critical inquiry and praxis advocated by the participants in Dill's study (Grzanka 2014).

The synergy of inquiry and praxis

In chapter 1, we briefly discussed how relationality constitutes a core theme of intersectionality that takes varying forms. We indicated that relationality uses many terms such as "coalition," "dialog,", "conversation," "interaction," and "transaction." Because this core idea of relationality traverses much intersectional inquiry and practice, we use this idea of relationality as central to this chapter. Here, the core idea of relationality refers to a synergistic relationship joining intersectionality as a form of critical inquiry and praxis.

The remainder of this chapter contains two very different cases of intersectional synergy. The first examines how using intersectionality as an analytic tool has resulted in more complex understandings of violence. Because violence against women has been such a powerful catalyst for intersectionality itself, and because violence seems increasingly ubiquitous within a global context, intersectional analyses of this topic are not only widespread but have also informed political activism and public policy. Using intersectionality as an analytic tool fosters a broader conception of how heterogeneous forms of violence contribute to social inequality and social injustice (Collins 1998b). Violence constitutes an important theme for seeing how the synergy between inquiry and praxis actually works within intersectionality.

The second case examines intersectional praxis in an unlikely location, namely, the critical praxis that shaped Muhammad Yunus's ideas about microcredit and rural poor people. This case is reminiscent of Latinidades, in that the term "intersectionality" is not central to Yunus's approach to microcredit. Instead, this case shows how critical praxis enabled selected dimensions of intersectionality to unfold.

Violence as a social problem

Kimberlé Crenshaw's groundbreaking article, "Mapping the Margins: Intersectionality, Identity Politics and Violence

Against Women of Color," argues that intersectional inquiry and praxis are both needed to address the social problem of violence against women of color (Crenshaw 1991). Crenshaw's article tapped into a deeper sensibility about the need for new explanations about the shape and effects of violence against women of color that reached out to scholars and practitioners alike. Solutions cannot be found by imagining women as one homogeneous mass, or by painting men as perpetrators, or by focusing exclusively on individuals or state power as sites of violence. Solutions to violence against women remain unlikely if violence against women is imagined through singular lenses of gender, race, or class. For example, gender-only lenses of male perpetrators and female victims, or race-only lenses that elevate police violence against black men over domestic violence against black women show the limitations of non-intersectional thinking.

When it comes to violence, using intersectionality as an analytic tool demonstrates the synergistic relationship between critical analysis and critical praxis. Three examples show how intersectionality shapes anti-violence initiatives. The organization of the One Billion Rising for Justice movement, our first example, illustrates how intersectional frameworks affect the social justice activities of ordinary citizens in many local settings. One Billion Rising for Justice is a global call to women survivors of violence and those who love them to gather safely in community outside places where they are entitled to justice – courthouses, police stations, government offices, school administration buildings, workplaces, sites of environmental injustice, military courts, embassies, places of worship, homes, or simply public gathering places. Women are encouraged to assemble at local places where they deserve to feel safe but too often do not. The movement calls upon survivors to break their silence by releasing their stories through art, dance, marches, ritual, song, spoken word, testimonies, and whatever way feels right. On February 14, 2013, one billion people in 207 countries rose and danced to demand an end to violence against women and girls. On February 14, 2014, they escalated their efforts, calling on women and men everywhere to "Rise, release, dance and demand justice!"

The case of One Billion Rising for Justice illustrates how the growth of global mass media has brought with it a more expansive conception of speech. This understanding of speech includes not just words but also a range of images, lyrics, gestures, and other forms of communication that collectively contribute to an ethos of violence. Some people experience the representations of black women and men within mass-media sites of entertainment, news, and advertising as resembling pornography or hate speech that targets women. Within black popular culture, for example, black women appear as targets of violence. This depiction works to desensitize viewers to the type of violence visited upon countless African-American women and to encourage African-American men (and those who emulate them) that it is their right to engage in such conduct. In the same way that pornography against women is recognizable because it links sexuality to violence, persistent media images of women as sexualized body parts and calls of "bitch in the street" create a climate of hate speech that fosters black women's abuse.

The website and the day of action of One Billion Rising for Justice centers on the needs of women and girls, yet no one woman or category of women stands for the billion. Instead, by using the site and the day to network seemingly unrelated projects, the site claims the multiplicity of experiences that women have with violence. The day of rising's call that women gather in currently unsafe spaces, both private and public, identifies women's work as deeply tied to patterns of violence against women. One Billion Rising for Justice also sheds light on how violence touches everyone's lives; it sees the necessity of organizing all people in support of women. The actions involve women from diverse backgrounds and their loved ones and allies. This is not an exclusionary movement. This movement occurs in a global context where many different groups see freedom from violence as part of a human rights discourse.

The activities of the Center for Intersectionality and Social Policy Studies at Columbia University provides a second example of how the synergy between intersectionality's critical inquiry and praxis shapes anti-violence initiatives. Spearheaded by the actions of Kimberlé Crenshaw, the Center was founded in 2011 to foster the critical examination of how social structures and related identity categories such as gender, race, and class that interact on multiple levels result in social inequity. The first of its kind in the United States, the Center serves an important role in facilitating intellectual dialog between innovative intersectionality scholars, developing cross-disciplinary research networks, integrating intersectional research and analysis into policy debates and social justice advocacy, and developing innovative academic programming and learning opportunities for law students at Columbia Law School and beyond.

The Center has served as the primary research support for the African American Policy Forum (AAPF) for both domestic and transnational affirmative action work in 2012 and 2013. This think tank connects academics, activists, and policy makers in the work of dismantling structural inequality and engaging new ideas and perspectives to transform public discourse and policy. The work of the AAPF promotes frameworks and strategies that address the bases of discrimination as they relate to the intersections of race, gender, and class.

Informed by the intersectional philosophy of its host center, the activities of the African American Policy Forum illustrate a synergy between inquiry and praxis. Violence against black men and boys was an important catalyst for the Policy Forum's actions. The Forum soon learned that addressing violence required a more broad-based initiative. The Policy Forum took the lead in analyzing My Brother's Keeper (MBK), President Barack Obama's racial justice initiative. Launched in February 2014, MBK is designed to address the problems of low achievement and lack of mentoring for young black and brown men. The exclusion of black and brown women from the project generated considerable disappointment and opposition. For many, this exclusion proved how easy it is to overlook intermeshing oppressions that shape the life chances of women of color. In a spirit of solidarity with women, in the months following the formation of MBK, 200 black men signed an open letter to President Obama to express their concerns on the exclusion of black girls and women from the MBK. The signatories have called for "an intersectional initiative" that would emphasize the "denunciation of male privilege, sexism and rape culture in the quest for racial justice." They argued that "the exclusion of girls and women from MBK will once again relegate Black girls and women to the space they have occupied for far too long in the journeys to racial and sexual equity – in the margins" (Thurman 2014). Cognizant of "the multiple forms of oppression experienced by Black women and girls," the men urged that "as a nation, we have to be as concerned about the experiences of single Black women who raise their kids on sub-poverty wages as we are about the disproportionate number of Black men who are incarcerated."

Two weeks after the release of the men's letter, more than a thousand women and girls of color signed a follow-up open letter addressed to the Obama administration calling for their inclusion in the MBK initiative. While praising "the efforts on the part of the White House, private philanthropy, social justice organizations and others to move beyond colorblind approaches to race-specific problems," the signatories expressed their dismay at the exclusion of women and girls of color from this critical undertaking. They argued:

> addressing the crisis facing boys should not come at the expense of addressing the stunted opportunities for girls who live in the same households, suffer in the same schools, and struggle to overcome a common history of limited opportunities caused by various forms of discrimination. We simply cannot agree that the effects of these conditions on women and girls should pale to the point of invisibility, and are of such little significance that they warrant zero attention in the messaging, research and resourcing of this unprecedented Initiative.[3] ("Why We Can't Wait" 2014)

The Center and the African American Policy Forum initiated a broad array of events that drew upon intersectionality as a form of critical inquiry to craft intersectionality as critical practice. For example, the #WhyWeCantWait campaign criticizing the My Brother's Keeper initiative speaks to their efforts to educate the public, organize relevant constituencies, and affect public policy. The African American Policy Forum engaged in conversations, released open letters, published a variety of op-eds, conducted television and radio interviews, and produced a series of nationally broadcast Webinars concerning President Obama's signature initiative. They built a broad-based national campaign calling for the inclusion of girls and young women of color – in addition to boys and young men of color – in the initiative with the belief that:

> any program purporting to uplift the lives of youth of color cannot narrow its focus exclusively onto just half of the community.

The African American Policy Forum has also moved beyond its initial critique of the MBK initiative to make a more forceful and carefully researched case that more attention be paid to black girls. Their 2015 report, *Black Girls Matter: Pushed Out, Overpoliced and Underprotected* (Crenshaw, Ocen, and Nanda 2015), is based on a new review of national data and personal interviews with young women in Boston and New York. Girls of color face much harsher school discipline than their white peers but are excluded from current efforts to address the school-to-prison pipeline: "As public concern mounts for the needs of men and boys of color through initiatives like the White House's My Brother's Keeper, we must challenge the assumption that the lives of girls and women – who are often left out of the national conversation – are not also at risk," said Kimberlé Crenshaw, the report's lead author.

Crenshaw argues that an intersectional approach encompassing how related identity categories such as race, gender, and class overlap to create inequality on multiple levels is necessary to address the issue of school discipline and the school-to-prison pipeline. The study cites several examples of excessive disciplinary actions against young black girls, including the controversial 2014 case of a 12-year-old in Georgia who faced expulsion and criminal charges for writing the word "hi" on a locker-room wall. A white female classmate who was also involved faced a much less severe punishment. According to the most recent data from the US Department of Education cited in the report, black girls in US schools were suspended *six times* more than white girls, while black boys were suspended three times as often as white boys.

The report recommends policies and interventions to address challenges facing girls of color, including revising policies that funnel girls into juvenile supervision facilities; developing programs that identify signs of sexual victimization and assist girls in addressing traumatic experiences; advancing programs that support girls who are pregnant, parenting, or otherwise assuming significant familial responsibilities; and improving data collection to better track discipline and achievement by race/ethnicity and gender for all groups.

A third case of anti-violence initiative also reflects the synergistic relationship between critical inquiry and praxis. More radical anti-violence organizations, such as the INCITE! Women, Gender Non-Conforming, and Trans people of Color Against Violence group, argue that institutionalized violence in all its forms has to be taken into account if one's struggle is to end violence against multiply oppressed groups. In INCITE!'s words, they aim "to end all forms of violence against women, gender non-conforming, and trans people of color and their communities." Their organization consists of local grassroots chapters and affiliates across the United States that work on police violence, reproductive justice, media justice, and similar particular political projects. Significantly, they use a framework of analysis and action called "dangerous intersections":

> Underlying our work is a framework we call dangerous intersections. That means women, gender non-conforming, and trans people of color live in the dangerous intersections of sexism and racism, as well as other oppressions. [...] Movements against sexual and domestic violence have been critical in breaking the silence around violence against women. But as these movements are increasingly professionalized and de-politicized, they're often reluctant to address how violence operates in institutionalized ways and against oppressed people. INCITE! recognizes that it is *impossible* to seriously address sexual and intimate partner violence within communities of color without addressing these larger structures of violence (including militarism, attacks on immigrants' rights and Indigenous treaty rights, the proliferation of prisons, economic neo-colonialism, the medical industry, and more). So our organizing is focused on places where state violence and

sexual/intimate partner violence intersect. (INCITE! n.d.; emphasis in original).

The One Billion Rising initiative, the efforts to intervene in public policy by the African American Policy Forum, and INCITE!'s grassroots organizing agree on the need to address violence and draw upon intersectionality to inform their actions. But the synergy of inquiry and praxis pursued in these cases differs dramatically. The wide differences of opinion that circle around the question of violence that also permeate understandings of anti-violence provide an important window for seeing the synergy between intersectionality's critical inquiry and praxis.

In chapter 1, we argued that power relations are to be analyzed both *via their intersections*, for example of racism and sexism, as well as *across domains of power*, namely structural, disciplinary, cultural, and interpersonal. Violence can be analyzed both via how it traverses intersecting systems of power as well as by how it is organized across domains of power. Across varying social contexts, the use or threat of violence has been central to power relations that produce social inequalities, for example, rape and domestic violence within sexism, lynching within racism, and hate crimes for LGBTQ people. An intersectional analysis reveals how violence is not only understood and practiced within discrete systems of power, but also how it constitutes a common thread that connects racism, colonialism, patriarchy, and nationalism, for example. By questioning how forms of violence within separate systems might in fact be interconnected and mutually supporting, intersectionality's analytical framework opens up new paths of investigation. Because violence has long been a topic of concern for feminists, anti-racist organizers, scholars, community organizers and practitioners across multiple fields of study, intersectional inquiry and praxis offers a more robust understanding of violence.

Finding intersectionality in unlikely places

The work of Nobel-prizewinning economist Muhammad Yunus is not typically seen as connected to intersectionality.

Yet Yunus's critical praxis in working with the poor and his scholarship that advances a new way of conceptualizing and remedying poverty has potential implications for intersectionality.

Yunus is known for creating the idea of microcredit, giving tiny loans to poor people, as a way of helping them. The significance of Yunus's alternative banking system not only helps poor people, it provides a critique of specific aspects of capitalism. Yunus acknowledges that "capitalism is in serious crisis," and identifies the crises in food, energy, and the environment as having a host of immediate economic and physical causes. He states quite clearly, "they all have one thing in common. They all reflect the inadequacy of the current economic system. In each case, we confront social problems that cannot be solved solely by the free market as it is currently understood" (Yunus 2009: 6). Pointing to the major upheaval of the 2008 collapse of large sectors of the global financial system, Yunus states, "[O]ne thing is clear. The financial system has broken down because of a fundamental distortion of its basic purpose" (Yunus 2009: 6).

For Yunus:

> poverty was not created by the poor, but is rather a result of the socioeconomic system we have designed for the world...reliance on flawed concepts explains why the interactions between institutions and people have resulted in policies that produce poverty, rather than alleviate it, for so many human beings. The fault of poverty therefore lies with the top of society, with policymakers and academics. It does not reflect any lack of capability, desire, or effort on the part of the impoverished. (Yunus 2007: 20)

That's a thumbnail sketch of the main ideas of Yunus's scholarship on poverty. We recognize that feminist critiques of Yunus's approaches to poverty raise important points. Yunus is neither a Marxist social thinker, a feminist critic nor an anti-racist scholar. Within prevailing practices of categorizing thinkers in order to engage their ideas as ideas, Yunus does not fit. The radical nature of Yunus's praxis is that he rejects a core framing assumption of capitalism, and, by doing so, creates the space for fresh ideas.

Our concern is less with the substance of Yunus's Nobel-prizewinning economics, or with the scaling up of his ideas in a global context, but rather with how the synergy of critical inquiry and critical praxis shaped his novel approach to poor people and the challenges they faced. We wondered what kind of critical praxis led Yunus to follow this particular line of inquiry. Many people study poverty, yet Yunus did not set out to be a poverty researcher. Many policy makers set out to remedy the poverty that stems from the global economic inequality that we discuss in chapter 1, yet Yunus apparently did not set out to remedy poverty. Yunus did not start out *within* existing interpretive frameworks of intersectionality: he did not advance a gendered analysis of global patriarchy and the feminization of poverty. Nor did Yunus engage capitalism on its own terms, as does the Marxist political economy. So how did he end up with a novel approach to poverty?

In a transcribed version of a talk he delivered at the City University of New York, Yunus describes how he became involved in his project of microcredit for the poor (Yunus 2014–2015). Yunus did not begin working with poor people as a poverty researcher, by identifying questions and arguments within existing frameworks and then "testing" them in the field. Instead, he describes how he started by noticing the poverty around him in rural Bangladesh. Yunus describes how his work began:

> It was not because I was doing a lot of research or that I was a serious faculty member…The circumstances in which I was in Bangladesh, in that university, in that situation, kind of forces you to do something. The situation was so terrible around me, around the campus, around the country. So you feel the desperation of the situation which pushes you into doing something…the university where I was teaching was located right next to villages…so you see the terrible conditions. It's a beautiful campus, but right outside, a terrible village. (Yunus 2014–2015: 87)

Yunus asked himself: "Can I make myself useful to one person, even for a day?" This small question sparked what sociologist C. Wright Mills describes as the "sociological imagination" of biography, history and society (Mills 2000). By beginning small and working from the bottom up of seeing small things, Yunus was able to think outside the box of prevailing economic theory and reframe his understanding of why people are poor. He did not abandon such theory but, rather, also learned to view the world as poor people saw it. With this new angle of vision, Yunus was able to generate new ideas and strategies that helped the poor.

Yunus began doing little things for the villagers near his university and, in the process, began to understand village life and the life of the people. This up close and personal, bottom-up perspective showed how loan-sharking within the village contributed to keeping poor people poor. As a trained economist, Yunus knew that loan-sharking was far bigger than this one village and that it occurred not only within Bangladesh but was a global problem (see, e.g., Bales 1999). Helping poor people under these conditions presented a seemingly unsolvable theoretical and political puzzle. He describes the moment of discovery of thinking outside prevailing economic assumptions:

> Suddenly, it came to my mind that I could do something! And it was a very simple idea, and I went right on ahead. The idea was: Why don't I lend the money so that people can come to me? Then they don't have to go to loansharks. Why just go on shouting and writing articles about loansharking? I can do something by lending my money. (Yunus 2014–2015: 87)

Yunus's strategy of lending his own money to villagers, trusting that they would pay him back, flew in the face of conventional economic theory and practice. Yet the villagers did pay him back. As he lent the returned money to new borrowers, he realized that he could no longer cover the loans with his own money. Poor people who were more economically stable due to the microcredit they received, initially from Yunus and subsequently from one another, became lenders to others who needed microcredit. Yunus had formed a new kind of bank that was based on different principles. The bank was not trying to eliminate poverty, but rather organized poor people to fund one another. Yunus's initial loans grew into the Grameen Bank, a village bank created in 1983 that by 2014 had eight-and-a-half million borrowers. Significantly, the bank was owned by the borrowers.

Relationships among lenders and borrowers differed dramatically from traditional banking. Yunus also describes how the philosophy of the village bank differs from conventional, big banks:

> Conventional banks require collateral, that's a big catch. You have to have lots of money to get lots of money from a bank. On the very first day we said forget it. If you're asking for collateral you are not going reach poor people because those are the people who don't have anything. So we reversed the whole thing; we don't ask for collateral. So how do you do that? We build a relationship between the people and the bank...the entire bank is based on trust. (Yunus 2014–2015: 88)

Yunus's philosophy of how he went about growing what eventually became a global initiative illustrates a synergy between a stance of critical praxis and critical inquiry. His decision to take action, his bottom-up approach to inquiry, complemented his knowledge as a trained economist. Yunus's approach also led him toward intersectionality, but not in traditional ways. Yunus's initial project was to find ways to help poor people within existing capitalist frameworks. But this impetus spurred connections between class and gender: "I just looked at the conventional banks...Once I learned how they did it, I just went ahead and did it the opposite way. And it worked...they go to the rich; I go to the poor; they go to men; I go to women; they go to the city center; I go to the remote villages" (Yunus 2014–2015: 88). The use of the categories of class, gender, and region did not precede his project, but rather emerged from within it, with their utility tested in how they worked. Yunus is using categories of class, gender, and age to solve problems, not to explain existing problems. Moreover, because there is no such thing as a generic poor person, or a generic woman, Yunus's project invoked the multiple, intersecting identities within intersectionality.

Yunus cannot be easily categorized within any one body of scholarship nor any prevailing methodology. His unique analysis and praxis bears further investigation because it touches on themes that also affect intersectionality. For one, Yunus engaged in a form of activist research without needing the framework of activist research or an identity as an "activist researcher" for guidance. His training within economics predisposed him *away* from direct action. Yet Yunus's actions over a thirty-year period of working with the Grameen Bank and its related social businesses resemble features of an activist-research tradition that seemingly had little influence on his project.

Activist scholarship is known by many names, among them, action research, participatory action research, collaborative research, grounded theory, public intellectual work, and engaged research. In the introduction to the edited volume, *Engaging Contradictions: Theory, Politics, and Methods of Activist Scholarship*, Charles Hale argues that research and political engagement can be mutually enriching, and he offers a wide range of disciplinary and interdisciplinary perspectives on how the two have been brought together (Hale 2008). As Hale points out, "the essays gathered here are intended to till a field, not to fill a container" (Hale 2008: 3). His survey of the field yielded a large number of works of the container variety – they attempt to stake out definitional ground and then establish rules, procedures, and best practices, often in the tone of "how-to" manuals. In contrast, the challenge of his edited volume is to "provide a general mapping of how people think about and practice activist scholarship, while leaving the research process fully open to contradiction, serendipity, and reflexive critique (2008: 3). The range of essays in the volume detail the heterogeneity of approach and theme that falls under the heading activist research.

Interestingly, the case of the Grameen Bank and its effectiveness in addressing poverty also resembles the principles of Participatory Action Research (PAR). PAR consists of systematic, empirical research in collaboration with representatives of the population under investigation, with the goal of action or intervention in the issues or problems being studied. PAR draws on the work of critical theorists, such as Paulo Freire, who stress the importance of oppressed people's interrogating and intervening in the conditions of their oppression. PAR is grounded in the epistemological belief that authentic understandings of social problems require the knowledge of those directly affected by them. Local knowledge is essential to all stages of PAR, and outside researchers, from a university for example, are not experts but collaborators who, like their local co-researchers, bring particular skills and knowledge to the research process (Brown and Rodriguez 2009: 1). There is no evidence that Yunus was aware of PAR or saw it as guiding his work. But the idea of working with poor people to define the problems that they face and implementing remedies that work (taking action), and evaluating action by its results (improving poor people's lives as a worthy goal) permeate this case.

The Grameen Bank project resembles some of the classic dimensions of PAR and differs from others. For example, most PAR projects focus on disenfranchised populations and have explicitly political aims. Yunus worked with a highly disenfranchised population yet, while the project had important political implications, its initial goal was not explicitly political. Microcredit does not fit within the prevailing frames of what makes actions political, yet its outcomes had political impact. Similarly, Yunus was a co-partner in working with poor women. Because research was not the primary goal but rather simply a part of the process of helping poor people, this form of activist research could just as easily be described as research-informed activism. The synergy is the strength in the formation of the Grameen Bank.

Next, co-researchers can be involved in many different stages of the PAR process. As PAR scholars Brown and Rodriguez (2009) explain, "Local coresearchers then have an essential role in the conceptualization, design, and implementation of the study, which can change based on factors like the needs of the population being studied, the findings, or the outcomes of the actions. Thus, the research process is more organic and dynamic than in conventional research, where the research design is predetermined and fixed" (Brown and Rodriguez 2009: 2). Comparing PAR to more traditional research methodology identifies some methodological challenges it faces, namely, criticisms that PAR is methodologically unspecified and overly optimistic (Brown and Rodriguez 2009: 4).

Yet the key feature that distinguishes PAR from more traditional research pivots on understandings of action. Action, which can take many forms – workshops, letter-writing campaigns, or influencing policy, for example – should bring about some positive change that is relevant to the study's objectives and findings, to the context in which action occurs, and to the needs, interests, and ways of knowing and communicating of people who participated in the study. The effectiveness of the intervention, which is informed by the data, is a vital dimension for evaluating the validity of PAR (Brown and Rodriguez 2009: 4). Here the Grameen Bank points to action within a sustained trajectory over a long period of time. This is not the episodic action of one study that uses PAR as a method, works briefly with disenfranchised people, then moves on to other methods to study poverty. Instead, Yunus's work with the Grameen Bank constitutes a methodology, a way of working at the synergy of inquiry and praxis that potentially enriches both.

3
Getting the History of Intersectionality Straight?

The histories that most people learn in school typically agree upon points of origin, key figures who played important roles, and noteworthy events that fostered some important outcome. Students take exams that test them on the so-called facts and write term papers on their meaning. These authoritative versions of history may be widely accepted, yet these straight-line renditions of history typically include some groups at the expense of others and emphasize certain experiences over others. People are taught to treat these histories as universal, yet these authoritative histories typically represent partial views of the world. For example, for years, the authoritative narrative of US history focused on the ideas and actions of propertied white men, leaving out everyone else. Certainly including people of color, women, LGBT people, poor people, and undocumented people was an improvement, but correcting the dominant history was not enough. Instead, writing and rewriting the American story reveals more complexity, multiple entanglements, and many intersecting individual and group narratives. What appeared to be straight was far from it.

Intersectionality's history cannot be neatly organized in time periods or geographic locations. Tying authors to particular decades and schools of thought, far from being neutral, divides history into periods which often leads to oversimplified explanations. Instead, this chapter asks, how do certain

histories about intersectionality's origins become authoritative at the expense of others? What kinds of intellectual and
political work do these legitimate accounts achieve in academic and activist settings? What does not getting the history
of intersectionality straight tell us about how power relations
influence intersectionality as a form of critical inquiry and
praxis?

Raising these questions from the outset, we stress that our
aim is not to set the history of intersectionality straight. This
chapter begins in the decades stretching from the late 1960s
to early 1980s, a period of social movement activism in the
United States that catalyzed many of the main ideas of intersectionality. Intersectionality's core ideas of social inequality,
power, relationality, social context, complexity, and social
justice formed within the context of social movements that
faced the crises of their times, primarily, the challenges of
colonialism, racism, sexism, militarism, and capitalist exploitation. In this context, because women of color were affected
not just by one of these systems of power but by their convergence, they formed autonomous movements that put
forth the core ideas of intersectionality, albeit using different
vocabularies.

Many contemporary scholars either ignore or remain
unaware of this period, assuming that intersectionality did
not exist prior to its naming in the late 1980s and early
1990s. Instead, they point to African-American legal scholar
Kimberlé Crenshaw's "coining" of the term as a foundational
moment for intersectionality. Crenshaw's work is very important. Yet we take issue with this view that intersectionality
began when it was named. Choosing this particular point
of origin erases the synergy of intersectionality's critical
inquiry and critical praxis, and recasts intersectionality as just
another academic field. During the 1990s, the period when
intersectionality became institutionalized within higher education, intersectionality's institutional incorporation was
neither smooth nor straight. Often conceived within some
narratives as the seeming advent of intersectionality, the
1990s make sense in relation to the immediate decades that
preceded them. These decades also established a context for
intersectionality's dispersal after 2000.

Intersectionality and social movement activism (1960s and 1970s)

The 1960s and the 1970s constitutes important decades for the elaboration of the core ideas of intersectionality. In the confines of racially and ethnically segregated neighborhoods and communities in the late 1960s, women of color were in conversation/tension with the civil rights, Black Power, Chicano liberation, Red Power, and Asian-American movements. Within these movements, women of color were typically subordinated to men, but also had a titular equality with men that was different than the problems they experienced with racial and class segregation. Importantly, the intellectual production and activism of black women, Chicanas, Asian-American women and Native women were not derivative of the so-called second-wave white feminism but were original in their own right (Roth 2004; Springer 2005). During this period, in the United States black feminists created their own political organizations, using the epithet "black feminist"; and Mexican-American feminists articulated a political subjectivity as Chicana and formed an autonomous Chicana feminist movement (Arredondo, Hurtado, Klahn, Nájera-Ramírez, and Zavella 2003; Garcia 1997a, 1997b).

During the 1970s, African-American women developed intersectional analyses within social movement settings and expressed their ideas in political pamphlets, poetry, essays, edited volumes, art, and other creative venues. Because African-American women had not only participated in but also assumed leadership positions within the civil rights and Black Power movements, they saw the importance of testing ideas within political contexts. Conversely, they used what they learned in social movements to frame analyses of social inequality. Although separated from Afro-Brazilian women by four decades, linguistic difference, and different national histories, African-American women understood that addressing the oppression they faced could not be solved by race-only, or class-only or gender-only or sexuality-only, frameworks. Thus early statements of intersectionality permeated black feminist intellectual production because other women of colour developed similar sensibilities and because a social context of social movement activism provided venues for working on these ideas (Collins 2000).

The core ideas of intersectionality appeared in several key texts. For example, 1970 volume *The Black Woman*, edited by black feminist author and essayist Toni Cade Bambara, stands as a groundbreaking publication that, using a variety of formats, assembled the ideas of African-American women from diverse political perspectives (Bambara 1970). Collectively, the essays point out how black women would never gain their freedom without attending to oppressions of race *and* class *and* gender. Written for the general public, as well as for academic audiences, the fact that the volume was published at all constitutes a significant break with politics that kept black women silent and represented by others. Despite its title, one representing the naming conventions of the times, there was no groupthink among the contributors to *The Black Woman*. Instead, this volume can be seen as one important, albeit overlooked, intersectional text that illustrates how intersectionality incorporated both inquiry and critical praxis.

Frances Beal's essay "Double Jeopardy: To Be Black and Female," published in 1969 as a pamphlet (Black Women's Manifesto), distributed by New York's Third World Women's Alliance, and reprinted the following year within *The Black Woman*, is a signature publication from this period. Beal lays out an intersectional argument to explain black women's lives. Beal starts with a powerful critique of capitalism and refers to racism as its "afterbirth" (Beal 1995 [1970]). Her approach is systemic: her double critique of patriarchy within the Black Power movement and of racism in the white women's liberation movement also criticizes capitalism. Beal's choice of words, the double jeopardy of race and gender, does not leave out capitalism but intentionally situates it on a different plane. Foreshadowing contemporary intersectional scholarship, Beal's analysis of intersectionality examines racism, sexism, and capitalism as social processes (Hong 2008: 101).

Beal's analysis of black women's life experiences, conditions, and subjectivities are firmly based on a conception of identity that is strongly associated with structural forces. She argues:

> It is idle dreaming to think of black women simply caring for their homes and children like the middle class white model. Most black women have to work to help house, feed and clothe their families. Black women make up a substantial percentage of the black working force and this is true for the poorest black family as well as the so-called 'middle class' family. [...] Black women were never afforded any such phony luxuries. Though we have been browbeaten with this white image, the reality of the degrading and dehumanizing jobs that were relegated to us quickly dissipated this mirage of "womanhood." (Beal 1995 [1970]: 147)

Beal is clearly aware of the dirty work of domestic service and agricultural labor that black women have been forced to do because of their location within the social relations of race, gender, and class, and builds her argument on this foundation.

Interestingly, despite Beal's contribution to black feminism as well as to the idea of intersecting oppressions, her ideas remain neglected within most narratives of intersectionality's history. Instead, the Combahee River Collective's (CRC) "A Black Feminist Statement" appears within histories of intersectionality that acknowledge social movement influences on intersectionality (Combahee-River-Collective 1995 [1977]). Originally written in 1977, the CRC Statement lays out a comprehensive framework that permeated black feminist politics for years to come. Reflecting many of the ideas of Beal's pamphlet, this text focuses on how systemic oppressions of racism, patriarchy and capitalism interlock. Unlike Beal's analysis, the CRC Statement also includes heterosexism and places more emphasis on homophobia.

The context for CRC's formation is important for understanding the significance of the Statement. Individual African-American women had expressed black feminist sensibilities for some time. But none had CRC's audience nor social movement setting. For example, the 1840s Sojourner Truth's "Ain't I a Woman" speech is a benchmark for intersectional sensibilities. Truth was an abolitionist and a feminist, yet delivered her most famous speech to an audience of white women.

Truth aspired to be included within feminism, yet the venue in which she delivered her most famous speech contributes to a long-standing perception among black women that feminism is primarily for white women. Anna Julia Cooper, whose brilliant book *A Voice from the South; By a Black Woman of the South* (Cooper 1892) has been reclaimed by black women as a core text of black women, had neither a community of black feminist intellectuals nor a social movement that could transcend the late nineteenth-century politics of respectability. Cooper developed an analysis of black women's experiences that saw intersecting oppressions of race, class, gender, and sexuality, but lacked the resources to make her voice heard (May 2007).

But CRC was different – not only were they a collective, a community of black feminists, they developed their intersectional analysis in the context of social movements for decolonization, desegregation, and feminism. A small group of black lesbian socialist feminists, among them Barbara Smith, Demita Frazier, and Margo Okizawa Rey, initially formed the Collective in 1973 as the Boston chapter of the National Black Feminist Organization (NBFO). Seeing how homophobia within the NBFO limited that organization, the group recognized the gap between their radical political vision for social change and that of the NBFO. They broke off from the parent organization and organized politically as radical socialist black lesbians. Barbara Smith's reflections describe the political and psychological value of autonomous organizing:

> Combahee was really so wonderful because it was the first time that I could be all of who I was in the same place. That I didn't have to leave my feminism outside the door to be accepted as I would in a conservative Black political context. I didn't have to leave my lesbianism outside. I didn't have to leave my race outside, as I might in an all-white-women's context where they didn't want to know all of that. So, it was just really wonderful to be able to be our whole selves and to be accepted in that way. In the early 1970s, to be a Black lesbian feminist meant that you were a person of total courage. It was almost frightening. I spent a lot of time wondering if I would ever be able to come out because I didn't see any way that I could be Black and a feminist and a lesbian. I wasn't

thinking so much about being a feminist. I was just thinking about how could I add lesbian to being a Black woman. It was just like no place for us. That is what Combahee created, a place where we could be ourselves and where we were valued. A place without homophobia, a place without racism, a place without sexism. (Barbara Smith interview in Harris 1999: 10)

Truth and Cooper were people of courage, yet in the absence of widespread collective black activism, neither could find CRC's space of freedom.

From the CRC's perspective, the homophobia within the National Black Feminist Organization required a new organization (Springer 2005: 130). The Statement clearly conveys that they view sexuality as a system of power (heterosexism) which is part and parcel of interlocking systems of oppression, and not an add-on: "A combined anti-racist and anti-sexist position drew us together initially, and as we developed politically we addressed ourselves to heterosexism and economic oppression under capitalism" (Combahee-River-Collective 1995 [1977]: 234). Smith has a sophisticated analysis of capitalism, a fact that is evident in the Statement itself.

Because authoritative histories of intersectionality often start in the 1990s, fifteen years after this Statement, they exclude important ideas that were laid out in this key text of intersectionality. For example, the Statement is the first document to frame identity through an intersectional lens and to present identity politics as a vital tool of resistance. Significantly, CRC's understanding of identity politics is built upon "the multilayered texture of black women's lives" (Combahee-River-Collective 1995 [1977]: 235) that framed the experiences that black women gained by their placement within intersecting power relations. Identity politics politicized a shared structural position through inquiry and praxis:

This focusing upon our own oppression is embodied in the concept of identity politics. We believe that the most profound and potentially most radical politics come directly out of our own identity, as opposed to working to end somebody else's oppression. [...] sexual politics under patriarchy is as pervasive in Black women's lives as are the politics of class and race. We [...] find it difficult to separate race from class from sex

oppression because in our lives they are most often experienced simultaneously. We know that there is such a thing as
racial-sexual oppression which is neither solely racial nor
solely sexual. (Combahee-River-Collective 1995 [1977: 234)

Contemporary renditions of identity politics generally miss
the fact that the identity politics articulated in the Statement
are collective and structural. Moreover, as Norman notes,
"the 'we' of the Statement, like the "we" arising from the
anthologies [such as *This Bridge Called My Back, Home
Girls, All the Women are White...*] as a whole, is not a
homogeneous subjectivity, but a collective space that accounts
for the particularities of location" (Norman 2007: 112). As
the following excerpt makes clear, systemic analysis is central
to the CRC's understanding of the compound nature of the
oppression they grapple with:

> We are actively committed to struggling against racial, sexual,
> heterosexual, and class oppression and see as our particular
> task the development of integrated analysis and practice based
> on the fact that the major systems of oppression are interlock-
> ing. [...] The synthesis of these oppressions creates the condi-
> tion of our lives. As Black women we see Black feminism as
> the logical political movement to combat the manifold and
> simultaneous oppressions that all women of color face. [...]
> We need to articulate the real class situation of persons who
> are not merely raceless, sexless workers, but for whom racial
> and sexual oppression are significant determinants in their
> working/economic lives. (Combahee-River-Collective 1995
> [1977]: 232, 235)

The analysis is not only systemic, pointing to race, gender,
sexuality and class oppression, but also integrated. By using
the terms "interlocking," "manifold," "simultaneous," and
"synthesis," the analysis treats oppression as resulting from
the joint operations of major systems of oppression that form
a complex social structure of inequality. The Collective also
emphasized crafting integrated analytical and political tools
in order to combat interlocking systems of oppression. The
key ideas encapsulated in the Statement operate on two
fronts: theory and politics. Theory is needed but cannot be
the end point, for there are political needs and struggles. The

experiences that emerge from political struggles can catalyze an enriched conceptual vocabulary for understanding inter-secting oppressions, yet unexamined experience is also not enough. The synergy of ideas and actions is important.

Multiple narratives of intersectionality

Given the historical discrimination against women of African descent, it is tempting to grant African-American women ownership over the seeming discovery of the then unnamed intersectionality. However, as stated earlier, in the United States, African-American women were part of heterogeneous alliances with Chicanas and Latinas, Native American women, and Asian-American women. Though their experiences and the social movements they engendered took different forms, these groups were also at the forefront of raising claims about the interconnectedness of race, class, gender, and sexuality in their everyday life experiences.

Chicanas were engaged in similar intellectual and political struggles to create space for their empowerment within the confines of social movement politics (Blackwell 2011). Chicana feminism came of age during the same decades of the 1970s and early 1980s within grassroots activism and in the work of Chicana writers: in 1973, writer and activist Dorinda Moreno edited an anthology of Chicana feminist writings titled *La Mujer – En Pie de Lucha*; and in 1976 and 1977 Marta Cotera published two major monographs for Chicana feminist thought and movement (Cotera 1976, 1977; Garcia 1997b: 8; Moreno 1973). In the early 1980s, Cherríe Moraga and Gloria Anzaldúa edited *This Bridge Called My Back*, an important collection of the writings of radical women of color from different ethnicities (black, Chicana and Latina, Native American, and Asian-American feminists). Like other pioneering anthologies by radical feminists of color of the 1980s, it incorporated articles, essays, testimoni-als, poetry, and artwork (Moraga and Anzaldúa 2015 [1983]). Gloria Anzaldúa's classic volume *Borderlands/La Frontera* not only influenced Chicana cultural theory, it became an important core text for studies of race, class, gender, and sexuality (Anzaldúa 1987). Anzaldúa's work on *mestiza* consciousness, *nepantla* (in-between space), and relationality became important sources of inspiration for the next generation of radical feminist and queer of color scholars and activists and their engagement with intersectionality. Irene Blea's work, *La Chicana and the Intersection of Race, Class, and Gender* (Blea 1992), two anthologies published in the early 1990s edited by Anzaldúa (*Making Face, Making Soul/Haciendo Caras: Creative and Critical Perspectives by Women of Color* [Anzaldúa 1990]) and by Norma Alarcón and colleagues (Alarcón et al. 1993) all contributed to the shaping of intersectionality as an analytical and political orientation within Chicana and Latina feminist thought.

This tradition of collective work, bringing together feminists of color from different ethnic, religious, linguistic, and racial backgrounds, as well as different sexualities and gender identities, in an anthology persists, for example, in the anthology of the Latina Feminist Group, founded in 1993, *Telling to Live: Latina Feminist Testimonios* (2001). This anthology illustrates the vision forged by radical feminists of color of the 1970s and 1980s who sought to foster cross-movement dialogs and engage creatively their differences (class, religious, ethnic, racial, linguistic, sexual, and national differences or different combinations of them), rather than muting them for the sake of (the myth) of unity. As Aurora Levins Morales puts it, they rely on a conception of "women of color" that "is not an ethnicity. It is one of the inventions of solidarity, an alliance, a political necessity that is not the given name of every female with dark skin and a colonized tongue, but rather a choice about how to resist and with whom" (Latina Feminist Group 2001: 100). Through their *testimonios* (testimonies or life stories), the contributors reclaim and regenerate the tradition of knowledge building based on their lived realities, politicizing their identities and fostering coalitional possibilities. As the collective authors point out in the introduction to the anthology, "*testimonio* has been critical in movements of liberation in Latin America, offering an artistic form and methodology to create politicized understandings of identity and community" (Latina Feminist Group 2001: 3).

Creating university courses and programs also played a noteworthy role during intersectionality's formative decades.

For example, University of California at Berkeley and San Francisco State University were important social locations for the emergence and structuring of Asian-American feminism. The launching of the first journal, *Asian Women*, in 1971, originated from the efforts of Asian-American women enrolled in college courses. Besides the *This Bridge* anthology, which included the work of Asian-American feminists, two anthologies published in the late 1980s were important for the formation of Asian-American feminism: *Making Waves* (Asian Women United of California [AWUC] 1989) and *The Forbidden Stitch* (Lim and Tsutakawa 1989) brought together the writings, including short stories, poems, and artwork, of Asian-American women from different ethnic and national backgrounds, specifically, Chinese, Japanese, Filipino, Korean, Vietnamese, and Indian. Other noteworthy examples include Esther Ngan-Ling Chow's article that invokes "cross-pressures" faced by American-Asian women and highlights the importance of a multiple lens; Chow's article examines lived realities of Asian-American women as part of organizing Asian-American feminism (Chow 1987). Lisa Lowe's essay on heterogeneity, hybridity, and multiplicity provides an original conceptualization of Asian-American differences (Lowe 1991). In the 1990s, Asian-American feminism, like Latina feminism, also developed affinities with transnational feminisms. These ties were valuable for questioning the taken-for-granted treatment of categories of nation, nation-state and nationalism within early intersectional thinking.

Indigenous feminisms have been particularly noteworthy in denaturalizing the legitimacy of colonial nation-states and white-settler societies. Indigenous feminist consciousness, as an acquired political standpoint, is not dissociated from questions such as those of indigenous sovereignty and the respect for treaties. The nexus of power they face includes colonialism as well as patriarchy, white supremacy, and poverty. Importantly, indigenous feminisms center anti-colonial practice within their organizing as well as in their discourses. They often express the aim of decolonizing the colonized mentality (interpersonal domain of power), which is captured in the anthology *Unsettling Ourselves* (Unsettling Minnesota 2009). Offering a counter-history of feminism to dominant narratives is a part of this decolonial work. Contesting dominant feminist frameworks that divide feminism into "waves," indigenous feminists argue that they did not appear suddenly during the third wave in order to bring diversity into mainstream feminism. As Andrea Smith, feminist scholar and activist, co-founder of INCITE!, aptly posits:

> This periodization situates white middle-class women as the central historical agents to which women of colour attach themselves. However, if we were to recognize the agency of indigenous women in an account of feminist history, we might begin with 1492 when Native women collectively resisted colonization. This would allow us to see that there are multiple feminist histories emerging from multiple communities of colour which intersect at points and diverge in others. This would not negate the contributions made by white feminists, but would de-center them from our historicizing and analysis. (Smith 2009: 159)

Indigenous/Native studies scholars were also at the forefront of efforts to bring sexuality and queer theory into the field but, unlike other critical conversations between theories/fields, theirs were particularly articulated with questions of indigenous sovereignty and oriented toward unsettling or queering settler colonialism (Driskill, Finley, Gilley, and Morgensen 2011; Rifkin 2011). Needless to say, the spirit presiding over such theoretical dialogs that nourish emergent queer indigenous studies is deeply infused with intersectional thinking and relationality.

Black women, Chicana and Latina women, Indigenous/Aboriginal/Native women, and Asian-American women have distinct histories, yet their activist and intellectual work has also been shaped by collaboration (for example, *This Bridge* anthology). These distinctive social movements by women of color developed systemic understandings of oppression and also focused on personal life experiences that privileged an individual and collective identity politics. For instance, in 1970, the Black Women's Alliance of New York City, in collaboration with the Puerto-Rican women's movement, launched the Third World Women's Alliance. They used the term "Third World" to display their solidarity with ongoing anti-colonialist and anti-imperialist struggles and their opposition to the Vietnam War. In their newsletter named *Triple*

Jeopardy and subtitled *Racism, Imperialism, Sexism,* they clearly identify "capitalism as the context for the triple jeopardy countenanced by women of color," and address the components of triple jeopardy "as systems, not individual identities, oppressions, or experiences" (Aguilar 2012: 421).

Examining how women of color in the United States approached the task of their own empowerment within and across different racial/ethnic communities and in different national contexts demonstrates varying patterns of how race/class/gender/sexuality were negotiated in the context of social movement politics. For example, African-American women and Chicanas confronted the task of incorporating gender into prevailing race/class arguments of the black and Chicano nationalist movements, as well as incorporating race and class into a feminist movement that advanced gender-only arguments. In this context, intersectional analyses concerning race/class/gender/sexuality were honed within and across multiple social movements.

Because they were situated in Britain and were often migrants from different places within the British Empire, women of color or "racialized" women in Britain faced a different set of concerns. They also founded an autonomous social movement forged around blackness as a coalitional political identity: in this context, "black" merged black African, South Asian, and Caribbean experiences of domination (Bryan, Dadzie, and Scafe 1997 [1985]; Mirza 1997). One of the most decisive influences on black women's politics in Britain, the Organization of Women of Asian and African Descent (OWAAD), active between 1978 and 1983, was organized "on the basis of Afro-Asian unity" that the use of the term "black" strived to forge into a coalitional political identity. This did not come without difficulties: internally, it meant finding ways of working with and through differences between women of African and Asian descent who were situated differently in relation to former colonial powers. As Beverley Bryan, Stella Dadzie, and Suzanne Scafe, all veterans of the OWAAD, have made clear: "When we use the term 'Black', we use it as a political term. It doesn't describe the skin colour, it defines our situation here in Britain. We're here as a result of British imperialism, and our continued oppression in Britain is the result of British racism" (p. 43). Despite their commitment to women's empowerment, the OWAAD also explicitly rejected the term "feminism": "We are not feminists – we reject that label because we feel that it represents a white ideology. In our culture the term is associated with an ideology and practice which is anti-men. We don't alienate men because they put down Black women, because we recognize that the source of that is white imperialist culture."

By the late 1970s and into the 1980s, the core ideas in social movement settings began to develop a shared vocabulary, or signifiers of intersectionality. One of the earliest vocabularies of intersectionality is "jeopardy," for example, Beal's (1995 [1970]), discussion of the double jeopardy of race and sex in the context of capitalism. Subsequent variations include "triple jeopardy" in the work of Beverly Lindsay (1979) and in activist publications like the aforementioned newsletter of the Third World Women Alliance (1970), and "multiple jeopardy" in the work of Deborah King (King 1988). Beverly Lindsay argues that the concept of triple jeopardy, namely, the interaction of sexism, racism, and economic oppression, constitutes "the most realistic perspective for analysing the position of black American women; and this perspective will serve as common linkage among the discussions of other minority women" (Lindsay 1979: 328), such as Native American, Chicana, and Asian-American women. Lindsay aims to find a common ground to foster collaboration among women of color. Working within sociology, King uses an array of noteworthy terms such as "multiplicative effects," "interactive oppressions," and "nexus" – a set of synthetically linked elements – which help her avoid the pitfalls of additive approaches and pave the way for the metaphor of intersectionality. There are many other signifiers of intersectionality in these formative years. We have already described CRC's use of terms such as "interlocking systems of oppression," "simultaneous," and "manifold" to describe what Patricia Hill Collins would later call in her book *Black Feminist Thought* "the matrix of domination" (2000). Our close reading of selected works from women of color's intellectual production during intersectionality's formative years uncovers its truly original combination: a way of interconnecting personal experiences and structural analyses of interlocking oppressions without skirting the meaning of life experiences, multiple identifications, and political communities.

What's in a name? Intersectionality's institutional incorporation (1980s and 1990s)

In the 1980s and 1990s, social movements seemingly disappeared, yet this does not mean that political protest disappeared. Activism persisted, although not in the forms it took in the 1960s and 1970s. In the era of visible social movements, people took to the streets and engaged in social protest such as marches, boycotts, press conferences, and demonstrations. They demanded changes in schools, housing, employment, health care, and policing. One important issue across social movements concerned how social institutions not only excluded many social groups from jobs, schooling, and housing but also discriminated against people when they were included. Much of this political activity occurred *outside* these major political institutions, often linked to a demand for fairness through inclusion.

In contrast, in the 1980s and 1990s, social institutions responded to these criticisms of exclusion by recruiting formerly excluded people. Whether willingly or under court order, schools and employers sought to remedy the discriminatory practices that upheld social inequality. One outcome was that political activists moved *inside* those same institutions, often recruited by the same businesses, schools, and government agencies whose exclusionary practices they had protested. People got elected to political office, found jobs at social service agencies, and moved into administrative positions in hospitals, schools, and government agencies. Moreover, these same people were often tasked with fixing the very problems of exclusion that they had identified within social movement settings.

Within colleges and universities, this transition from visible social movement politics to institutional incorporation had important implications for intersectionality as a form of critical inquiry and praxis. African-American women, Latinas,

Asian-American women, women from indigenous groups, poor and working-class white women who had been involved in social movement activism found themselves inside the very same institutions that had formerly excluded them. Within higher education, during the 1980s and 1990s, formerly excluded groups entered colleges and universities as graduate students, instructors, assistant professors, university staff, and administrators. Not all of these political actors brought social movement sensibilities and experiences with them. But many did. Women of color and their allies brought with them ideas such as the multiplicity of oppressions, the importance of identity politics, and the significance of structural trans-formation that shaped their understanding of institutional incorporation into the academy. Like the women in Dill's study of race, class, and gender scholars (see chapter 2), these groups brought a sensibility of "working at the intersections" with them. In essence, social movements themselves may have moved into abeyance, yet this constituted a strategic political shift (Taylor 1989).

Had social movements not fought for the inclusion of women and people of color in colleges and universities, con-ceptions of intersectionality advanced by social movement actors were unlikely to have emerged within the academy. Alice Walker, Angela Davis, Nikki Giovanni, Barbara Smith, and other important figures within black feminism and inter-sectionality had lived experiences with social movements. Gaining access to academic positions enabled African-American women directly to bring ideas from black feminist politics with them into the academy through the dual streams of black feminism and race/class/gender studies. Major works by African-American women that established the ground-work for what came to be known as intersectionality included June Jordan's *Civil Wars* (Jordan 1981), Audre Lorde's classic volume *Sister Outsider* (Lorde 1984), and Angela Davis's groundbreaking volume *Women, Race and Class* (Davis 1981). In works such as these, one can see how black women's intellectual production contained an explicit analysis of the interconnectedness of race, class, gender, and sexuality as systems of power that were explicitly tied to varying social justice projects catalyzed by their involvement in social movement politics (Collins 2000). Gloria Anzaldúa's book *Borderlands/La Frontera* was also immensely important during this period of incorporation, providing important categories of analysis such as *mestiza* consciousness and *nepantla* (in-between space) (Anzaldúa 1987).

When black feminists and similar political actors from social movement politics entered academic environments, they not only brought ideas that were honed in social movement settings. They also encountered academic norms that were antithetical to many of these ideas. Ideas from social movement settings, such as the significance of social inequality as an important subject of study, attending to interconnected power relations, and the value of social justice as an ethical framework, simply did not match prevailing norms of bona fide scholarship. When black feminism, Chicana feminism, and similar social justice initiatives became incorporated into the academy, their primary focus on social justice, which had been taken for granted within social movement politics, could no longer be assumed. Within social movement settings, the Combahee River Collective, for example, had no need to make a case that social justice mattered – they began their analysis with this assumption. In contrast, institutional incorporation for race/class/gender studies meant defending the social justice and political sensibilities of heterogeneous social movements within an academic context with its own sensibilities concerning politics and ethics.

The initial naming of the field as race/class/gender studies reflected the unstable relationships among various social movements, each of which was engaged in trying to figure out its relation to the other, now occurring within colleges and universities. By this expansion into the academy, "race/class/gender" found itself fighting for space and legitimacy within prevailing academic politics. As academic incorporation progressed, the strategies and arguments associated with race/class/gender studies shifted. Survival within academia meant recasting the dynamic, messy politics associated with social movements into race/class/gender studies as a more recognizable field of academic study. Initially, race/class/gender studies and similar interdisciplinary projects aimed to transform the academy (Dill, Zambrana, and McClaughlin

2009; Parker, Samantrai, and Romero 2010). Yet, over time, it became apparent that institutional transformation would be easier to imagine than to achieve.

This interim phase of race/class/gender studies in the 1980s confronted the dilemma of holding fast to forms of critical inquiry and praxis honed within social movements, yet adhering to the norms of academia. Race/class/gender studies also confronted new challenges in the academy. First, colleges and universities staunchly resisted the incorporation. Recall Dill's observation that incorporation was "done in the face of indifference and hostility. Scholars engaged in building programs in women's studies, ethnic studies, and in lesbian, gay, bisexual, and transgender studies have had their intellect, their scholarship, their professionalism, and even their sanity questioned" (Dill 2009: 229). Second, the relations between various study programs were far from harmonious. The various new fields of study often inherited distinctive histories and bodies of scholarship explaining social inequality, and the concept of race/class/gender challenged these approaches. Some of the early attempts at coalition building within the academy faced the intellectual and political challenges of trying to work across the boundaries that separated these fields. For example, the classic article "The Cost of Exclusionary Practices in Women's Studies" analyzes some of the issues of intersections of race and gender within women's studies (Zinn, Cannon, Higginbotham, and Dill 1986). How would this field with the placeholder name of race/class/gender negotiate these far-reaching, dynamic, and often contested concerns? Finally, could race/class/gender studies continue its intellectual growth without some sort of common framework? How would the emerging area of sexuality studies work with this interdisciplinary endeavor? An umbrella term could serve as a marker to distinguish critical projects drawing from social movement sensibilities from those that did not.

Using the term "intersectionality" to name the field seemingly addressed these challenges. A new umbrella term might enable coalition building among the exponentially growing study area of race, class, and gender. Naming the field might also help legitimate the kind of scholarship produced within these areas by making it more compatible with academic norms of discovery, authorship and ownership. Attributing the discovery of the term "intersectionality" to Kimberlé Crenshaw fits these academic norms (Crenshaw 1989, 1991). Via her authorship of two journal articles, Crenshaw is credited with naming intersectionality as a credible form of inquiry. The language that is used to describe her work, namely, that Crenshaw "coined" the term, fits within academic norms of ownership of cultural capital.

Stock stories of the emergence of intersectionality routinely claim that Kimberlé Crenshaw "coined" the term "intersectionality" in her *Stanford Law Review* article "Mapping the Margins: Intersectionality, Identity Politics, and Violence against Women of Color" (Crenshaw 1991). Like law students and legal scholars who helped launch the field of critical race studies, Crenshaw was ideally positioned to write this particular article. She was familiar with social movements both outside and inside the academy. Her grounding in law provided an expansive view of law both as a site of repression and as a site of social justice. She also saw the possibilities offered by the so-called linguistic turn within social theory in the 1990s. Legal arguments are narratives, a particular kind of storytelling that is linked to structural power relations.

Because Crenshaw's 1991 article is most often cited as the point of origin for intersectionality, it constitutes a pivotal document in marking the translation of understandings of intersectionality emanating from black feminism and similar social justice projects, and understandings of intersectionality within the academy. Yet a close reading of Crenshaw's 1991 article serves to bridge understandings of intersectionality as a form of critical inquiry and praxis honed within social movement settings, and intersectionality as a legitimate field of academic inquiry. Stated differently, Crenshaw seemingly "coined" the term "intersectionality," but her groundbreaking work did far more than this. Crenshaw's article identifies an important marker that shows not only intersectionality's growing acceptance in the academy, but also how this acceptance subsequently reconfigured intersectionality as a form of critical inquiry and praxis.

Several features of Crenshaw's 1991 article foreshadow subsequent focal points within intersectionality, some of which have been warmly embraced, others of which remain points of contention within the field (for an expansive discussion of these ideas, see Collins and Chepp 2013). First, Crenshaw focuses on the experiences of women of color, a devalued group from the perspective of the academy, as well as within broader US society. Crenshaw argues that the experiences of women of color are important in and of themselves, but become especially significant in understanding and remedying important social issues. Crenshaw works within the tenets of standpoint epistemology, acknowledging that experience matters, not simply in incorporating the experiences of individual knowers, but also in seeing women of color as differentially placed as knowledge-creators (Collins 1998a: 201–28). Distinctive angles of vision and challenges accompany differential social locations, a theme developed via Crenshaw's attention to the different experiences that women of color have with domestic violence. All discourses come from a particular standpoint, yet those of women of color are often obscured.

Second, Crenshaw places herself within her narrative where she self-identifies as a "black feminist." Via this move, Crenshaw signals a particular epistemological stance for scholars, especially scholars of color, who engage in black feminism, race/class/gender studies and/or intersectional knowledge projects. Experience and embodied knowledge are valorized, as is the theme of responsibility and accountability that accompanies such knowledge.

Third, Crenshaw argues that the needs of women of color cannot be met by looking at one category of analysis. Crenshaw's innovation lies in building her argument from the ground up from the experiences of women of color and then showing how multiple systems of power are inseparable in the ways they impact their lives. Mutually constructing systems of power produce distinctive social locations for individuals and groups within them. In this case, women of color's multiple identities position them differently within complex social inequalities than white men or white women.

Fourth, Crenshaw's article expresses a social justice ethos that assumes that more comprehensive analyses of social problems will yield more effective social actions in response. Why write this article on women of color and violence at all, if not to provide some insight for social justice initiatives?

Fifth, Crenshaw's article contains an emphasis on relationality. By introducing the term "intersectionality," Crenshaw questions the nature of the relations between and within the entities that are intersecting. Crenshaw draws from the ideas of women of color developed in actual social movements who came to see that this issue of relationships was crucial – it was not enough to have a common enemy; rather, they had to figure out patterns of interconnectedness. Crenshaw's argument carries this nuance in that she includes several groups under the umbrella category "women of color," with attention to the specificities and commonalities of their experiences with domestic violence. Because they had to figure out how various individuals and social movements might work together, this attentiveness to relationality and its significance for coalitional politics is significant.

To sum up: Crenshaw's article: (1) identifies several main ideas of intersectionality that reappear across intersectionality as a form of critical inquiry, for example, relationality, power relations, and social justice; (2) demonstrates how to use intersectionality as an analytic tool; and (3) marks an important transitional moment within intersectionality's history. In other words, it shows what persisted, what became muted, and what disappeared (Collins 2015).

Kimberlé Crenshaw's "coining" of the term turned out to be a pivotal moment for intersectionality, but not in the way that is currently understood within an emerging canon of intersectionality's history. Across numerous journal articles, one sees the same language of "coining" repeated verbatim. These practices not only routinely neglect the writings and activities of many people who came before Crenshaw, but they also misread the full extent of Crenshaw's arguments. They also ignore Crenshaw's subsequent work which has advanced intersectionality as a form of critical inquiry and praxis (see, e.g., the discussion of Crenshaw's work with the African American Policy Forum in chapter 2 and her involvement within a global human rights setting in chapter 4). Crenshaw builds upon the ideas of Combahee not only to name intersectionality, but also to: (1) draw links between individual identity and collective identity; (2) to keep a focus on social structures; (3) to theorize from the ground up (versus from the top down) the case of violence against *women of color* as a set of experiences with structural, political, and representational links; and (4) to remind readers that the purpose of intersectional scholarship lies in its contributions to social justice initiatives. Crenshaw is clearly advocating for intersectionality as a social justice construct, not as a theory of truth disconnected from social justice concerns. Yet this aspect of Crenshaw's work is increasingly neglected.

Crenshaw's 1991 article may have been so well received, in part, because it demonstrated the ability to fuse the sensibilities of social movement politics and its commitment to social justice initiatives with sophisticated theoretical perspectives, in particular, the growing significance of postmodern and post-structuralist analyses within the late-twentieth-century US academy and beyond. Crenshaw thus spoke to two primary audiences within academia. First, her work spoke to activists/scholars whose social movement sensibilities embraced the social justice ethos of intersectionality, for example, race/class/gender scholars and those in the emerging field of critical race studies. Second, the post-structuralist, narrative dimension of her analysis was also well received by scholars who saw the value of narrative traditions and truth-telling. Crenshaw's piece thus aimed to challenge academic norms. Yet, for many of its readers, it also fit comfortably within them.

Crenshaw's article provides a useful snapshot of an important moment of transition for contemporary canon formation when intersectionality as an ostensibly novel construct travelled into the academy and had to adapt to its new social context. Ironically, as the structural contours of social movement politics of the 1960s and 1970s receded into the past, intersectionality's incorporation into the academy in the 1990s seemingly uncoupled intersectionality from its social justice moorings and overshadowed understandings of intersectionality as critical praxis. Intersectionality as a form of critical inquiry and praxis shifted from bottom-up knowledge projects, reflected in Crenshaw's ability to draw from grassroots politics, to top-down knowledge projects whose structural contours were increasingly shaped by the normative practices of the academy.

When the term "intersectionality" began to be used in the 1990s, it seemed to be a good fit for this emerging form of critical inquiry and praxis that worked in border spaces between social movements and academic politics. Yet naming also raised a new challenge that was associated with straightening intersectionality's history. Contemporary renditions of intersectionality's past increasingly bypass altogether the heterogeneous forms that intersectionality took during the period of social movement politics. Instead, they confine themselves to locating a point of origin in the early 1990s *within* the academy, typically by identifying Crenshaw as intersectionality's foremother, and then constructing a straight-line narrative from that point of origin. Intersectionality seemingly didn't exist until it was discovered by academics and named and legitimated within the academy. Via institutional amnesia that rewrites history, entire categories of people who were central to intersectionality's inception become erased from the intersectional canon.

What might explain intersectionality's patterns of incorporation, especially its rapid reception after it got a name? One would think that during the pivotal decades where neoliberalism gained legitimacy, an increasingly market-oriented university would not welcome women's studies, race/class/gender studies, black studies, ethnic studies, and similar projects that criticized the academy. Paradoxically, the opposite happened. Through incorporation, universities seemingly suppressed the transformative and potentially disruptive dimensions of these critical projects (Bilge 2014).

Here, returning to the varying ways that intersectionality can be critical, as discussed in chapter 2, becomes important. Some scholars see intersectionality as a tool for critical intervention and use intersectionality as an analytic tool to facilitate important institutional changes within their universities and related social institutions. For example, Canadian sociologist Olena Hankivsky supports "diversity mainstreaming," arguing that integrating intersectionality into all stages of health policy formation fosters holistic equality in health policy-making processes (Hankivsky 2012). Likewise, in assessing an Equality and Diversity Mainstreaming program in Northern Ireland, Bagilhole (2010) argues that intersectionality is useful for avoiding prevailing gender-first approaches. Some scholars argue that intersectionality would benefit from a better disciplinary integration, for instance in political science (Hancock 2007a, 2007b) and in the sociology of stratification (Walby 2007; Yuval-Davis 2011b). Others are more skeptical about the positive outcomes of institutionalizing intersectionality, suggesting that incorporation depoliticizes and co-opts intersectionality (Erel, Haritaworn, Rodriguez, and Klesse 2008). Yet many scholars see institutionalization as a complex issue that should be tackled with caution.

Other scholars point out specific problems with intersectionality's institutional incorporation. Some claim that the forms of black feminism and intersectionality that are increasingly institutionalized within the academy are no longer critical enough (Alexander-Floyd 2012; Bilge 2014). Yet such criticism does not imply that counter-histories, such as the one presented here that connects intersectionality to social movements, romanticize intersectionality's pre-institutional period as if it were unaffected by power's operations of capitalism and the state.

We make no effort to resolve these tensions but point instead to certain strategies that might help. In this chapter, we offered a critical reading of intersectionality's history by claiming at the outset that there is no one legitimated story. We also presented a critical reading of intersectionality's legitimated history that shows the effects of how what's missing shapes contemporary understandings of what intersectionality is becoming. For instance, the close readings presented here of Beal's race and gender analysis as embedded in capitalism, the robust identity politics as holistic social justice praxis advanced in the works of the CRC, and Crenshaw's understandings of intersectionality as a form of critical inquiry and practice illustrate how different histories of intersectionality might foster different contemporary understandings of what intersectionality is. In this chapter, we examine lesser known texts precisely because their framing assumptions are being lost on a new generation of intersectionality scholars and practitioners. In many cases, people are simply unfamiliar with the works from this period prior to intersectionality's naming, in part because their history of intersectionality begins with Crenshaw's coining, and in part because intersectionality itself has grown so exponentially.

The fundamental dilemma of institutional incorporation lies in the tension between aiming to bring about institutional transformation, yet being aware that one is changed in the process of trying. In his discussion of Cultural Studies' institutional trajectories, Stuart Hall asks an important question:

> what happens when a field [...] defined as a political project, tries to develop itself as some kind of coherent theoretical intervention? Or to put the same question in reverse, what happens when an academic and theoretical enterprise tries to engage in pedagogies which enlist the active engagement of individuals and groups, tries to make a difference in the institutional world in which it is located? (Hall 1992: 284)

Intersectionality's institutional incorporation also requires attending to both continuities and breaches between the ways that intersectionality has been understood and practiced at different stages of its development in different national and institutional contexts.

What difference can and does intersectionality make in higher education? How is intersectionality itself changed when it tries to change the institutional practices of the academy? Like other forms of critical inquiry and praxis that initially cast a critical eye on the academy, intersectionality confronts the ongoing challenge of being disciplined by normative academic practices (Bilge 2014). Put another way, within the neoliberal university, intersectionality has been invited to settle down within, instead of unsettling, the established frames of knowledge production and dissemination. Does this shift represent a seemingly successful absorption of intersectionality that suppresses its initial social justice commitment? Or does it reflect the strategic choices of social justice-oriented knowledge projects that have found new ways to survive within an increasingly conservative academy?

4
Intersectionality's Global Dispersion

The year 2000 marked an important milestone for the global dispersal of intersectionality. In the new millennium, intersectionality entered an era of internationalization by moving into international diplomacy and human rights governance. Intersectionality also gained wider academic acceptance within and beyond the English-speaking world, earning it the label of a fast travelling theory (Knapp 2005). Today, digital and social media constitute one of the most vibrant scenes of intersectionality where a new generation of activists, artists, and scholars debate its intellectual and political significance.

By examining three important channels of diffusion and cross-fertilization, this chapter explores this broad dispersal of intersectionality as a form of critical inquiry and praxis. First, the chapter traces intersectionality's global dispersal within human rights and equality policy arenas. An important shift has occurred, one where intersectional analyses of social inequality no longer occur solely within national policy frameworks. Instead, human rights perspectives increasingly draw upon intersectionality as an analytic tool to address social inequality within a global context.

Second, by focusing on intersectional scholarship, the chapter builds on earlier conversations about intersectionality's entrance into the academy and its institutional incorporation. Intersectional frameworks have changed the terms of scholarly conversation across many fields of study. Because intersectional scholarship is too vast to be surveyed here, the chapter identifies some important issues to consider.

Finally, intersectionality has travelled into digital media. New information and communications technologies (ICTs) have changed the terrain of intellectual production and political action for individuals, nation-states, businesses, and social movements. Intersectionality has become a hotly debated topic on the Web. We present a small sample of this material.

Overall, this chapter examines how intersectional frameworks have travelled into three very different interdependent venues that place different emphases on inquiry and praxis. Stated differently, these three cases illustrate the synergy between intersectionality as a form of inquiry and as critical praxis.

Intersectionality and human rights

The preparations for the 2001 United Nations World Conference Against Racism (WCAR) in Durban, South Africa played an important role in intersectionality's dispersal in human rights venues. In May 2000, the first United Nations Preparatory Committee that took place in Geneva included representatives from Brazil, India, Portugal, United Kingdom, Israel, Guatemala, Philippines, Mali, and Uganda. This committee invited Kimberlé Crenshaw to present a position paper and organize a training workshop (Crenshaw 2000). Following the Geneva meeting, references to intersectionality in the international arena became increasingly common. For example, in December 2000, the Citizen's Conference Against Racism and Preparatory Intergovernmental Meeting of the Americas in Santiago, Chile, also preparing for WCAR, introduced intersectional frameworks into UN human rights agendas. Other groups also prepared for Durban by commissioning background papers, some of which contributed to intersectionality's dissemination in UN human rights venues. For example, a background paper commissioned by the International Gay and Lesbian Human Rights Commission analyzed intersectional oppression in relation to race and sexual orientation.

Kimberlé Crenshaw's involvement in preparatory work for the World Conference Against Racism made a major contribution to intersectionality's dispersal in global venues. Crenshaw's background paper was crucial for the history of intersectionality:

> it marks the inclusion of intersectional theory, research, and politics at the highest levels of international diplomacy. Though it may be an overstatement to call this "mainstreaming," because the uptake of Crenshaw's recommendations have been mixed, the consideration of intersectionality at the level of the UN and in more than rhetoric signifies an undeniable degree of political legitimacy and recognition for the movement. Furthermore, Crenshaw's work for the UN (among other human rights and social justice organizations) embodies key tenets of Black feminists' original configuration of intersectionality as an activist project for social transformation. (Grzanka 2014: 16–17)

The importance of Durban for intersectionality's global reach cannot be overstated. Imagine some 10,000 delegates from all around the world, with women in the majority, learning about each other's struggles. Representatives from the South African landless movement, the Dalit struggle in India for the rights of lower-caste groups, indigenous movements, and the Intifada, the Palestinian uprising against the Israeli occupation, all attended. These representatives brought multi-issue frameworks that reflected the complexity of their lived experiences and political struggles. Whether the term "intersectionality" was used or some other terms captured its essence, intersectionality gained a global platform for dissemination and development.

The full title of the conference, The United Nations World Conference against Racism, Racial Discrimination, Xenophobia, and Related Intolerance, was itself historic. The term "related intolerance" linked racism to its intersections with poverty, gender discrimination, immigration, and homophobia. After decades of struggle to gain recognition for the gendered impacts of racism, xenophobia, and violence, this meeting was the first UN-sponsored conference against racism to include "related intolerance" (Blackwell and Naber 2002: 240).

By 2000, the core elements of intersectionality were already present within the international human rights arena (Yuval-Davis 2006). The World Conference Against Racism drew upon the ideas expressed in the 1948 Universal Declaration of Human Rights. Intersectionality seemingly aligned with existing UN policy prescriptions for equal rights and anti-discrimination. Article 1 of the 1948 Declaration affirms that all human beings "are born free and equal in dignity and rights"; and Article 2 states that everyone "is entitled to all the rights and freedoms set forth in this Declaration without distinction of any kind, such as race, colour, sex, language, religion, political or other opinion, national or social origin, property, birth or other status."

Feminist activism for women's rights, as well as feminist preparations for the 2001 World Conference Against Racism and the activities of the conference itself, were important in heightening interest in intersectionality within UN circles (Grzanka 2014; Yuval-Davis 2006). The World Conference Against Racism could build on prior UN conferences on the status of women. The Beijing Declaration at the Fourth World Conference on Women (1995) constitutes one of the earliest translations of the idea of intersectionality, though not the term, into UN language. The declaration asks governments to "intensify efforts to ensure equal enjoyment of all human rights and fundamental freedoms for all women and girls who face multiple barriers to their empowerment and advancement because of such factors as their race, age, language, ethnicity, culture, religion or disability or because they are indigenous people" (United Nations 1995).

In many countries, in particular those with substantial racial/ethnic diversity, preparations among women's organizations for WCAR drew more attention to internal differences and tensions, as well as to the exclusions of dominant strands of feminism prevailing in the country. The Afro-Brazilian Women's movement was engaged in a long-standing effort to bring a black feminist movement into being and grappled with issues of dealing with both the Black Movement and the mainstream Brazilian feminist movement (Carneiro 2002). Just as the Afro-Brazilian movement developed its own analysis of its own needs and goals, one that drew upon intersectionality as inquiry and critical praxis, other local, regional, and national women's groups engaged in similar projects. These movements aimed to address the social problems associated with global social inequality. They recognized the particular constellations of power relations of race, class, gender, sexuality, religion, age, ability, and citizenship categories in their specific social contexts. And this recognition enabled many of them to negotiate the political differences that separated them. The Afro-Brazilian women's movement is not unusual in this regard, but it does provide a closer look inside the political projects of groups as they prepared for WCAR.

Despite these differences, or perhaps because of them, the preparations for the conference paid off. Article 119 of NGO Forum Declaration at the 2001 World Conference Against Racism included a definition of an intersectional approach to discrimination:

> [It] acknowledges that every person be it man or woman exists in a framework of multiple identities, with factors such as race, class, ethnicity, religion, sexual orientation, gender identity, age, disability, citizenship, national identity, geo-political context, health, including HIV/AIDS status and any other status are all determinants in one's experiences of racism, racial discrimination, xenophobia and related intolerances. An intersectional approach highlights the way in which there is a simultaneous interaction of discrimination as a result of multiple identities. (WCAR NGO Forum 2001)

This statement marked a watershed moment for intersectionality's global dispersal. Yet the gains of Durban were larger than its declarations and official documents. The process enabled feminists around the globe to articulate race, gender, and poverty with human rights (Falcon 2012).

Incorporating intersectionality into an overarching global human rights framework gave nation-states a more defined mandate to revisit their equality policies. Across different ideological perspectives, e.g., neoliberal, democratic, or socialist, governments constitute primary sites where human rights policies and practices take form. In 2000, the European

Union (EU) adopted legally binding directives about discrimination on the grounds of race and ethnicity, as well as of age, disability, sexual orientation, and religion (Krizsan, Skjeie, and Squires 2012: 2). The adoption of these new directives fostered the spread of a new institutionally integrated approach to discrimination. Across Europe, different national bodies use intersectionality as an analytic tool to shape their public policies concerning equality. In the United Kingdom, the incorporation of gender, race, disability, sexual orientation, religion or belief, and age into equal opportunities and diversity legislation has led to the creation of a new single equality body for Great Britain (England, Scotland, and Wales) (Bagilhole 2010). The adoption of new directives prompted equality policy reforms in many countries – some of them creating new equality bodies that would enforce equality legislation on all prohibited grounds of discrimination. The British Equality and Human Rights Commission, for example, gathers under one roof efforts to challenge discriminations based on gender, race, disability, age, religion or belief, and sexual orientation or transgender status. Policy analysts often look to intersectionality as a new institutional model to address multiple or complex inequalities. Thus mainstreaming intersectionality is a significant step forward within the equality policy arena because it helps avoid the dominant single-issue, gender-first approach (Bagilhole 2010; Hankivsky 2007).

A closer look: intersectional frameworks and human rights policy

The policy prescriptions of the UN's trajectories and the national policies of EU nation-states show how intersectionality as a form of critical inquiry and praxis is being negotiated on the macro-level of analysis. But putting teeth into policies and legislative mandates requires thinking through how people try to use intersectional frameworks. A closer look at one of many meetings within a global human rights context where people try to figure out how to use intersectionality reveals how challenging using intersectional frameworks can be.

In 2013, approximately 25 people from diverse backgrounds in law, advocacy, and academia assembled in a conference room at the Center for Reproductive Rights at Columbia University's Law School. They had been invited to attend a one-day symposium on "Intersectionality in the Inter-American Human Rights System (IAHRS)." The talent around the table was remarkable, including representatives from organizations such as Wangki Tangni, created to serve the needs of the Miskito community in Nicaragua, Disability Rights International, Amnesty International, Programa de Acción por la Igualdad y la Inclusión Social (Colombia), as well as representatives from law school programs such as the International Women's Human Rights Clinic at the City University of New York Law School, the Human Rights in the US Project, and the Center for Gender and Sexuality Law projects at Columbia University Law School.

The meeting itself was convened by Tracy Robinson (Jamaica) and Rose-Marie Belle Antoine (St Lucia), two elected commissioners representing the Inter-American Commission on Human Rights (IACHR). Robinson and Antoine were responsible for specific areas that would help IACHR monitor compliance of nation-states covered by the Organization of American States (OAS) with inter-American human rights treaties. The Commission was often the first point of contact for petitioners who might pursue human rights claims before the court. As rapporteurs to IACHR assigned to different areas of interest, the two commissioners supervised different areas of human rights concerns. Robinson oversaw activities dealing with the rights of women, as well as the rights of lesbian, gay, bisexual, trans and intersexed persons. Antoine served as rapporteur for claims dealing with the rights of Afro-descendants and against racial discrimination as well as the rights of indigenous peoples. The issue that became clear to both Robinson and Antoine was that many human rights claims did not fall squarely into any one of their four areas. Both commissioners recognized that the ways that gender, sexuality, race, and ethnicity were understood within the courts limited their ability to bring redress for human rights violations. They decided to work together; the meeting was one step in that process.

Robinson opened the meeting by identifying three important themes that would help commissioners to be more effective in addressing human rights issues. First, she pointed to the need for more effective tools for identifying discrimination. In a world where petitions for human rights violations could be brought under various categories, it was difficult to conceptualize what discrimination meant. When discrimination is legally framed either by sex, gender, or race, how does one best serve people who bring claims that touch on more than one ground of discrimination? Second, Robinson identified the need for better assessments of pain, suffering, and injury. What types of pain and suffering are appropriate for bringing a human rights claim? In what ways do questions of human dignity matter? A third issue concerned the search for appropriate reparations and remedies to victims of human rights abuses. What are state responsibilities if harm has been documented and suffering has occurred?

Commissioners Robinson and Antoine recognized the limitations of a strictly legal statement of human rights, and that the protected categories gained meaning both through intersectional frameworks and their effects on praxis, for example, remedies for people who are harmed. The meeting attendees were charged with the task of analyzing how intersectionality's emphasis on the ways in which axes of social division work together and influence one another might shape human rights. How might intersectionality contribute to better conceptualizations of discrimination, suggest ways to address the damage done by intersecting oppressions, and provide guidance for remedies or redress for human rights violations?

As the day unfolded, participants engaged Robinson's questions, primarily by discussing specific cases that shed light on various dimensions of intersectionality and human rights. Participants presented cases for discussion in sessions on gender and sexuality; gender and race, ethnicity, and migration; and gender and indigenous people. A closer look at actual cases revealed recurring themes. Across many of the cases, actual violence, the threat of violence, variations of state violence, and denial of human dignity re-emerged as core themes. Human rights violations had occurred against women who were raped, or children who were removed from their families by state action, or indigenous people who were displaced from land. Vulnerability was not an absolute category – whereas women were central to the cases selected for presentation, it was clear that the generic category of woman obscured more than it revealed. Specifically, some women were more vulnerable than others if they were indigenous, black, poor, and young. The categories of ethnicity, race, economic status, and age did not line up pristinely.

The cases under consideration showed the success of the Human Rights Court, as well as the challenges of using intersectional frameworks. One could see the workings of intersecting systems of power in shaping the lives of people who had experienced human rights violations as well as the significance of court remedies. For example, the 2005 case of *Dilcia Yean and Violeta Bosico v. Dominican Republic* claimed human rights violations for two girls of African descent who were rendered stateless by the Dominican Republic's citizenship policies. Born in the Dominican Republic to mothers who were also born in the Dominican Republic, the girls had Haitian fathers and Haitian maternal grandfathers. The Dominican government rejected the girls' mothers' efforts to register their daughters' birth certificates that are required for most things in the Dominican Republic (e.g., cell-phone contracts, school, and marriage). Because no domestic remedies existed in Dominican courts, the case came before the international court. The court also sought guidance concerning three cases that involved the rape of young girls. The three cases of *Rosendo Cantú et al. v. Mexico* (1994–2001), *Fernández Ortega et al. v. Mexico* (2001–2010), and *Ana, Beatriz and Cecelia González Perez v. Mexico* (2002–2010) showed how indigenous peoples became subject to violence during the militarization of Guerrero and Chiapas in Mexico. Recognizing that compensating the individual victims was not enough, two of the cases granted significant reparations at the community level.

The complexities of cases such as these suggested that addressing Commissioner Tracy Robinson's three issues required far more than a one-day meeting. Participants at the meeting faced the challenge of analyzing human rights law and practice in order to see: (1) what intersectionality means and what it requires in terms of government obligations;

(2) how it has been applied in practice; and (3) how it can and should be reflected within the IAHRS (through decisions, reports, recommendations, and remedies ordered by the Inter-American Court and the Inter-American Commission). These ideas obviously could not be developed in one day, but the fact that the meeting was held at all provides an important angle of vision on ongoing initiatives within intersectionality as a form of critical inquiry and praxis.

Several features of the meeting highlight the significance of contemporary efforts to examine links between human rights policies, state-based equality policies, and intersectionality's potential contributions. First, intersectionality has expanded beyond the civil rights framework suggested in Crenshaw's early articles (Crenshaw 1989, 1991) to a human rights framework within a transnational context, as explored in her position paper for the Durban conference (Crenshaw 2000). The human rights community is moving beyond civil rights advocacy that petitions the nation-state for redress to human rights advocacy that appeals to international and intergovernmental organizations such as The Hague International Criminal Court. The focus on social issues appears to be the same. What appears to be different is the recognition that the state can no longer lay claim to solving social issues as understood within intersectional frameworks.

Second, the engagement of intersectionality and human rights has potential implications for sharpening conceptions of social issues as potential human rights violations. Advocates for important social issues such as citizenship rights, reproductive justice, the exploitation of child labor, mass incarceration and prisoners' rights, environmental justice, and migrants' rights can claim the ethical protection of the UN Declaration of Human Rights and pursue remedies in organizations such as the Inter-American Commission on Human Rights (IACHR). Human rights-based frameworks can come with their own sets of problems, such as placing too much reliance on judicial processes or seeing social injustice as an individual versus a collective matter. This is why examining the specific social context of the Symposium on "Intersectionality in the Inter-American Human Rights System" is so important – the social actors around the table recognized the complexities of collective social harm, as well as the limitations of their own ability to remedy harm. As leaders of advocacy organizations, legal scholars, and community organizers, they collaborated in order to see how multiple points of view could produce results.

Third, a significant feature of efforts to develop human rights initiatives informed by intersectionality concerns how people aim to incorporate the ideas of intersectionality into their fields of practice, often by embracing a critical praxis approach. For example, neither lawyers nor heads of advocacy groups nor grassroots activists who attended the Symposium had all the answers. The meeting affirmed the need for collaborative work that takes seriously the points of view of stakeholders on a particular social issue.

Finally, this case exemplifies intersectionality's emphasis on social justice. People who work on violence against women come to grasp that solutions cannot be developed by seeing women as a homogeneous group, or by focusing either on interpersonal relations or on state power as sites of violence. Thus intersectional analyses help illuminate important global trends in the matters of social justice, understanding intersecting power relations, and human rights. Stated differently, intersectionality as a form of critical inquiry cannot flourish by separating itself from its critical praxis.

Intersectionality's dispersal in scholarship

The evidence of intersectionality's presence within academia is everywhere. By the early 2000s, heightened interest in intersectionality fostered numerous journal articles, special editions of journals, edited volumes, and undergraduate anthologies. Because interest in intersectionality has grown exponentially and expanded in so many directions, many scholars and practitioners are unaware of the breadth of intersectional scholarship. Intersectionality's widespread scholarly dispersal and its effects on academic production, disciplinary traditions and boundaries is a vast subject. Intersectional scholarship takes many forms: books and dissertations that cover a broad range of themes,[1] anthologies and edited volumes for undergraduate courses and the general public,[2] peer-reviewed and scholarly journal articles,[3] and a number of special editions of scholarly journals across various academic disciplines.[4]

The *term* intersectionality is certainly being dispersed. Yet one important question facing intersectionality concerns how this dispersal influences the scholarship in the academy. What are some important issues to consider in thinking through patterns of intersectionality's dispersal in scholarship?

One important issue concerns how scholars across academic disciplines and interdisciplinary fields use intersectionality as an analytic tool to rethink important social issues and institutions. Earlier case studies demonstrate how using intersectionality as an analytic lens creates new interpretations of topics such as the FIFA World Cup as a benign sporting event, mainstream perceptions of capitalism (chapter 1), and conceptions of violence that bring together inquiry and praxis (chapter 2). Each illustrates how the questions at hand shape the kind of intersectional analysis that ensues. We also highlight the importance of how ideas that develop within local and global social contexts of praxis, for example, Bonnie Thornton Dill's study of the institutional incorporation of race, gender, and class studies in higher education (chapter 2), the neglect of the ideas of the Combahee River Collective within intersectional scholarship (chapter 3), and honing the meaning of intersectionality in a global human rights framework (this chapter), also make important contributions to scholarship. As we move through this book, we provide additional examples of using intersectionality as an analytic tool. If we assembled our examples and included more, we would find many different intersectional approaches, most tailored to the questions, histories, and pathways taken by various fields. There is no one intersectional framework that can be applied to each field. Rather, varying academic fields of study take up different aspects of intersectionality in relation to their specific concerns.

In some cases, intersectionality provides new direction for rethinking existing areas within a traditional discipline. Take, for example, the ways in which US sociology engaged themes of race, class, and gender. Because American sociology developed in a political and intellectual context of race and gender segregation, the overall organization of the discipline, as well as the core themes and practices of its first hundred years, perceived race, gender, and class as different and seemingly unrelated axes of social division (Collins 2007). Sociological subdisciplines of class, race, and gender understood each area as distinctive and typically paid scant attention to one another. For example, if the study of marriage and the family was "covering" women, why should the subfield of race and ethnicity concern itself with gender? If African-American experience was studied within race, there was no need to include race as a major explanatory framework in either mainstream studies of social stratification or Marxist critiques of it. If the whiteness of immigrant groups was taken as the norm, the assumptions of whiteness that underlay the construct of US ethnicity need not be studied. Rather, class cleavages associated with varying levels of assimilation and upward social mobility could form the focus of investigation. As a result, these long-standing distinctions between sociological subdisciplines of class, race, and gender shaped their analyses of social inequality. Because the sociologists associated with stratification (class), race, and gender worked within social conditions that were segregated, this logic of separation shaped their organization. Thus studies of stratification/class, with their emphasis on dominant understandings of work and occupations, largely reflect the widespread tendency to equate white male experiences with society overall. For race and ethnicity, questions of culture prevailed, especially concepts of assimilation drawn from the experiences of white ethnic groups. For gender, white women found themselves either restricted to the so-called helping profession of social work and/or relegated to their so-called natural sphere of family by studying family. Preoccupied with the level of interpersonal family dynamics, gender analyses remained contained by the language of social psychology and individual social interaction. Overall, the non-intersectional approach of each area limited its ability to consider the ways in which other areas might shape its distinctive concerns.

Intersectionality pushed the boundaries of sociology within the discipline to examine connections between race, class, and gender, as well as sociology's ties with other disciplines. By the 2000s, sociologists had begun to produce important work that used intersectionality as an analytic tool. For example, sociologist Evelyn Nakano Glenn accomplished a sociological synthesis of race, class, gender, and nation in her ground-breaking book *Unequal Freedom: How Race and Gender Shaped American Citizenship and Labor* (Glenn 2002). Yet the path to this work was not easy. Glenn describes how she cobbled together strands from different fields of study and intellectual traditions for her scholarship:

> As I struggle to formulate an integrated analysis of gender, race, and class, I have relied on a historical comparative approach that incorporates political economy while taking advantage of the critical insights made possible by poststructuralism. I use a social constructionist framework, which considers how race, gender, and class are simultaneously constituted in specific locations and historical periods through "racialized" and "genderized" social structure and discourse. I try to inhabit that middle ground... by looking at the ways in which race, gender, and class are constituted *relationally*. (Glenn 1998: 32; emphasis added)

In this passage, Glenn provides a backstage look at the changing contours of what it meant to do intersectionality within social science. Glenn's work synthesizes areas within sociology – she brings sociological traditions of race, class, gender, and nation together. But she also realizes that interdisciplinary engagements would strengthen her approach to race, class, gender, and nation. She draws upon a "historical comparative approach that incorporates political economy," a decision that points her toward history, especially labor history and workers' rights. Glenn also takes advantage of the "critical insights made possible by poststructuralism," an area of social thought that stresses narratives. One important contribution of post-structuralism lay in reviving interest in a "social constructionist framework," one that is closely aligned with intersectionality's emphasis on power relations. Significantly, Glenn points to the practice of working relationally.

A second issue to consider related to intersectionality's dispersal in scholarship concerns how placing interdisciplinary fields and intersectionality in dialog can raise issues for both. For instance, scholars in critical disability studies use intersectionality to criticize the whiteness of the canon and epistemology of the disability studies field. Conversely, disability studies are used to tackle the absence or the perfunctory use of disability in intersectionality scholarship. This kind of critical cross-conversation has the potential to expand and enrich intersectionality theoretically and epistemologically. For instance, Nirmala Erevelles's work provides an original conceptualization of disability's entanglements with axes of power (2011). Her approach provides a complex frame of relationality in which disability works as an ideological cornerstone for understandings of race, gender, and sexuality. Erevelles situates this complex frame of relationships within global class relations and capitalist modes of production.

Similarly, queer of color scholars use intersectionality to supplement both intersectionality and queer theory (see, e.g., Battle, Cohen, Warren, Fergerson, and Audam 2002; Cohen and Jones 1999; Ferguson 2012). They use intersectionality as an analytic tool to criticize queer theory for its implicit whiteness and its rejection of identities as important political categories. Instead, queers of color see the politically strategic use of collective identities as well as their psychic importance for queer and trans people of color in a racist society with racist LGBTQ communities. Conversely, queer scholars of color use queer theory to challenge the normativity that is found in some intersectionality scholarship. This entails understanding how the term "queer" unsettles the very idea of normal behavior – "queer" hence becomes a set of actions, a verb, not something one is or has. Foregrounding antinormativity in intersectionality creates space for new questions about how power operates but also for understanding how social hierarchies can be resisted. This understanding of queer also makes it difficult for dominant groups to normalize intersectionality, to assimilate it into "business as usual." In this sense, these thinkers "queer intersectionality" itself (Bilge 2012).

A third issue to consider related to intersectionality's dispersal in scholarship concerns how dispersal fosters new debates among scholars. Take, for example, the issue of intersectionality's connections to gender and feminism. In North America, where there is a tradition of critical race theory, intersectionality has evolved more holistically, not exclusively as a gender theory. This North American social context that privileges race and nation explains how many scholars take up issues of gender and social class. For example, over the past decade, considerable intersectional scholarship has focused on Hurricane Katrina and its aftermath. The majority of scholars who take up intersectionality as an analytic lens on Hurricane Katrina emphasized its class and racial politics, pointing to government action or inaction as a marker for nation (see, e.g., Hartman and Squires 2006; Johnson 2011). Gender has been part of the analysis, but it has not been a determining feature of the Hurricane Katrina analysis. Gender need not be central to intersectional analysis. In 2012, for example, *Ethnic and Racial Studies* published a special edition devoted to the theme "Class, Nation, and Racism in England and Britain." In a framing essay titled "Thinking Across Domains," the editors aimed to refocus attention on British national identity and its connection to white racism and to British understandings of class.

At the same time, intersectionality remains strongly associated with women and gender studies, primarily because women's studies faculty and students have been standard-bearers for advancing intersectionality as a form of critical inquiry and praxis in the academy. Despite this prominence, has the attention paid to gender within intersectionality created unexpected problems for intersectionality itself? When Kathy Davis, a prominent feminist thinker, published an article titled "Intersectionality as a Buzzword: A Sociology of Science Perspective on What Makes a Feminist Theory Successful," her article defined intersectionality as a feminist theory (Davis 2008). Is intersectionality a form of feminist theory, similar to socialist feminism, liberal feminism, or lesbian feminism? Or do feminist theories themselves constitute a gendered analysis that is better categorized under the umbrella of intersectionality?

The ways in which intersectionality is tied to gender are neither obvious nor smooth. This is especially true in Europe, where it has become a cliché to declare intersectionality the brainchild of feminism (Bilge 2013). Take the call for papers for the *Italian Review of Sociology* for its planned special issue on intersectionality (March 2016) under the editorial direction of two senior sociologists, Enzo Colombo and Paola Rebughini. The call presents intersectionality as follows: "The notion of intersectionality has been present in international debate for at least twenty years, but only in recent times this concept has spread beyond the field of gender studies where it was originally elaborated." What is notable is that these sociologists acknowledge the potential of intersectionality for disciplinary sociology provided that its analytical range be extended: "The idea of intersectionality represents nowadays an important analytical device in sociological theoretical debate and research not only in gender studies and discrimination, but also in the investigation of social stratification and social agency."

Finally, dispersal within the academy raises important definitional debates concerning what counts as intersectionality (Collins 2015).[5] A renewed focus on methodology constitutes one outcome of these definitional debates within intersectional scholarship. Students, faculty, and scholars who aim to use intersectionality as an analytic lens wonder whether the methods they are using are in fact "intersectional." For graduate students and researchers, the core question concerns *how* intersectionality can be conceptualized *within* a particular research design that is simultaneously attentive to the core themes of intersectionality and that makes a good faith effort to deploy intersectionality as an analytic tool in the face of such uncertainty.[6]

These definitional debates are far from benign because they speak to what counts as intersectional scholarship and what criteria determine what counts. Seemingly simple questions can foster big controversies. For example, does gender always have to be present for intersectional scholarship to be intersectional enough? Does race always have to be included? Does a study that uses more social divisions, for example, class and sexuality and age and ethnicity, provide a superior approach than a study that uses fewer categories?

Digital debates: intersectionality and digital media

New information and communication technologies (ICTs) have been a game changer for both individuals and social movements. The development of Web 2.0 and the spread of applications that go beyond the display of static content foster interactive communities of users who can add, edit, and update content. By transforming the practices and blurring the boundary between producer and consumer, the rise of digital and open media has opened up new spaces for debate. Not surprisingly, a term as visible and contentious as intersectionality has become the object of heated debates in digital spheres. Hence, intersectionality has a noteworthy digital presence, particularly on social media platforms, which provide substantial opportunities for users to create content. Here we examine intersectionality's dispersal through digital media by a close look at three related trends: (1) debates within cyberfeminism that question intersectionality's accessibility to people outside the academy; (2) analogies that seem associated with intersectionality, such as "gay is the new black"; and (3) the shape of a Twitter campaign launched by women of color that criticized the racial politics of feminism and the gender politics of African-American social and political thought.

Intersectionality and cyberfeminism

The contested treatment of intersectionality within cyberfeminism constitutes one site of digital controversy. Digital media, especially social media platforms such as Facebook and Twitter that create web-based communities, have changed the face and the average age of feminism. For many feminist groups, writers, and activists, feminism is taking on new forms that have a strong digital presence. In an article in *Bluestockings Magazine* titled "Is the '4th Wave' of Feminism Digital?," Ragnar Jónsson contends that digital media, including the blogosphere, digital news media, and social media networks, have entirely changed "the operations, economics, communications, readership, outreach and presentation of feminism" (Jónsson 2013). Despite this expansion, until the early 2000s, cyberfeminism was largely perceived as a set of practices launched by an "educated, white, upper-middle-class, English-speaking, culturally sophisticated readership" within digital media, with references to the intersection of gender and race "exceedingly rare within both cyberfeminist practices and critiques of them"

(Fernandez, Wilding, and Wright 2003: 21). Cyberfeminist debates assumed that, because they are viewed as a gender homogeneous category, by implication, digital technologies had to mean the same thing to all women across differences of race, class, and sexuality (Daniels 2009: 103).

More recently, this cyberfeminist perspective on gender and feminism has come under scrutiny, mostly by the steady online presence of feminists of color who have become the key advocates and developers of intersectionality. The popularity of digital magazines and especially of blogs run by feminists of color, such as *Colorlines, The Feminist Wire (TFW), Racialicious, the Crunk Feminist, For Harriet, Black Girl Dangerous*, and *Janet Mock's Blog*, shows the vitality and relevance of intersectionality as a form of critical inquiry and praxis for the social justice projects advanced by women, queer/gender non-conforming and trans persons of color. Individuals from these groups offer a wealth of intersectional analyses of topics as varied as popular culture (*Racialicious*), housing justice, Black History Month (*For Harriet*), and President Obama's My Brother's Keeper initiative (*the Crunk Feminist*), or #BlackLivesMatter (*TFW*).

Within cyberfeminism, debates over intersectionality underscore feminist fault lines that divide along racial lines, although they masquerade occasionally as class divisions, for example, when intersectionality became swept up in feminist reactions to Caitlin Moran's bestselling autobiography (*How to Be a Woman*, 2011). Defenders of Moran's book decided to show the superiority of Moran's "easy-and-fun" populist feminism by using intersectionality as a straw man. They framed intersectionality as an elitist term, as an "esoteric theory" that was too abstract and abstruse for those outside the ivory tower. Ironically, this charge against intersectionality, made mostly by young white feminist bloggers, is diametrically opposed to white feminist academics' criticism of intersectionality, more prevalent in Europe, that intersectionality is not a "mature theory," and that it should be "elevated" theoretically (Bilge 2013). Via these strategies, white feminists devalued intersectionality: for its lack of theorizing and for its excess of theorizing, the first argued by disciplinary feminists in the academy and the latter by (self-declared) populist cyberfeminists.

In an October 2012 *New Statesman* article titled "In Defence of Caitlin Moran and Populist Feminism – Some Educated Women Seem to Want to Keep Feminism for Themselves and Cloak it in Esoteric Theory," two young white British cyberfeminists defend Moran's book by bashing intersectionality. The authors of the article, Rhiannon Cosslett and Holly Baxter, founding editors of online magazine *The Vagenda* and the *New Stateman*'s regular feminist blog, The V Spot, argue that "issues of race, class, religion, sexuality, politics and privilege often end up fracturing feminist dialogue, most regularly causing disagreements between those armed with an MA in Gender Studies and a large vocabulary to match, and those without." For them, intersectionality could not achieve "genuine equality" because, unlike Moran's easy and fun prose, ordinary women found it inaccessible. They argue:

> In the last few weeks some have been bandying about the oft-quoted phrase 'my feminism will be intersectional or it will be bullshit'. We would suggest that anyone with an interest in genuine equality for all adapt that phrase to 'my feminism will be comprehensible or it will be bullshit.' Achieving 'intersectionality' is impossible unless you can communicate clearly, with everyone. Moran at least speaks a language that we all understand. And how many other feminists can you credit with that? (Cosslett and Baxter 2012).

Ironically, in their criticism of intersectionality, the authors misappropriate the work of a feminist of color, Flavia Dzodan (2011), "My Feminism will be Intersectional or It will be Bullshit!", without due credit.

Following the controversy that their article raised, in a November 2013 *Guardian* column titled "I'm a Half-Arsed Accidental Feminist," Cosslett reasserts intersectionality's alleged inaccessibility. Now she claims to reject the word, not the idea:

> Part of our work with the Vagenda has involved visiting schools and universities to chat to young women about just what it is about feminism they find so distasteful. They told [. . .] that feminism is angry and scary and difficult and 'not for them', and that feminists aren't feminine or sexy and that they hate men. Frankly, anyone who doesn't think feminism

has an image problem or doesn't need "rebranding" [...] can't see the nose in front of their face. [...] After talking to these young women, we wrote a column criticising academic feminists' use of alienating terms such as "intersectionality" on the basis that most people don't understand them. "Intersectionality" basically means taking into account the way different systems of oppression – race, class, disability, sexual orientation – relate to one another. The article raised issue with the language, not the concept, but because we deigned to criticise the method of communication, we were deemed racist. (Cosslett 2013)

Flavia Dzodan (2014) documents how this tactic of "rejecting the term, not the concept" has become common within white cyberfeminism, particularly among gatekeepers. By rejecting the term "intersectionality," these feminists strip women of color of their conceptual tools and reinforce cultural cloning – "speak our language, use our words" – which also keeps white feminist issues/vocabularies at the forefront of feminist discourse and action:

At the core of this rejection of the word but not "the concept" is a rejection of knowledge produced and developed by Black women and other Women of Color. Since in the face of overwhelming evidence these white feminists cannot deny that racism is alive and kicking, then they will do the next best thing: deprive us of the use of words that help us explain how we are uniquely affected by these power structures. [...] *at the core of this denial resides an erasure of our tools, the very fabric of the theories and knowledge that explain our lives.* [...] "Use our words because otherwise our issues will not be front and center." (Dzodan 2014; our italics)

The critique of intersectionality among white feminists that took hold of digital media in 2013 and continued in 2014 (particularly acute in the British context) was self-fashioned as a commitment to democratize feminism. Misreading intersectionality as a privileged tool, feminism would be improved by discarding intersectionality, and, by implication, all who advocate for it. One peculiar example from this cyberfeminist debate provides a feel for how threatened some feminists apparently are by intersectionality. In a vitriolic article entitled "Don't You Dare Tell Me to Check My Privilege", columnist Julie Burchill argues:

> intersectionality is actually the opposite of socialism! Intersectionality believes that there is 'no such thing as society' [*à la* Margaret Thatcher!] – just various special interests. [...] Intersectionality, like identity politics before it, is pure narcissism. [...] Here's hoping that the in-fighting in-crowd of intersectionality disappear up their own intersection really soon, so the rest of us can resume creating a tolerant and united socialism. (Burchill 2014)

These two examples show that a new framing is in progress – one that reverses the positions of the privileged and the marginalized within the feminist movement. No longer disenfranchised, women of color become the oppressors of uneducated white women via their alienating word – intersectionality – or get in the way of the socialist dream with their intersectional anthem and flawed identity politics.

Is gay the new black?

Another site of digital controversy concerns the resurrection of the tendency to draw parallels between the experiences of oppressed groups for the purpose of advocating on behalf of one's own group. Under this logic, one need not actually have the experiences of oppression but can appropriate them in the abstract in defense of one's own disadvantage. For example, the claim "gay is the new black," a new analogy that revamps the old ones and breaches the most basic premise of intersectionality: analogies such as these erase multiply disenfranchised groups. On the surface, this kind of analogy can seem benign, the first step in intersectional engagement where two sides recognize one another's struggles in a move toward solidarity. When Brazilian protesters chant "the love is over, Turkey is right here," and Gezi protesters proclaim "Everywhere is Taksim, resistance everywhere," these groups reference each other's struggles as part of a growing transnational solidarity. But this analogy means something entirely different. If gay is the new black, then what about black gay people? Or black lesbians? Or transgender Latinos? Intersectional scholars have argued that this kind of framing through analogy obscures the experiences of people who fall between the cracks of the analogy, the case, for example, of LGBTQ people within African-American communities (Cohen 1999).

After the *New York Daily News* published an opinion article by John McWhorter entitled "Gay Really is the New Black" (McWhorter 2013), the "gay is the new black" debate gripped the internet. McWhorter's piece generated substantial internet controversy and even earned its own hashtag #GITNB. Yet the catchphrase "gay is the new black" has a longer history. It emerged as a rallying cry within white-dominated gay activism in the context of California's passage of Proposition 8, which would ban same-sex marriage, and get repeated on the cover of the December 16, 2008 issue of *The Advocate*, the flagship gay publication. The cover proclamation, "Gay is the New Black: The Last Great Civil Rights Struggle," compared gays' fights for same-sex marriage with the African-Americans' civil rights movement. This assertion relies on a long-standing analogical thought pattern that equates heterosexism to racism.

Criticizing this kind of analogous thinking has been a cornerstone of intersectional thought and praxis. In the nineteenth century, African-American women Sojourner Truth, Anna Julia Cooper, and other activists and educators denounced comparisons of women and blacks. During the 1960s and 1970s, black women criticized their erasure from multiple social movements, an exclusion that catalyzed black feminism. Yet this analogical thinking that categorizes people as being only one thing, continually resurfaces. For example, during the 2008 US electoral campaign, reporters repeatedly asked African-American women the question: "Are you going to vote for Barack Obama or Hillary Clinton? And why?" This question barely masks the real one: "Are you going to vote for Obama because he's black like you or Clinton because she's a woman like you? Which part of yourself is most important?"

Significantly, proclaiming 'gay is the new black' buys into the post-race myth that fallaciously declares that racism has lapsed, so we may self-congratulate and move to the next checkbox. "Racism is fixed. Next up? Gay rights." Seemingly progressive claims like Gay Is The New Black (#GITNB) develop therefore new (anti-intersectional) analogies from the old patterns, which uphold, instead of challenging, the post-racial and post-feminist hegemony espoused by both liberal and conservative forces.

Race, gender, and Twitter

Our last digital debate returns to patterns of exclusion with pre-existing political groups, namely, the lack of race consciousness in mainstream feminism, and the lack of gender consciousness in African-American social movements. In the summer of 2013, black feminist bloggers launched Twitter hashtags that went massively viral. First, there was #SolidarityIsForWhiteWomen started by writer Mikki Kendall, followed by #BlackPowerIsForBlackMen initiated by Jamilah Lemieux, digital news and life editor of the magazine *Ebony*. The first was born out of Kendall's frustration with the complicity of influential white "digital feminists," such as Jessica Valenti, the founding editor of the blog Feministing.com, the most widely read feminist online publication with a readership of more than six hundred thousand. Despite Schwyzer's persistent smear campaign against outspoken feminist bloggers of color, white cyberfeminists helped Hugo Schwyzer, a self-declared "ally" of feminism, build his platform and access to major feminist digital media outlets. Kendall (2013) wanted a Twitter shorthand to stand for how often feminists of color are told that racism "isn't a feminist issue." She wanted it to initiate a discussion between people impacted by Schwyzer's bullying and white feminist complicity with it.

Unexpectedly, the hashtag became a huge success on Twitter, expanding on other social media and inspiring further initiatives taking issue with other intersectional erasures, for example, Lemieux's #BlackPowerIsForBlackMen targeted (hetero)sexism and misogyny that black women face within black male-led social movements; the hashtag #NotYourNarrative started by Rania Khalek and Roqayah Chamseddine to criticize western media's portrayal of Muslim women; or #NotYourAsianSidekick launched by Suey Park in support of Asian-American feminism. Park affirms having started the hashtag because she is "tired of the patriarchy in Asian-American spaces and sick of the racism in white feminism." Clearly, the reasons behind the launching of these hashtags resemble the catalysts that encouraged the Combahee River Collective and Afro-Brazilian women to ground a movement in collective identity politics.

As these cases illustrate, social media-savvy young feminists of color increasingly use intersectional frameworks to challenge various forms of the intermeshed oppressions they face. Intersectionality has become for many contemporary black feminists "the primary tool through which we articulate our understanding of how social inequalities are created and sustained, a key concern being that such an analysis should become normative practice for the wider movement rather than a niche concern of a minority constituency" (Okolosie 2014: 90). Social media, particularly Twitter and the feminist blogosphere, play an important role by providing platforms for feminists of color who hitherto rarely had access to larger audiences. Gaining popularity on social media can also prompt the careers of these black feminist bloggers, helping them publish in more traditional venues.

As exemplified by these debates, intersectionality's increasing and often contested visibility on social media provides important opportunities to examine intersections of class, race, sexuality, gender, and age in action. If the innovation and popularization of ICTs have transformed feminism by increasing young women's participation in digital feminist activism and media-content production, the questions of who among digital feminist activists has access to major social media outlets, who is authorized, who is disenfranchised as divisive, or elitist, or unhelpful to the feminist cause, suggest enduring racialized power dynamics. Certainly, intersectionality has notable social media presence, or to borrow the title of a *Ms Magazine* article: "Social media minds the intersectional gap" (August 16, 2013). Yet the resistance, even downright hostility, which some white feminists express toward intersectionality in the name of populism or socialism indicates a tricky interaction wherein racism masquerades as class politics.

It would be a major mistake to look at only formal venues, such as human rights or similar public policy venues, or the academic journals and conferences of higher education, to assess the actual and potential impact of intersectionality's dispersal. Intersectionality's digital vitality provides ample evidence of its significant appeal and utility to a new generation of people who face multiple marginalization, but who have access to and skills in ICTs. Online communities of color, most often women, queer, and trans people of color, constitute an important force in contributing to intersectionality's digital vitality. The people and communities who were historically most disenfranchised within US social institutions were the same people who facilitated intersectionality's emergence. In the same way, and perhaps building on this legacy, the very same individuals and groups who face discrimination and injustice in a global context criticize contemporary social injustice. And they are making this happen by relying to a large extent on their skilful use of new digital media.

5
Intersectionality and Identity

Students, faculty, teachers, and activists across many venues have used intersectionality as an analytic tool to create more expansive understandings of individual and collective identities. Chapter 3 examined how the Combahee River Collective used identity as part of their process of empowerment. Their strategy of seeing identities as constructed and multiple was a core feature of their political analysis. These early expressions of identity within intersectionality exist today in many forms. For example, the scholarly essays, personal narratives, ethnographic inquiry, and creative writings in *Critical Articulations of Race, Gender, and Sexual Orientation* point out how complex sexual identities emerge within various configurations of interlocking systems of oppression (Howard 2014). Similarly, the essays in *Critical Autoethnography: Intersecting Cultural Identities in Everyday Life* investigate the complex entanglements between interpersonal experiences of gender, sexuality, race, ethnicity, and ability, and how they relate to larger systems of power, oppression, and social privilege (Boylorn and Orbe 2014). For many, this focus on the social construction of identities has been a space of individual and collective empowerment.

Yet there is another widespread tendency within intersectionality, especially intersectional scholarship, which merits analysis precisely because identity has been so central to intersectionality. Increasingly, many people who are involved in intersectionality understand it as a theory of identity. Take, for example, how the introduction to the special issue of a journal devoted to "Race, Class, and Gender" summarizes this perspective: "Another attribute of this special issue is the extent to which it expresses intersectionality – a multifaceted perspective acknowledging the richness of the multiple socially-constructed identities that combine to create each of us as a unique individual" (Lind 2010: 3). Certainly, intersectionality does value the richness of multiple identities that make each individual unique. But intersectionality also means much more than this. To understand intersectionality primarily as a theory of individual identity, often with the goal of criticizing it, overemphasizes some dimensions of intersectionality while underemphasizing others.

Much is at stake for getting the relationship between identity and intersectionality right. To explore these connections, this chapter analyzes the connections between the politics of identity and intersectionality as a form of critical inquiry and praxis. First, because questions of the connections between identity and intersectionality extend beyond contemporary debates within the academy, the chapter begins not with academic debates but rather with hip hop. Given the amount of attention devoted to identity debates among scholars, it is useful to examine a different project of critical inquiry and praxis that occurs primarily outside the academy but that may have important ties to intersectionality.

Second, the chapter examines selected dimensions of contemporary scholarly debates concerning the connections of identity and intersectionality. Because the tone of academic debates about identity often reflect efforts to disavow the relevance of identity and of intersectionality for meaningful social justice projects, the chapter focuses on one particular strand of these debates, namely, scholarship that criticizes intersectionality because of its ties to identity. Here, social context matters. Scholars who criticize the ties between identity and intersectionality may advance provocative arguments, but they typically do so from within colleges and universities of the Global North. There are many points of view on identity and intersectionality. Yet this small but highly visible group has a relatively loud voice.

Finally, the chapter concludes with three important ideas concerning identity that might be useful for intersectionality. None of these ideas is new, but they might help intersectionality sustain its focus on social justice.

Hip hop, intersectionality, and identity politics

When it comes to the theme of identity, intersectionality and hip hop share some noteworthy similarities. Because people who experienced discrimination of race, class, age, sexuality, and citizenship have been central to the creation of both hip hop and intersectionality, it stands to reason that significant parallels might exist between these two forms of critical inquiry and praxis. Specifically, putting intersectionality and hip hop in dialog potentially provides another angle of vision on the identity politics of both.

The theme of identity has certainly been important for intersectionality. The Combahee River Collective (CRC) provided one of the clearest expressions of the politics of identity articulated during a foundational moment of intersectionality. The CRC Statement constitutes one of the sharpest elaborations of the kind of identity politics within intersectionality. To briefly review CRC's central tenets regarding identity politics: (1) CRC members understood identity as multiply shaped by their shared social location as African-American women within interlocking systems of oppression; (2) they conceptualized identities as political projects that are achieved through consciousness-raising about shared life conditions within structures of power; (3) they envisioned black feminism as the logical political movement to combat the manifold and simultaneous oppressions that they faced as black women; and (4) CRC identified the importance of building collective identity as a political project for women of color and other disenfranchised groups like themselves. The Statement clearly views identity politics as a vital tool of resistance against oppression and relies unambiguously on an understanding of identity as a political location, not an essence (Alcoff 2006: 15). This is the conception of the politics of identity that Crenshaw had in mind in her important article on intersectionality (Crenshaw 1991).

Hip hop expresses a similar sensibility concerning identity, yet in less explicit forms than intersectionality. Regardless of the lyrics, rap music is a form of powerful personal expression where youth claim a voice that emphasizes individual identity. In today's global context, youth are positioned to craft an identity politics that criticizes the social issues that they face under neoliberalism. Young people are often among the first to see the interconnections among systems of power that put them at risk, primarily because they experience the contours of growing global social inequality in their everyday lives. Because they are young and experience social inequalities that are associated with age as a system of power firsthand, children, teenagers, and young adults have a special vantage point on intersecting social inequalities of ethnicity, religion, gender, sexuality, and race. They know that their neighborhoods receive inferior services and special policing. They see how their schools have less experienced teachers, old and dilapidated buildings, and outdated textbooks. They know that jobs for teenagers are minimal, and that the legitimate jobs that do exist pay little and have few benefits. Race, class, gender, and citizenship categories disadvantage many groups under neoliberal policies, yet, because age straddles all of these categories, young people's experiences of social problems are more intensified.

Within and despite the commercialization of rap by major corporations, many hip hop artists have focused on the myriad social problems faced by youth. The practices associated with hip hop, for example, rap lyrics that criticize the police and schools, tagging public space with graffiti, and refusing to follow the rules, disrupt the neoliberal status quo. Originally seen as "noise," hip hop is increasingly seen as a form of cultural politics that complements the traditional politics of voting and holding-office (Clay 2012; Rose 1994). Youth are too young to vote and they rarely have the skills and time to get elected to public office. So where do they take their protest? When youth confront schools, labor markets, and other social institutions as part of the structural domain of power, and experience policing of the disciplinary domain of power, they turn to other venues for political expression.

Music, dance, poetry, and art of the cultural domain of power and personal politics of the interpersonal domain grow in significance. Both the cultural domain and the interpersonal domain focus on the significance of identity. In hip hop, teenagers and young adults tell the story of their own lives, the truths of their own experiences. Hip hop is not identity politics in the abstract. Rather, hip hop constitutes an important space for developing the kind of collective identity politics that informs contemporary intersectional praxis (see, e.g., Chun, Lipsitz, and Shin 2013; Crenshaw 1991; Terriquez 2015).

When it comes to the links between politics and identity, intersectionality and hip hop grapple with a similar set of challenges that shape the politics of identity within each area. First, intersectionality and hip hop both experienced rapid growth as their ideas were dispersed within different global venues. Both were places where collective identity politics of disenfranchised groups moved into public space. This dispersal may have been important to the construction of collective identity itself. By the early 2000s, hip hop's global dispersal surpassed intersectionality's travels. Mass media and digital space have been crucial to hip hop's dispersal within global urban spaces. The spread of hip hop to become a global phenomenon comes both through the commercialization and marketing of its major figures and through bottom-up initiatives by youth whose identity narratives reflect their local conditions. Youth identity politics occupy this contested space between the conformist pressures of neoliberalism and the participatory ethos of hip hop, especially evident in spoken word, where everyone has a voice. In this fast-paced digital era, the aesthetics and politics of hip hop have been disarticulated and rearticulated by youth in multiple places. Because each local neighborhood or city has its own particular history and story, hip hop takes different forms and advances distinctive issues. There is no hip hop leader or archetypal form of hip hop. Instead, hip hop constitutes an assemblage of loosely linked local projects, where the meaning of local is constantly reshaped by social media itself.

A truly global phenomenon, hip hop's geopolitical dispersal has gone far beyond its US origin story. Youth use hip hop as a form of cultural politics to analyze important social issues in North America, the Caribbean and Latin America, Asia, and Africa. For example, Muslim youth use hip hop to protest the West's war on terrorism (see Aidi 2014). Similarly, the Aboriginal hip hop group A Tribe Called Red supports the Idle No More movement (see Shingler 2013). The Black Atlantic constitutes another important axis of hip hop's dispersal. Migration of African, Middle Eastern, and South Asian populations has created new social problems for youth who often don't see a place for themselves either in sending countries or their new nations. The heterogeneity of youth experiences means that the issues raised by youth can look like one another on some dimensions but not on others. For example, because issues faced by youth living in the segregated suburbs outside French cities resemble those of urban youth living inside US cities, Francophone hip hop and US hip hop have a similar vibe. In contrast, youth who live in small cities and villages, where rural realities are different, often draw upon local cultures to adapt hip hop as an art form to express their identity politics.

Second, intersectionality and hip hop both recognize the significance of identities for political consciousness and behavior. Not only do they both offer alternative analyses of social problems, they point to reframing identities as an important component of politics. Hip hop communities understand personal identity narratives as highly influential in people's everyday lives, especially when responding to social problems. In his ethnography, *5 Grams: Crack Cocaine, Rap Music, and the War on Drugs*, Bogazianos argues that hip hop provided an alternative narrative for drugs that, in turn, contested public policies of criminalization that demonized and locked up youth of color. Bogazianos advances a novel thesis of how hip hop accomplished this: "What rap, ethnographic literature on crack dealing, and research on America's declining violence rates suggest is that youth, indeed, have been engaged in very serious efforts to monitor, train, and restrain *themselves*" (Bogazianos 2012: 12). In other words, because youth saw the dangers of the stereotypical identities that were manufactured for them, they used rap music to resist these identities. Bogazianos suggests that the decline of crack markets and the associated declines in lethal violence that began in the early 1990s were "seriously influenced by the cultural stigma that youth in communities most affected by crack cocaine attached to its users, derogatorily referring to them as 'crackheads' " (Bogazianos 2012: 4). Stated differently, not only did youth advance an alternative analysis of crack use but creating, politicizing, and censuring the identity of a crackhead was an important part of their political response to drugs. Youth had to craft their own self-defined identities, an important task for disenfranchised people who consistently have to create meaningful identities in response to stereotypes that are imposed from above.

Third, hip hop and intersectionality both reject views of identity that pit the individual against the collective. Instead, both highlight how collective political consciousness emerges when people see how their individual life experiences are connected to broader social forces. Hip hop's narratives contain a critique of many of the social processes that intersectionality also contests, but do so via an unabashed claiming of a collective identity politics as a vehicle of social commentary. For example, youth of color, especially in urban settings, are well aware of the effects of the defunding and neglect of public education on their lives. In urban areas, this educational neglect serves as a catalyst for outpourings of narratives from young people about forms of social injustice. The themes within hip hop are often raw, pointing to the effects on young people's lives of policies decided elsewhere. Initially created by poor and working-class African-American, Afro-Caribbean, and Latino youth as a mechanism to express their experiences with and feelings about the economic, social, and political challenges in their lives, hip hop has grown far beyond critique to provide a space for an emerging identity politics.

Spoken-word poetry constitutes an important site where the content of youth identity narratives reflects an infusion of intersectionality's narrative of multiple identities. In spoken word venues, individual artists share experiences of sexual assault, racial profiling, being too poor to afford clothes, homophobic violence, being kicked out of families, being rendered homeless, and the terrible conditions of their public schools. Yet they do so not in the privacy of hidden conversations, but in public venues, in supportive communities that they create and maintain. Spoken word becomes a place of healing from the injuries of varying combinations of forms of oppression. But the narratives of spoken-word poetry do not exclusively emphasize anger or sadness. As part of a broader expansion of hip hop to include artists from multiple genders, sexual orientations, religious backgrounds, and even ages ("old school" rap happens too), spoken word events demonstrate the significance of art as a place of love, healing, and intimacy.

Finally, and significantly, intersectionality and hip hop both face the challenge of how to cast a self-reflexive eye on their respective identity politics. Colleges and universities have been important sites for intersectionality's emergence and institutionalization, a placement that has elevated scholarship as the visible face of intersectionality's cultural politics. In contrast, hip hop's institutional terrain consists of the music industry, an institution with a more visible history of exploiting artists. Hip hop's visibility within television, music, and fashion raises questions about cultural politics as a form of political activism. In many ways, the manipulation of identities and identity politics is more visible within the music videos of mass-media venues than within the textbooks and research articles of more respectable academic venues. The culture industry knows the power of its own practices. As a genre, hip hop confronts capitalist marketplace relations that are part of neoliberalism from a seemingly different vantage point – hip hop has been immensely profitable. Similarly, intersectionality faces the same pressures to turn intersectionality into a hot commodity for academic consumption.

Hip hop may have the potential to foster a collective identity politics that embraces a critical consciousness, but does it actually do so? Scholars and hip hop practitioners alike have criticized rap in particular for promoting hyper-masculinity, misogyny, and homophobia. Analyzing *Billboard*'s top rap songs certainly provides evidence for this point of view. Yet the issue is to engage the contested politics of gender, sexuality, class, and ethnicity within hip hop, not criticize it as a whole. More nuanced analyses by scholars and artists who want to develop hip hop as a form of critical inquiry and praxis bring more complex intersectional analyses to the forefront (see, e.g., Clay 2008; Pough 2004).

Scholarship that uses intersectionality as an analytic tool to study hip hop highlights sheds light on hip hop's identity politics. In *Hip Hop Desis: South Asian Americans, Blackness, and Global Race Consciousness*, Sharma provides a fascinating and nuanced analysis of identity politics of Desis youth in hip hop (Sharma 2010). Sharma examines how middle-class South Asian youth, or Desis, navigate the terrain of race, class, gender, and immigrant status in the United States. Sharma examines how Desis craft identities in response to a mix of factors: (1) relationships with their parents who want them to retain Indian culture and middle-class lifestyles; (2) their varying social locations within diverse South Asian communities where being Indian and middle class privileges them; and (3) the neighborhoods where they live, which can be white or racially mixed. Sharma traces how hip hop provides an alternative space for Desis youth who use hip hop to carve out new identities within these contested politics. The complexities of Sharma's analysis lie in her attention to how Desi women within hip hop flip the scripts of gender and sexuality. She also interrogates issues of ownership over hip hop, illustrating that, while Desis see the connections with black people and global racism, they creatively employ hip hop for new projects.

In his ethnography, *Hip Hop Underground: The Integrity and Ethics of Racial Identification*, Anthony Kwame Harrison provides another angle of vision on the identity politics that is associated with hip hop, in this case an analysis of a diverse community of youth who identify as black, Latino, white, mixed, and/or LGBT (Harrison 2009). Harrison's ethnography of kids involved in underground hip hop in the Bay Area, or "West Coast underground hip hop," sees "the erosion of barriers that have traditionally separated hip hop performers from audience members, or producers from consumers." Harrison finds a cultural community constructed across multiple racial, ethnic, sexual, and gender identities, a new place provided by hip hop. Moreover, this community is also political because it challenges prevailing power relations to craft a more democratic community (Collins 2010).

Imani Perry offers a more cautious analysis of hip hop's identity politics, pointing out how the norms of participatory democracy and neoliberal marketplace competition lie at the heart of this form of cultural politics. Perry's analysis of the contradictions within hip hop bear striking resemblance to those within intersectionality: "the combination of democracy ('Speak your piece') and meritocracy ('Be the best MC') that exists in hip hop is threatened at every turn" (Perry 2004: 7). She describes hip hop as a democratic space in which expression is more important than the monitoring of the acceptable. Hip hop rejects the silencing impulse about taboo topics that exists in various segments of American popular culture. This impulse to silence the disenfranchised not only occurs outside African-American communities, but also within them. Hip hop resists the silencing of certain politics, ideologies, sexual preferences, or other controversial matters. Hip hop may create a space of intellectual freedom, but Perry also points to the complexities within this space:

> Hip hop may be democratic, but it is not, as a musical community, inherently liberatory. There are particular artists with liberatory agendas, who by their words protest racism, sexism, classism and thereby enlighten. But hip hop is not "liberation music." The ideological democracy inherent in hip hop prevents the kind of coherent political framework necessary for it to be characterized as such. (Perry 2004: 6–7).

As is everything else, hip hop too is a contested site of politics with its own specific form of identity politics.

Intersectionality and identity debates in the academy

Given the centrality of identity politics within both intersectionality and hip hop, contemporary academic debates about identity can seem strangely out of touch. Were the treatment of identity politics within academia just a matter of scholarly debate, exploring hip hop as a form of cultural politics would have been unnecessary. Yet because intersectionality has long been associated with identity politics, and shunned within some academic circles by the same token, intersectionality as a form of critical analysis and praxis has much at stake in getting this question of identity right. Here we focus on criticisms of intersectionality to ask what kind of identity do these critics assume to be associated with intersectionality? And if intersectionality is so compromised by its identity politics, should intersectionality divorce itself from any identity-related concerns and investigations?

Academic scholarship that focuses on identity as a *defining* feature of intersectionality typically offers a more narrow understanding of identity than those presented thus far in this book. Some critics construe intersectionality as inherently flawed due to overemphasis on identity, and even recommend abandoning intersectionality together. Others also point to the overemphasis on identity within intersectionality, counselling intersectionality scholars to pay less attention to it. Both strands of criticism see intersectionality as giving too much explanatory power to identity to explain social phenomena and political processes.

One criticism of intersectionality concerns the overuse of personal identity as a category of analysis. In other words, because too much attention is given to identity, intersectionality underemphasizes structural analyses, especially materialist analyses of class and power. Yet a careful read of intersectionality scholarship, past and present, reveals that these criticisms of intersectionality and identity become tenable only by ignoring the centrality of structural analyses that have characterized intersectionality from its beginning. For example, Beal's work, the CRC Statement, as well as the explicit focus on institutional transformation of key figures who introduced intersectionality to the academy suggest that, when it comes to questions of identity, intersectionality has long emphasized a combination of structural and cultural analyses. For example, Nirmala Erevelles approaches disability by focusing on "the actual social and economic conditions that impact (disabled) people's lives, and that are concurrently mediated by the politics of race, ethnicity, gender, sexuality, and nation" (Erevelles 2011: 26). This is one example of many that illustrate that materialist analyses remain salient within intersectionality.

A related criticism sees intersectionality as being overly concerned with conceptions of identity that do not acknowledge difference. *Essentialism* conceptualizes individuals as having unchanged, fixed, or "essential" identities that they carry around with them from one situation to the next. In contrast to these essentialized, individual identities, individuals can be seen as having multiple "subjectivities" that they construct from one situation to the next. In other words, people have many choices and considerable agency about who they choose to be. Much intersectional scholarship supports this perspective on human subjectivity: individuals typically express varying combinations of their multiple identities of gender, sexuality, race, ethnicity, and religion across different situations. Social context matters in how people use identity to create space for personal freedom.

This criticism of essentialism has also been applied to collective or group-based identities. Critics claim that collective identity can also have a negative effect on group politics when it suppress differences within a group. For example, if hip hop elevates African-American men as the essential identity for this form of cultural politics, it limits its political horizons because it ignores women, Desis, Aboriginal rappers, and Muslim rappers. The criticism of essentialism and collective politics has some validity. In fact, it is one that has been raised by scholars who use intersectionality as an analytic tool. For example, Cathy Cohen's important book *The Boundaries of Blackness: Aids and the Breakdown of Black Politics* presents a compelling analysis of how essentialist thinking that ignores the needs of LGBT African Americans, sex workers, and other groups within African-American communities compromised political responses to HIV (Cohen 1999). Rather than maligning identity politics writ large, Cohen challenges African Americans to draw upon more complex, intersectional notions of community and politics. Within the space of developing a collective identity politics, the challenge to all groups is to self-regulate and try to identify and oppose the essentialist tendencies of their projects.

Yet challenging groups to avoid essentialist pitfalls in developing collective political projects is not the focus of criticisms. Rather, critics deploy a scorched-earth policy of doing away with identity politics altogether in the name of eradicating the negative effects of essentialism. Yet being attentive to power relations that produce social inequality means that deconstructing identities within a situation of social inequality will have a disproportionate effect on poor people, women, racial groups, young people, undocumented immigrants, and similar groups who are disadvantaged within intersecting systems of oppression.

These strands of criticism that conflate intersectionality with identity seem to understand intersectionality as a type of identity studies. Consider Robyn Wiegman's claim that "intersectionality circulates today as *the* primary figure of political completion in US identity knowledge domains" (Wiegman 2012: 240). By this, she suggests that intersectionality is an important framework for thinking about politics within areas that are considering how identity is important for knowledge. She claims that intersectionality "is ubiquitous in identity-based fields of study" (2012: 2). This makes sense if one assumes that intersectionality is primarily, if not solely, about identity. Accepting the first part of the claim as valid, namely, that intersectionality is about identity, opens the door for the second part. Exactly which identities have been central to intersectionality in the past and which are central now? Associating intersectionality with African-American women, Latinas, the poor, and similarly disempowered people makes intersectionality into an inferior form of identity studies because the people at its center are inferior. Most likely, this interpretation is not Wiegman's intent, but the initial conceptual slippage puts this kind of argument on the path to this outcome. In other words, the problem is not an over-focus on identity. Rather, intersectionality focuses on the wrong kind of identity, one deemed too particular: that of black women (e.g., Nash 2008). Here intersectionality as identity studies is viewed as "exclusionary" or "parochial," given its focus on black women, women of color, or disenfranchised people, where it should better aspire to "universalism" (e.g., Hutchinson 2001).

This raises the question of whether the criticism that identity is an overused category of analysis within intersectionality, a claim that there is "too much identity in intersectionality," is actually claiming that there is "too much *identity politics* in intersectionality." In other words, criticizing identity becomes a way of criticizing identity politics without directly confronting the many groups who have historically laid claim to it. In light of the robust understandings of identity politics that influenced social movement understandings of intersectionality as a form of critical inquiry and praxis, taking a closer look at the three main criticisms of identity politics is important.

First, identity politics is branded as separatist and fragmentary. Intersectionality becomes guilty by association: it allegedly breaks groups into ever-smaller sub-groups – "the infinite regress problem" (Ehrenreich 2002). This view endorses fragmentary understandings of social organization, when it acknowledges the existence of the social at all. This charge of infinite fragmentation often uses identity politics as a foil to defend the concept of class and class politics against intersectionality (which is seen as being about culture). According to its critics, intersectionality weakens class struggle by turning people's attention toward cultural matters. This shift away from traditional politics of protesting the policies of the state serves global capitalism (Mitchell 2013). Influential leftist intellectuals not only meet identity politics with great distrust, they grossly caricature it. For example, philosopher John D. Caputo's charge against identity politics builds on important Marxist philosophers like Alain Badiou and Slavoj Žižek:

> [T]here is the proliferation of identity politics, of women's rights, gay rights, the rights of the disabled, of anti-Jewish or anti-Hispanic or anti-Italian defamation organizations, and so on, which both Badiou and Žižek treat with great cynicism. Žižek recently quipped that he wanted to start up a necrophiliac rights group. Each segment of identity politics creates a new market of speciality magazines, books, bars, websites, DVDs, radio stations, a lecture circuit for its most marketable propagandizers, and so on. By creating an endless series of proliferating differences, of new speciality markets, cultural identity fits hand in glove with the ever-proliferating system of global capital. (Caputo 2009: 6)

In another example, materialist feminist Eve Mitchell targets intersectionality, which she conflates with identity politics, in order to recenter a class analysis: "Since identity politics, and therefore intersectionality theory, are a bourgeois politics, the possibilities for struggle are also bourgeois. Identity politics reproduces the appearance of an alienated individual under capitalism and so struggle takes the form of equality among groups at best, or individualized forms of struggle at worse" (Mitchell 2013).

Second, critics argue that identity politics values cultural recognition over economic redistribution. In other words, groups claiming identity politics want recognition of their own narrow interests rather than having a broader commitment to the social good. This claim circumvents a vast literature documenting how disenfranchised groups tackle the issue of social justice on both fronts and view cultural empowerment (race, gender, sexuality) and economic redistribution (class) as inseparable. Out of necessity, women of color integrated their claims for equality, recognition, and redistribution. Separating them was practically or analytically impossible when racism and sexism always structured the specific form of class exploitation that they face (Bhandar 2013). Treating these claims as separable and arguing that oppressed groups can favor one over the other does not match empirical evidence from political projects such as the contemporary Afro-Brazilian women's movement. Concretely, by categorizing gender and race-based claims as cultural and dissociating them from economic justice claims, this criticism fails to address the ways in which economic injustice relies on gendered and racialized structures in historically specific ways.

A third criticism of identity politics is that it fosters victimhood politics. In other words, people who claim identity politics are basically clinging to some sort of victim status – as women, or blacks, or disabled – as the basis of their separatist claims for recognition. Their political claims are based solely on victimhood, nothing else of value. Interestingly, within left-wing criticism of identity politics and, by implication, intersectionality as it gets equated with identity politics, bashing identity politics on the basis of its alleged victimhood culture brings together Marxists and postmodern leftists, two strands of thought that don't generally see eye to eye. Within Marxist critique, the victimhood argument is linked to class struggle and how identity politics purportedly serves the interests of global capitalism. Surprisingly, the postmodern left presents an especially scathing criticism of identity politics. For instance, political scientist Wendy Brown argues that identities invariably subjugate people and cannot be viable in emancipatory politics. For Brown, identities are "wounded attachments" that trap poor people, black people, LGBTQ people, and women in a cycle of rehashing their injuries and blaming their oppressors. Identity-based political movements thus rely on a compulsive repetition of traumatic events, holding us captive of our oppression. She speculates: "particular constituents [...] of identity's desire for recognition [...] seem to breed a politics of recrimination and rancor, of culturally dispersed paralysis and suffering, a tendency to reproach power rather than aspire to it, to disdain freedom rather than practice it" (Brown 1995: 55). In brief, identity politics disempowers oppressed people because it encourages them to cling to the status of victim.

Collectively, these arguments against intersectionality's claims to identity only work within narrow understandings of intersectionality that simultaneously emphasize intersectionality as a form of abstract inquiry and neglect intersectionality as a form of critical praxis as it actually happens. This book's expansive understanding of intersectionality provides an intellectual context for these particular criticisms of intersectionality and identity politics. It suggests that identity politics has had an opposite effect. For example, the case study of why black women in Brazil felt they needed a black women's movement speaks to this use of identity. The living identity politics of this group were decidedly not separatist: they valued both cultural recognition – namely, respect as Afro-Brazilian women – and economic redistribution in Brazil. They also eschewed victimhood politics of begging more powerful groups for intellectual and political guidance.

Several studies provide empirical evidence that confirm how disenfranchised people use identity politics for political empowerment. This empirical work both uses intersectionality as an analytic tool and refutes the main points of the depiction presented above of the identity politics within intersectionality. In the following three studies, researchers underscore how identities are primarily understood as a collective political subjectivity and conscious coalition that also leaves room for individual identity.

The ethnographic work of political scientist José E. Cruz counters the three major criticisms of intersectionality's identity politics: identity politics are separatist; they value cultural recognition over economic redistribution; and they incite victimhood politics. His study of Puerto Rican politics in Hartford, Connecticut, the oldest and largest concentration of Puerto Ricans in the United States, demonstrates how identity-based political organizing, rather than causing isolation or wallowing in victimhood, encouraged greater political mobilization and citizen involvement (Cruz 1998). The Puerto Rican Political Action Committee of Hartford mobilized Puerto Rican identity as "a code that structured their entrance into mainstream society and politics" (Cruz 1998: 6). Their demands neither fragmented the political setting, nor artificially separated cultural recognition from economic redistribution.

Similarly, Kalpana Kannabiran's analysis of Dalit feminist resistance within India's National Federation of Dalit Women not only invalidates the critiques of identity politics, but also the postmodernist assumption that intersectionality is deeply flawed by essentialism. Kannabiran shows how the Dalit women's movement mobilized a collective identity that was forged "in several struggles at once" (Kannabiran 2006: 68) and that sought to create solidarities and dialog with other women's rights movements. Talking about "the intersectional articulation of the Dalit women's political position" (Kannabiran 2006: 67), Kannabiran views this identity as a creative expression of a political standpoint shaped by multiple and interrelated systems of oppression: religiously sanctioned casteism, patriarchy, capitalism, state, and religion. Vulnerabilities and violence generated by this organization of power are also multiple and interrelated: higher caste aggression perpetrated both by men and women, Dalit male aggression, patriarchal violence within the family and community, sexual assaults by men of higher castes, economic exploitation of both Dalit men and women by dominant caste-owned capital (e.g., landowners and factory owners), and the complicity of the state and its institutions. Kannabiran's work shows how, through identity-based resistance and struggle, Dalit women forged solidarities among race, caste, and gender at the local, national, and international levels. Moreover, they did so by using international soft-law mechanisms, as well as the theoretical framework provided by "intersectionality in race theory" (2006: 68).

Edwina Barvosa-Carter's historical account of the emergence of Latino/a identity in 1970s Chicago also refutes the understandings of identity politics offered by intersectionality's critics (Barvosa-Carter 2001). Her work shows how this new ethnic identity was a "politically strategic formation," enabling the members of two discrete ethnic groups, Mexicans and Puerto Ricans, to collectively understand themselves as "members of a single, larger, internally diverse, and *politicized* ethnic group" (2001: 21; italics in original). This new identity helped them collaborate across their differences to fight discrimination. Hardly a homogeneous ethnic identity, Latino/a signifies a political coalition aware of multiple differences – not only those between Mexicans and Puerto Ricans, but also those within them. "In the process, Latino/a identified people both engaged a new identity and retained the identities they already had – including national, sexual, gender, age, ideological, class, professional, and other identities" (2001: 21).

Overall, scholars who consider intersectionality as flawed because of its ties to identity typically rely on understandings of identity and intersectionality that neglect how intersectionality as a form of critical praxis operates across many different venues. Instead, their criticisms constitute theoretical approaches to power and politics that remain plausible in the abstract. For Marxists, identity means being apolitical and obscuring class as the most fundamental oppression. For those who embrace postmodern anti-categorical thinking, intersectionality's identity conceptions are essentialist and exclusionary. Thus, in many of these critiques, identity gets either associated with bad politics or dissociated from politics in ways that resemble the decoupling of intersectionality from social justice. Yet, taking a more holistic approach to intersectionality, one that attends to intersectionality's critical praxis, creates space to rethink this relationship between intersectionality and the politics of identity.

Then what kind of identity for intersectionality?

The mainstream criticisms leveled against intersectionality's identity politics, namely, that intersectionality fosters separatism, overemphasizes cultural recognition, and exaggerates victimhood, could just as easily be targeted at hip hop. But when it comes to the identity politics of hip hop, these criticisms falter. As a form of cultural politics with tremendous global reach, hip hop can hardly be accused of being separatist. As a genre, hip hop contains numerous demands for better schooling, adequate housing, stopping police violence, and jobs. These kinds of social problems can only be met with some form of economic redistribution. Thus hip hop's cultural politics do not demand simple cultural recognition from the mainstream. Instead, hip hop uses identity politics as an important vehicle to criticize the lack of recognition of the social problems faced by disenfranchised youth. As for victimhood politics, what would be gained by youth who kept their victimization to themselves? The power of the voice in spoken word and rap lies in sharing stories not only of victimization, but also of triumph, struggle, disappointment, and a range of human experiences. Who benefits from the suppression of identity politics advanced by disenfranchised groups? And this is exactly the question that intersectionality must ask concerning its own practice.

Instead of dissociating intersectionality from these negative depictions of identity and identity politics, a more productive approach lies in examining how understandings of the politics of identity can constitute *a starting point for intersectional inquiry and praxis and not an end in itself.* Rod Ferguson captures this sensibility of identity as a starting point for intellectual and political action: "women of color feminism had to express a politics of negation and difference in which identity was a point of departure since the gendered and sexual regulations of national liberation proved that women of color, in general, and lesbians of color in particular could not take comfort in the presumed accommodations of nationalism" (Ferguson 2004: 130).

When it comes to intersectionality as a form of critical analysis and praxis, how might reclaiming identity politics speak to contemporary challenges of understanding social inequality and fostering social justice? This book cannot do justice to the heterogeneity and richness of scholarship that takes up varying aspects of this question, but it has made a consistent effort throughout this entire book to cite it. Three important understandings of identity have potentially important implications for intersectionality, namely, identities as strategically essential, identities as de facto coalitions, and transformative identities.

First, identities mobilized in political struggles of disenfranchised groups are not fundamentally fixed and unchanging but, rather, are *strategically essentialist* (Spivak 1996). Strategic essentialism is about the politics of performing different multiple identities from one context to the next. Drawing on the work of US-based postcolonial scholar Gayatri Spivak, strategic essentialism is best thought of as a political practice whereby an individual or group foregrounds one or more aspects of identity as significant in a given situation.

Rejecting criticisms of intersectionality as essentialist creates space for subordinated groups to use identity politics for political goals. In her 1994 essay, Chicana lesbian feminist Emma Pérez explains how unequal power relations and knowledge hierarchies shape strategic essentialism:

> I essentialize myself strategically within a Chicana lesbian countersite as a historical materialist from the Southwest who dares to have a feminist vision of the future. My essentializing positions are often attacked by a sophisticated carload of postmodern, post-Enlightenment, Eurocentric men and by women who ride in the back seat, who scream epithets at those of us who have no choice but to essentialize ourselves strategically and politically against dominant ideologies that serve only to disempower and depoliticize disenfranchised minorities. [...] As 'disenfranchised others' essentializing ourselves within countersites thwarts cultural and political suicide. (Pérez 1994: 105)

Strategic essentialism animates both the power analysis required for coalition building, namely, having a platform of some sort around which individuals and groups can coalesce. Black women in Brazil were able to incorporate so many different groups into their movement because they had shifting alliances with many groups. One sees in their work the use of strategic essentialism as an important legitimate political tactic in a struggle for social justice.

Second, and relatedly, identities are important for seeing how coalitions work. Conceptualizing identity as inherently coalitional creates space for coalitional possibilities among individuals, as well as new directions for understanding groups. This linking of identity politics and coalitional politics is not new. Anna Carastathis points out its presence in Crenshaw's work (Carastathis 2013). Carastathis examines how Crenshaw uses intersectionality as a framework to conceptualize identity-based groups as de facto coalitions, "or at least coalitions waiting to be formed" (Crenshaw 1991: 1299). Crenshaw writes, "[r]ecognizing that identity politics takes place at the site where categories intersect thus seems more fruitful than challenging the possibility of talking about categories at all" (1991: 1299). For Crenshaw, seeing identity as already coalitional creates possibilities for political organizing that attends to intersecting power differentials within the group.

Crenshaw argues that this recognition of "the intersectional experiences of women of color disenfranchised in prevailing conceptions of identity politics does not require that we give up attempts to organize as communities of color. Rather, intersectionality provides a basis for reconceptualising race as a coalition between men and women of color [...] or a coalition of straight and gay people of color" (Crenshaw 1991: 1299). Understanding identity as a coalitional location stresses in-group and inter-group power differentials. In other words, conceptualizing identity *coalitionally* highlights the coalitional labour *already at work* within the group before deploying it for building inter-group alliances.

Finally, conceptualizing identities themselves as transformative constitutes another important understanding of identity with implications for intersectionality. Arguing that transnational feminist solidarities require a rethinking of identity politics, Allison Weir insists on the necessity of a shift to an ethical and political model of identity: a relational model that is pragmatic but also transformative: it "focuses on what matters, what is meaningful for us – our desires, relationships, commitments, ideals" and can take change into account: "a model of *transformative identity politics*" (Weir 2008: 111; emphasis in original). For Weir, this approach seeks to elaborate "a model of *identification in coalition* that can take account of our locations in power relations" (2008: 122; our emphasis).

This idea of a transformative identity politics comes closest to capturing the spirit of identity politics within various expressions of intersectionality. Many women of color point to the transformative possibilities of an individual identity that becomes formed within, and itself shapes, broader social phenomena. As pioneering Mohawk scholar, lawyer, and activist, Patricia Monture-Angus argues:

> Some Aboriginal women have turned to the feminist or women's movement to seek solace (and solution) in the common oppression of women. I have a problem with perceiving this as a full solution. I am not just woman. I am a Mohawk woman. It is not solely my gender through which I first experience the world, it is my culture (and/or race) that precedes my gender. Actually if I am object of some form of discrimination, it is very difficult for me to separate what happens to me because of my gender and what happens to me because of my race and culture. My world is not experienced in a linear and compartmentalized way. I experience the world simultaneously as Mohawk and as woman. It seems as though I cannot repeat this message too many times. To artificially separate my gender from my race and culture forces me to deny the way I experience the world. Such denial has devastating effects on Aboriginal constructions of reality. (Monture-Angus 1995: 177–8)

Identity is central to building a collective we. Identity politics rests upon a recursive relationship between individual and social structures, as well as among individuals as an existing collective or a collective that must be brought into being because they share similar social locations within power relations. A transformed individual identity is potentially transformative and long-lasting. Once people are changed on the individual level, they are likely to remain so. Focusing on the self, on its wholeness, provides a major impetus for individual and collective empowerment.

6
Intersectionality, Social Protest, and Neoliberalism

In 2015, without much coverage by international media, the Spanish government adopted the Citizens' Security Law that allowed police unprecedented discretionary powers over freedom of association and protest. The new law imposed fines up to US$650,000 for unauthorized demonstrations near transportation hubs or nuclear power plants, and up to US$30,000 for activities during protests such as filming, photographing police, or failing to show ID. The law also cracked down on simply gathering without authorization in front of universities, hospitals and other government buildings. Banned from demonstrating outside parliament, Spanish activists launched an ingenious strategy of popular resistance: they used holograms to stage the world's first virtual protest. The *NoSomosDelito* ("We are not crime") movement, an association of more than a hundred different organizations, invited supporters around the world to participate in the pioneering event by simply webcamming their faces via the campaign website. During the hour-long hologram demonstration, more webcam faces were posted than could be used. Passing the law did not make international headlines, yet this virtual demonstration, using more than two thousand virtual images sent across the world, did.

Spain is one of many democracies that have embraced coercive policies, or police repression and other punitive state action, as a way to control both social unrest and the fear of it. Since 2012, a number of democratic governments have implemented legislation designed to stifle peaceful public protest and the right to assemble in public places. For example, France has banned pro-Palestinian demonstrations, and police in Australia now have the power to ban protesters from appearing in public spaces for a year. If Mexico's congress-approved *ley antimarchas* is ratified by the state-level governments, it will amend the Mexican Constitution to make any unauthorized gathering illegal. In the United States, protesting near government buildings, political conventions, and global summits, except in heavily policed so-called free-speech zones, has been a federal crime since 2012. In Baltimore, many protesters of the killing of Freddie Gray were held without charge for over 48 hours, and were denied phone calls and access to lawyers. Following the formation of the #BlackLivesMatter movement in New York City, the Police Commissioner, in addition to demanding a machine-guns-armed special unit of a thousand police for the exclusive task of monitoring protests, also sought to modify the law to make resisting arrest a felony.

Rising social unrest in the face of growing economic inequalities is hardly surprising. Yet the use of force as a response to social protest by democracies points to an erosion of the bond of trust between citizens and their governments. An Oxfam survey in six countries (Spain, Brazil, India, South Africa, the United Kingdom and the United States) shows that the majority of people believe that laws are skewed in favor of the rich, and that, when laws are designed and rules bent to benefit them, "wealth captures government policymaking" (Oxfam 2014: 2–3). "We are the 99 percent," the slogan of the Occupy movement, captured this growing sentiment of discontent. Growing global social inequalities promise to be a flashpoint for changes both in how nation-states grapple with neoliberalism, as well as in how people who bear the costs of neoliberal policies respond.

This chapter examines how intersectionality fosters more robust understandings of two interrelated phenomena. The first involves global social protest against social inequalities that bubbles up in local settings and that finds new forms of organization via social media and social networking. The phenomenon links together the social problems of global social inequality, local, grassroots community organizing, new uses of cyberspace for purposes such as forums about intersectionality, and the cultural politics of youth.

The second phenomenon is closely related to the first. Local social protests take aim at nation-states that implement unpopular neoliberal policies. Many democratic states have taken a coercive turn, namely, they increasingly use force to compel their citizens to obey. A constellation of terms describe this coercive turn, among them, the "security state," the "coercive surveillance state," the "police state," the "carceral state," or quite simply the "neoliberal state." These coercive policies take myriad forms from one nation-state to the next. Mass incarceration, the militarization of police, and the securitization of immigration constitute social policies deployed by nation-states in ways that reflect the particularities of their populations, histories, and neoliberal aspirations. Using intersectionality as an analytic tool to analyze these interdependent phenomena sheds light on the global networked structure of global social protest and neoliberal policies.

Intersectionality and global social protest

Using intersectionality as an analytic tool suggests unexplored commonalities among social protests that appear to be particularistic, uncoordinated, scattered, and local. Global social protests against economic inequality and social disenfranchisement are linked within the neoliberal world order. The neoliberal world order relies on a global system of capitalism that is inflected through unequal relations of race, gender, sexuality, age, disability, and citizenship. This global organization of power also operates through increasingly repressive nation-states. If universal theories of capitalism that relied on class-only explanations of economic inequality are limited, theories of global political protest that embrace single-issue organizing may be similarly parochial.

The growing awareness of economic inequalities has been an important catalyst for global waves of social protest. Between 2009 and 2015, popular uprisings against various injustices spread across the globe. These protests had many names, reached out to various and sometimes contradictory constituencies, and were not unified by a single ideology or target. They were singular in their historical specificities and geopolitical stakes, and took different internal forms within each country. Despite their differences, intersectionality sheds light on several common features of these seemingly scattered protests.

They usually started small, sometimes even with an action by one individual, which went viral and was coordinated through social media. In 2011, the self-immolation of a fruit vendor to protest police harassment and corruption in the small town of Sidi Bouzid, Tunisia, and the rapid and widespread dissemination on social media of a related video recorded on a mobile phone ignited the Arab Spring, a wave of rebellions across the Arab world. In 2012, Attawapiskat chief Theresa Spence's hunger strike to draw attention to the ongoing erosion of treaty and Indigenous rights in Canada sparked the Idle No More movement that also quickly gained momentum through social media, rallies, and teach-ins.

In some cases, their initial targets were highly local or specific issues such as the rising cost of public transportation (Brazil), tuition fees in higher education (Quebec, Chile, United Kingdom), saving an urban green space from shopping-mall construction (Turkey), or protesting police corruption in a local market (Tunisia). These initial protests often resonated with larger public discontent with specific government policies, namely, political corruption, authoritarian governing styles, and social inequalities that resulted from unearned benefits. For example, the 2014 anti-World Cup protest spread across a hundred Brazilian cities via social media. Initially critical of the exorbitant expenditures of public money on stadium construction, protest groups rapidly addressed other social issues, ranging from housing and evictions, the right to peaceful protest, health and education reform, and demilitarization of police that was part of Brazil's legacy of dictatorship.

In other cases, from the outset, protests took aim at much broader social issues. Financial speculation and real-estate bubbles (the Occupy movement); national debt, austerity measures, and unemployment (*Indignados* in Spain and *Aganaktismenoi* [outraged] in Greece, UK Uncut movement);

political corruption (Brazil, Mexico), authoritarianism, and lack of democracy (Arab Spring, Hong Kong); and human rights violations (Arab Spring), narco-state violence (Mexico), Indigenous rights, colonization, and environment (Idle No More in Canada and the Chilean student movement in defense of Mapuche rights) have all been themes within global social protest. Increasing wealth disparities and growing unemployment/underemployment were common themes.

The catalysts for these protests came from many sources – cutbacks in public funding for schools, health care, and other social services, rising prices for transportation, housing, and food, and a growing youth unemployment rate that left entire categories of youth without prospects for meaningful work. Yet punitive state action, specifically police violence, ignited many of these protests and contributed to the public outcry against police response. Police violence has been central to the unfolding of the protests in many contexts: in Greece, Spain, Egypt, Turkey, and Mexico, at various locations of the international Occupy movement, as well as the international student movement from Chile, to Quebec, to the United Kingdom.

A defining feature of these seemingly scattered local protests is how participants imagine them as part of a broader transnational struggle on which they keep themselves informed. In Turkey, one of the slogans of the Gezi protests – "Everywhere is Taksim, resistance everywhere" – captures how the site of local resistance, Taksim Square in Istanbul, is envisioned as a transnational space of resistance. This transnational sensibility permeates slogans as chanted by Brazilian protesters in São Paulo: "The love is over, Turkey is right here," or echoed in the title of an open letter penned by Egyptian protesters: "From Taksim and Rio to Tahrir, the smell of the teargas" (Tugal 2013: 157, 160). These actions illustrate one facet of what social movement literature calls globalization from below. This phrase refers to a *transnational political imaginary*, namely, a way of imagining political action that goes beyond local face-to-face organizing and beyond national politics to encompass a broader transnational focus. Social issues are seen as bigger than any one specific location – the case, for example, of seeing climate change as a man-made social problem that cannot be solved by any one country alone. For social justice movements, this concept of a transnational political imaginary enables them to see their local issues as part of global resistance.

This transnational political imaginary draws from intersectional understandings of the interrelatedness of these protests. The specific histories of disenfranchisement associated with racism, sexism, class exploitation, and ethnic subordination that shape one another in specific social contexts are no longer understood as separate events but, rather, are connected. The necessary, but not sufficient, condition for this transnational political imaginary to emerge is its communicative possibilities via digital and mobile technologies and social media platforms that are outside mainstream media which either censure or negatively portray these movements.

A second feature of these movements is their use of digital technologies, so much so that they can be viewed as digitally mediated social movements. Manuel Castells refers to them as networked social movements and highlights how they use both cyberspace and urban space for mobilization (Castells 2015: 221). From citizen-made mobile-phone videos broadcast on YouTube to the use of social media platforms such as Twitter and Facebook, protesters use new technologies to provide updates on protests and to share vital information, for example, which roads to avoid, what to do in case of arrest, and home remedies against teargas. Digital technologies have been an integral part of local movements, but they have also played a major role in linking them nationally and transnationally. Digital and social media helped create a sense of belonging to an imagined global community of resistance and facilitate cross-fertilization between movements in terms of style, tactics, inspiration, and use of art, as well as of building international audience and support. For Turkish sociologist Cihan Tugal, given that the countries shaken by these waves of social protest display starkly different dynamics, "it is technology (and more broadly style) rather than social factors that link the uprisings to each other" (Tugal 2013: 157).

A third commonality among these movements is their intersectional understandings of the social problems they address. In his detailed empirical study of several of these movements, Manuel Castells argues that "they often express an acute consciousness of the intertwining of issues and problems for humanity at large, and they clearly display a cosmopolitan culture, while being rooted in their specific identity" (Castells 2015: 221). Intersectionality helps politicize the initial catalyst, be it the defense of an urban green space or the cost of public transportation, in that social protest becomes a rallying platform for an array of differentially disenfranchised groups. This intersectional sensibility is also expressed in efforts to create an inclusive political identity for the movements (e.g., Lopez and Garcia 2014 for the Spanish *Indignados*) or the propensity for horizontal coalitions instead of federations.

Collectively, global social protest embraces a transnational political imaginary that relies on digital media for communication among differently disenfranchised groups. Intersectionality enables these groups to see the interconnectedness of the issues that concern them, as well as their own placement within global power relations. But these same digital media also provide tools for organizing. As a result, political activism is both local and transnational in ways that reflect the constraints and possibilities of the new neoliberal world order. Social protest, while intense and episodic, becomes the catalyst or base for community organizing. When local groups gather together within a nation-state or develop transnational networks that are linked to the immediacy of specific protests of different kinds across national settings, social movements take on new transnational forms. New communications technologies make this kind of community organizing possible beyond neighborhoods, workplaces, or geographic regions. Such new technologies not only expose the similarity of issues, for example, the coercive state and securitization that take heterogeneous form, they provide new tools for combining grassroots, civil society organizations, and broader social movements.

The Rana Plaza tragedy

The global social protest unfolding in the aftermath of the Rana Plaza tragedy in Dhaka, Bangladesh illustrates how using intersectional frameworks can shed light on global social protests and political activism. In 2013, the fire and collapse of Rana Plaza, a building housing dozens of garment factories, killed 1,129 workers and injured 2,500 others. It is now considered the deadliest incident in the global history of the garment industry. Less deadly tragedies are so common in sweatshop factories across the Global South that they barely make the headlines.[1] It took a tragedy of this magnitude to initiate some change in the garment industry.

The garment industry has a long history of labor exploitation and unsafe working conditions, punctuated by egregious tragedies that, like Rana Plaza, can catalyze activism. For example, in 1911 in the United States, the Triangle Shirtwaist Company factory in New York City burned, killing 145 workers, overwhelmingly young immigrant women. Nearly all of the workers were teenaged girls who did not speak English, working 12 hours a day, every day, for US$15 a week. When the International Ladies Garment Workers Union led a strike in 1909 demanding higher pay and shorter and more predictable hours, the Triangle Company was one of the few manufacturers that resisted. It hired police to imprison the striking women and bribed politicians to look the other way. The danger of fires in factories like Triangle was well known, but the levels of corruption in both the garment industry and city government ensured that few precautions were taken. The deaths from the Triangle tragedy were largely preventable – most of the victims were trapped behind locked doors on the eighth floor. The fire was over in 18 minutes. Forty-nine workers had burned to death or been suffocated by smoke, 36 were dead in an elevator shaft, and 58 died from jumping to the sidewalks. The workers' union set up a march on April 5 on New York's Fifth Avenue to protest the conditions that led to the fire. It was attended by 80,000 people. It also fostered legal reforms that were important to preventing similar disasters in the future.

The Rana Plaza collapse shows similar signs of becoming a rallying cry for the contemporary anti-sweatshop movement where garment workers grapple with very similar working conditions. Thousands of women workers took action worldwide to commemorate the second anniversary of the fire and collapse at Rana Plaza. On April 24, 2015, the national chapters of the World March of Women from around the world took part in a global 24-hour feminist action[2] to commemorate this deadliest tragedy with their rallying slogan, "Rana Plaza is everywhere." It took a catastrophe of this magnitude in a country that has the world's second-largest national garment industry to garner international attention and revitalize the contemporary anti-sweatshop movement.

Tragedies such as the Triangle Shirtwaist Factory fire and the Rana Plaza collapse catalyzed both global protests and organizing for workers' rights. The anti-sweatshop movement, as part of a more general call for workers' rights, reveals important ways that people protest growing social inequality, namely, building a transnational political imaginary as a way of understanding how women workers are exploited in the garment industry.

Using intersectionality as an analytic tool sheds light on how some of the key features of the Rana Plaza collapse led to global social protest. First, because the Rana Plaza collapse highlights how capitalism and nation-state policies converge to shape the social inequalities in the global garment industry, intersectionality suggests new avenues of investigation for social protest. In chapter 1, we introduced FIFA as part of a global entertainment, sports, and tourism industry where the working conditions of the players on the field represented a small part of how the industry actually operated. The globalized garment industry is also part of the World Cup industry, for which it produces apparel and souvenirs. The striking gap between factory workers' wages and high-priced World Cup paraphernalia drew increased attention, through media coverage, to global economic inequalities and the garment industry.

Social protest focused not solely on the tragedy of Rana Plaza, but also on the working conditions of the people who died in the collapse. Within global capitalism, the garment industry presents an especially bad version of the erosion of workers' rights. Employers located the Rana Plaza factories in Bangladesh because they were drawn to the country's cheap, abundant, and seemingly obedient workers. Bangladesh's favorable regulatory climate also contributed to the factory's working conditions. Lax regulations enabled violations of shoddy construction or unsafe conditions for workers to be overlooked. Despite certifications of compliance with international labor standards, actual compliance is minimal. As a result, the jobs in these factories lack fair pay, job security, and safe working conditions. The Rana Plaza tragedy highlights the poor working conditions in sweatshops. Factory managers routinely block windows and doors, do not provide fire exits, stifle trade unions, and violate workers' rights through practices such as a 70-hour or longer week and restricted toilet time.

Second, the garment industry relies on workers who are multiply disadvantaged within systems of gender, age, race, and citizenship status. This case shows how these systems of power intersect to produce social locations of disadvantage for workers and privilege for managers and owners. The garment industry contains a highly feminized workforce, relies on child labor in some countries, uses race and ethnicity as markers for the kinds of people it hires, and favors undocumented migrant workers. This means that workers are drawn from populations who are disadvantaged within intersecting systems of oppression. Their poverty, illiteracy, gender, age, immigration status, race, caste, or ethnicity make them more vulnerable to capitalist exploitation and violence, specifically physical and sexual abuse. The garment industry exploits these gender and ethnic inequalities, as well as immigration status and age differences, for profitability.

Third, protests by workers are likely to be met with punitive responses. When garment workers slow down production, organize strikes, or unionize to protest their extremely poor working conditions and low wages, companies often respond by firing people and intimidating workers through threats, violence, and arrests (Armbruster-Sandoval 2005: 3–4). Factories often relocate to other countries where laws are more favorable to sweatshop conditions and where labor is cheaper. More importantly, these labor practices are not new.

Labor practices in the garment industry have deep historical roots and reach across national borders. One can draw a straight line between the young women workers in the Triangle Shirtwaist factory to those in Rana Plaza. Garment factories relocated from New York City to the less regulated and unionized climate of the US South, Haiti, and similar countries of the Central American and the Caribbean, to the cheaper labor and lax regulation of countries in South Asia. Within traditional frameworks of neoclassical economics, these historical patterns are simply the cost of doing business in an increasingly global marketplace. Yet intersectional frameworks that pay attention to how intersecting power relations have shaped this particular industry provide a more nuanced argument about the connections between which people become workers in the garment industry (interpersonal domain), how managers control and exploit workers (disciplinary domain), the location of factories in countries with cheap labor and lax government oversight (structural domain), and social norms that send young women into factories to help support their families (cultural domain).

Fourth, in this context, the magnitude of the Rana Plaza tragedy has served as a powerful catalyst for coalitions among activists for workers' rights and consumer activism. The power of social media and digitally mediated consumer activism has revitalized unionism, enabling workers to push for legally binding plans and to pressure multinational brands to sign. In a *Guardian* article (April 24, 2014), Christy Hoffman explains how, for years, the global labor movement and NGOs tried in vain to create an independent safety inspection regime for the Bangladesh garment industry. It was only after Rana that they were able to progress. Two global trade unions and a number of Bangladeshi unions, with more than 160 brands from 20 countries in Europe, North America, Asia, and Australia, signed a legally binding agreement that covered approximately half of all Bangladeshi factories for the export market and two million workers. It was the first time that such an agreement between global trade unions and multinational brands was reached. The scope of the Rana Plaza disaster has invigorated consumer activism, especially among college students who became exposed to patterns of labor exploitation that produced their college T-shirts and trademarked school gear. Moreover, the lists of multinational companies that refuse to sign any agreement and those declining to pay compensation to victims' families and injured survivors of the Rana Plaza collapse circulate on social media, generating consumer activism such as boycotts and petitions.

A new wave of consumer activism has seemingly emerged in the Global North, one that is increasingly concerned with the economic conditions of workers and the environmental impacts of consumed products. Since its beginnings in the late 1960s and 1970s, consumer activism in the Global South has been attentive to social justice issues (Hilton 2009). More recently, consumer activism in the Global North has grown. In the age of digital media, information about working conditions travels widely and rapidly, and it can influence consumer choices. Coordinated action by consumers who boycott companies that do not take responsibility for their effect on social welfare and the environment can encourage multinational brands, which make huge profits through their production via subcontracting to factories in the poorest countries, to use the power they have to positively change working conditions and wages.

The impact of consumer activism in an age of digital media cannot be underestimated. For example, after one million people signed a petition, the Italian company Benetton agreed to pay into a fund for Rana Plaza survivors, basically paying compensation to workers who were not its direct employees. In a *Guardian* article (April 10, 2015), Tana Hoskins quotes Bettina Musiolek, an activist with the Clean Clothes Campaign who had worked for garment workers' rights for 20 years. Musiolek stated: "there was not one single moment or one case that established this relationship of brands paying for people who are not their employees. It was a process over the last 15–20 years of civil society campaigns or human rights campaigns that defined the responsibility of brands and retailers." Clearly, public pressure from consumer boycotts and bad publicity changed the climate for the garment industry. The initial Rana Plaza compensation fund of US$8.5 million constituted a small victory for activists long involved in the anti-sweatshop movement. This amount cannot adequately compensate the thousands of victims, but it can serve as an agenda item for this ongoing social movement.

Finally, the question persists of how the global, anti-sweatshop movement will sustain transnational solidarities, especially across differences of nation, gender, age, sexuality, race, and ethnicity. This social movement engages garment workers, community-based organizations, labor unions, consumer leagues, women's groups, students' associations, and faith-based groups, as well as various NGOs (Armbruster-Sandoval 2005: 2). It also comprises several intermeshed sites of political activism already mentioned: grassroots politics, civil society organizations, digital activism, and social movements.

Intersectionality raises new questions for understanding the kind of global social protest associated with the Rana Plaza collapse, the contours of the global anti-sweatshop movement, and global social protest generally. How might the emerging transnational solidarities of global social protest inform intersectional understandings of political praxis? How might political projects operating at different levels and/or having different priorities, for example, the anti-sweatshop movement and consumer activism, find value in intersectionality's analytical and political sensibilities? What are the possibilities for coalition politics for a situation as complex as the Rana Plaza collapse and the social inequalities it upholds?

The coercive turn in nation-states

Intersectional analyses of global social protest show the links between local and global social networks. Yet the Rana Plaza collapse occurred within Bangladesh, a particular nation-state whose national policies, forms of governance, and specific history all contributed to the forms of local protest in Bangladesh and the global social movement in which those protests participated. In this sense, the particular governance structures of nation-states constitute important sites that link local and global politics.

Despite differences in the forms of government, political traditions, and history, government responses to social protest and to waves of social uprisings have been strikingly similar, namely, police repression and other punitive state action. When it comes to responding to social protest, the leaders of authoritarian and liberal democratic states alike often expand police-state techniques that build largely on counter-terrorism and warfare (Tugal 2013: 158, 160). For example, a proposed New York City Police Department anti-terror unit asked to carry machine guns during public protests. The urban revolts reveal the extent of the punitive turn taken by many democratic nation-states where law enforcement methods and practices, acquired in decades of wars on drugs, on terror or on insurgency, have become commonplace. From Cleveland to Kolkata, amplified powers of militarized and increasingly privatized police are exerted most heavily on the most structurally disenfranchised populations whose social location within interlocking systems of oppression makes them vulnerable to violence.

Intersectionality sheds light on various facets of this process, namely, the booming punishment industry, differential policing for minority and poor communities, the refinement of surveillance techniques, and the militarization of police. First, nation-states emphasize punishment and make it profitable through varying strategies of mass incarceration. In many democratic states, the number of incarcerated people has grown substantially over the past two decades. The increased sentencing for a multitude of offenses and growing prison populations reflects the punitive turn in state policies. The prison population doubled between 1993 and 2012 in Britain. In France, it increased by 50 percent between 2002 and 2012, a period that coincides with the 2007 introduction of longer mandatory minimum sentencing. Although the crime rate has been decreasing over the past two decades, Canada's prison population is now at its highest level ever. The federal budget for the Correctional Service of Canada has increased by 40 percent to US$2.6 billion in the past five years (M. Brosnahan, "Canada's prison population at all-time high," *CBC News*, November 25, 2013).

In Brazil, the growth of the prison population has been massive since 1990, resulting in the fourth-largest prison population in the world after the United States, China, and Russia. The so-called war on drugs carried out through discriminatory policing practices such as racial and class profiling also plays an important role in the increase in incarceration in Brazil. Roughly 25 percent of inmates are incarcerated on drug charges, the majority of whom are petty dealers who come from poor backgrounds. In Brazil, too, racialized youth from poor urban neighborhoods or favelas have been the primary target of anti-drug legislation and aggressive policing. In its ongoing war on drugs, the Brazilian government has killed many favela youth or has put them in jail or provisional detention for minor crimes without implementing safeguards to avoid their brutalization or their absorption into organized crime.

Intersectional frameworks point out how the coercive turn taken by neoliberal states has fallen heavily on populations who are disadvantaged by race, class, gender, sexuality, disability, religion, and migration status. Within globalized cities, urban sanitization or revitalization policies can lead to the criminalization of so-called slums and the expropriation of the poor viewed as "eyesores" and the "casualties" of development (Amar 2011). In India, for example, the urban homeless population has grown exponentially since the 1990s, primarily due to massive dislocations prompted by development projects and lack of employment in rural regions. The homeless are criminalized by the state, harassed by brutal police evictions, deprived of most basic facilities, such as shelter, running water, and sanitation, and ostracized as "outsiders" or "invaders." In response, with the help of NGOs, the urban homeless are mobilizing to claim basic human rights in a struggle many consider as one of the key new social movements in contemporary India. Within this urban homeless movement, women play a major role and make "gender specific demands concerning livelihood, sexual and reproductive health, child care, privacy, security and rehabilitation" (Chakravarti 2014: 117–18). Homeless women face different sets of problems to homeless men, such as sexual assaults. For Paromita Chakravarti, there is need to find common ground across class and caste lines and between diverse movements led by disenfranchised urban women on issues related to access to the city and citizenship. The homeless women's movement should dialog "with other street-based urban women's mobilizations like that of roadside vendors, sex-workers or movements demanding women's safety in public spaces like 'Take Back the Night' which are gathering strength in Indian cities following the Delhi gang rape" (Chakravarti 2014: 118).

Intersectional frameworks are useful in explaining how the organization of power impacts the types and outcomes of police action for different population groups. The policing tactics applied to African Americans in the United States illustrates these patterns. For example, the 2014 killing of Eric Garner by the Staten Island police cannot be dissociated from his intersectional location vis-à-vis power structures. Garner was a large black male street vendor selling unauthorized cigarettes. The police officer who choked him to death, and who was subsequently exonerated by the court for doing so, saw Garner as an especially dangerous black thug, and not as he was – an unarmed man repeatedly saying "I can't breathe." Tanisha Anderson, a black woman, was killed by the Cleveland police while she was having a "mental health episode." Her mother called 911, asking for help for her daughter, yet when the police arrived they slammed Anderson to the ground in a fashion that caused her death. Tanisha Anderson's death reflects her social location within intersecting systems of power: a 37-year-old black woman with mental health problems whose family likely wouldn't have called 911 had they access to private health care. For the intervening police officers, Tanisha Anderson wasn't someone in need of care but a threat: an agitated black woman. The force of stereotypes such as "black thug" or "crazy black woman" is literally lethal when coupled with police powers in a society structured by intersecting forms of racial and gendered dominance.

Intersectional frameworks examine the ways in which public policies uphold social inequalities. Take, for example, how Australia's asylum policies are militarized. A *New York Times* article, "Australia's Rigid Immigration Barrier" (Appleby 2015), outlines the Australian navy's authority to intercept and return boats carrying asylum seekers to countries like Indonesia, where they live in legal limbo, and Sri Lanka, where they may face government prosecution. Those who successfully reach Australian shores are relocated to offshore remote locations. This is the so-called Pacific Solution, a legislation enabling the Australian government to offshore asylum seekers on Manus Island, Papua New Guinea, and Nauru, where conditions are extremely poor. Implemented between 2001 and 2007 and interrupted in 2008, offshoring practices persist. In 2013, Australia reached a Regional Resettlement Arrangement with Papua New Guinea, which allowed the Australian Defence Force to divert all "unauthorised maritime arrivals," namely, people without visas, to mandatory unlimited detention on Manus Island with no possibility of settling in Australia. Asylum seekers are detained there in a military base under dreadful conditions and face harsh treatment by employees – as evidenced by the death of a young Iranian man after being attacked by a group of employees during a riot. Hunger strikes and suicide attempts among the detainees are not uncommon. As of March 2015, 124 children were in immigration detention in Australia, 103 on Nauru.

Australia's offshore detention practices on Manus Island resemble the US offshore detainment of suspected terrorists at Guantanamo, Cuba. Both sites operate in a legal vacuum, a globally unregulated no-man's-land where the United States exercises unchecked state power outside its national borders. Detainees become "out of sight, out of mind, out of rights" (McCulloch and Pickering 2008: 229). The carceral state operates, as evidenced in these cases of containment, through in-between spaces where criminalized populations, refugee claimants, or people suspected of terrorism are placed in a state of indeterminacy vis-à-vis their most basic human rights.

The case of Lucía Vega Jiménez illustrates various facets of police repression and other punitive state action as governmental responses to social protest and other perceived threats. On December 1, 2013, Lucía Vega Jiménez finished her night shift as chambermaid at a Vancouver hotel. She took the SkyTrain home, but she never made it there. During a routine fare check, the Transit Police (TP) stopped the 42-year-old Mexican worker because she failed to provide proof that she had paid. When the TP officer who initially stopped her for lack of fare heard her foreign accent, the officer contacted the Canadian Border Security Agency (CBSA). The Transit Police turned Jiménez over to the CBSA on suspicion of being illegally in Canada. Jiménez had 20 days of detention, first in a maximum-security prison, then at the immigration holding center several stories below Vancouver International Airport. During her detention, she received neither proper legal aid nor mental health care. Instead, what looked like deliberate neglect cost her the right to contest her deportation. Evidence shows that the CBSA hampered due process by withholding vital procedural information from her. Forty-eight hours after her deportation date was set, she committed suicide.

By looking at Lucía Jiménez's story through intersectional frameworks, we see how race, class, gender, and immigrant status interconnect as categories of power. Ms Jiménez's appearance made her the target of profiling policies. A TP officer later testified that he decided to contact the CBSA to check Ms Jiménez's identity because she "had an accent" and that he believed "she wasn't originally from Canada." She was racially profiled by an armed TP officer. Her criminalization was an ideological dimension of intersecting power relations. Her detainment for several weeks in a maximum-security prison shows the extent of criminalization of undocumented migrants. Each year, some eleven thousand undocumented migrants, including children, are criminalized by the CBSA. Her detainment also calls attention to the existence of subterranean holding cells under the gleaming Vancouver International Airport where Jiménez committed suicide. Harsha Walia, co-founder of the Vancouver chapter of No One Is Illegal, soberly points out in a *Mainlander* article (October 6, 2014):

> During the last month of her life, every institution that Lucia came into contact with was most interested in law enforcement and least interested in her safety. Though this is not shocking to anyone familiar with the immigration system, the facts that are emerging about what happened to Lucia while in custody are illuminating to those unfamiliar with how immigration enforcement really operates.

Moreover, the government apparently tried to cover up the suicide. Documents released by the CBSA, under the Access to Information Act, suggest that the agency deliberately withheld information from reporters and the public about Ms Jiménez's death.

This case shows how disciplinary practices also operate through intersecting power relations of race, class, and gender. The expansion of police powers, even beyond actual police forces, is one way that democratic governments regulate people's daily lives. Specifically, the Transit Police's responsibility is to track fare evaders on public transport, yet here the TP acted as if they were border police, turning public transit into a de facto border. Every day, at various SkyTrain stations and bus stops in the Greater Vancouver area, the Transit Police

– the only armed transit police force in Canada – profile people of color and turn those suspected to be illegal migrants over to the CBSA. According to Transportation Not Deportation, a community campaign calling for an immediate end to the Transit Police's collaboration with the CBSA, the Vancouver area Transit Police reported 328 people to the CBSA in 2013, one in five of whom faced a subsequent immigration investigation which can lead to deportation. Lucía Vega Jiménez was one of them.

But the most significant power dynamic of this case, and the one most closely tied to the main ideas of this chapter, involves the structural power relations of nation-states that have adopted neoliberal philosophies. Lucía Vega Jiménez's treatment illustrates how global capitalism, immigration, and state violence work together to categorize Jiménez and others who share her position as disposable people (Bales 1999). From the point of view of oppressed groups, the ways in which nation-states disenfranchise, dehumanize, and render them disposable are everywhere. Policies and practices such as mass incarceration, the criminalization of the homeless by imposing fines for sleeping outside, evicting poor people from their homes in the name of urban revitalization, and blocking doors and windows in sweatshop factories to ensure that workers cannot leave constitute a chain of similar events that collectively illustrate how nation-states organize the combined work of global capitalism and securitization.

Immigration policies are crafted and implemented by nation-states. While nation-states routinely draw upon different dimensions of neoliberalism, they do not embrace the same dimensions of neoliberal philosophies nor implement the ones that they do in the same way. Common trends across the Global North include the expansion of border checkpoints and border-security staff within borders. For instance, in the United Kingdom, the 2014 Immigration Act enlists employers, health-care providers, educators, and landlords, to act as border guards in their everyday lives. Those on the receiving end of this surveillance risk constant ID checks and discrimination in housing, education, employment, and public services. Like Vancouver's Transit Police, by enforcing seemingly fair laws that have unjust outcomes, various service providers participate in border patrol proxy via loose interpretations that reflect racist biases and stereotypes. Thus converting ordinary citizens into proxy immigration law enforcement resonates with other forms of neoliberal surveillance and privatization.

Overall, there is evidence of a globalized state security apparatus, with many participating nation-states, which produces long-term captive populations, making the prison industrial complex one of the fastest-growing business sectors in the world. By linking seemingly discrete phenomena, using intersectionality as a form of critical inquiry and praxis potentially sheds light on the relationship between the growth of coercive neoliberal states, global capitalism, and configurations of social divisions and hierarchies based on class, gender, sexuality, race and ethnicity, disability, religion, nationality, and location. Intersectional analyses of the connections between immigration, securitization, and the carceral state illustrate yet another way of using such frameworks to analyze important social phenomena.

Securitization: a problem for everyone?

Developments such as the booming punishment industry, differential policing for minority and poor communities, the refinement of surveillance techniques by expanding the network of people with police powers, and the militarization of police all demonstrate how liberal democratic states respond to social protest. They are actively investing in neoliberal policies of securitization.

The term "securitization" emerged in the late 1990s in the Copenhagen School for Peace Studies to describe "how political speech acts or media representations produce subjects of politics that are used to transfer everyday social, economic and cultural governance into the realm of emergency police enforcements and military occupations" (Amar 2011: 306). With this shift, ever-larger groups within a population who become designated as a problem for, rather than as subjects of, justice are increasingly targeted, monitored, policed, and incarcerated. The neoliberal state thus retreats from regulating markets and providing social services but intensifies its practices of surveillance and control of individuals' everyday lives. The concept of securitization is useful to understand this shift – for instance how social protest can be conflated with terrorism and contained with counter-terrorism policing practices.

Securitization has many facets. For example, the differential policing of urban neighborhoods seems designed to secure the borders in order to contain poor people of color rather than protect them. Securitization can also refer to a population. For example, youth is a global population most vulnerable to policies of securitization, regardless of citizenship status. Like Jiménez, youth can be routinely stopped by the police, adults, and mall security guards and questioned about their behavior. Adults who are treated like children – women, people of color – resent it, because this treatment shows unequal power relations.

The securitization of migration refers to processes through which enforcement measures identify transnational migrants and asylum seekers as problem groups, ostensibly to protect national security. Because they arrive without having been selected by governments, asylum seekers are often associated with illegality, disorder, and fraud. Depictions can range from the more benign "they are bogus refugees, queue-jumpers" to the downright hostile belief that "they are criminals." This depiction posits asylum seekers as a security threat, a representation that makes their detention acceptable. The shift in border management regimes is manifest in the adoption of border enforcement strategies to deter refugee claimants, undocumented migrants, and visa over-stayers. Such strategies include the construction of fortifications like the US–Mexico border fence; detention in maximum security prisons; and the creation of no-man's-lands where asylum seekers are unable to claim their rights under refugee protection conventions and receiving states can skirt their protection obligations.

Forms of immigrant detention operate across the Global North to repel, deter, and contain so-called illegal migrants including asylum seekers (who are doing nothing illegal according to the Geneva Convention) from the Global South. These countries include the United States, the UK, Australia, Canada, France, Sweden, Denmark, Finland, Belgium, Spain,

Portugal, Ireland, Germany, Austria, Greece, and the Netherlands. There is a global punitive trend targeting asylum seekers – a trend championed by Australia, which instituted a program of mandatory, prolonged, and even indefinite detention unprecedented amongst countries in the Global North (McCulloch and Pickering 2008: 226, 228, 239).

By casting a new light on the intermeshed relationship between securitization and the coercive state, scholars and activists can use intersectional frameworks to criticize these practices. For example, Liat Ben-Moshe uses intersectionality to reconsider the terms of the mass incarceration debate by re-questioning who counts as incarcerated, and to reconceptualize the linkages between medical/psychiatric institutionalization and imprisonment not simply as analogy but as a deep interconnection in their logic, historical enactment, and social effects. Considered from a perspective that redefines what counts as incarceration, it becomes clear that US incarceration rates have long been extremely high – and that many spaces can become sites of incarceration. Likewise, scholars and activists using intersectional frameworks help unpack how state surveillance and violence disproportionately impact racialized transgender and gender nonconforming people. Mainstream racial justice or migrant rights movements often overlook the needs of this group, arguing that "trans issues" are not significant or representative of their constituencies.

Intersectional frameworks can also shed light on how progressive politics can shore up the security state and population control. Some strands of feminism unwittingly contribute to the expansion of a state's repressive powers and the criminalization of society through the types of action they favor to address violence against women. This is the case when they advocate for state-driven, pro-criminalization strategies and call for increased policing, prosecution, and imprisonment, as well as anti-prostitution and anti-trafficking legislation (Bumiller 2008). Relying on her ethnographic fieldwork, Elizabeth Bernstein (2010) argues that there is collusion between "carceral feminism" and militarized humanitarianism within the contemporary feminist anti-trafficking movement. Preferred political remedies seem to be carceral politics and securitized state apparatuses. As Bernstein points out:

The feminist anti-sex-trafficking movement along with aboli-tionist feminism calling for the criminalisation of demand for prostitution (clients) are not really reflective of *intersectional praxis*. Community accountability in this context means lis-tening to sex workers, being attentive to their needs as they articulate them, not calling for repressive state action. By validating the carceral state in matters such as 'sex work' or 'trafficking', these feminist actions espouse state-sanctioned sexual moralism and politics of respectability (white, middle-class, and heteronormative). As such, feminist respectability politics feeds into the security state's border politics through the 'war against human trafficking' – feminists can thus unwittingly sanction the deportation of migrant sex workers in the name of rescuing them from 'prostitution'. (Bernstein 2010: 54; our italics)

Finally, intersectionality as a form of critical inquiry and praxis can help raise community accountability as a norma-tive principle, so that the interlocking nature of oppression faced by groups is not lost in racial justice, or gender and sexual justice initiatives. Community accountability is also a significant guideline for non-oppressive research practices that intersectionality scholars need to engage.

7
Intersectionality and Critical Education

Critical education has long been important for intersectionality. Across classroom settings, religious communities, mass-media venues, village schools, living rooms, or street corners, education has the potential to oppress or liberate. In this context, the emancipatory potential of education is far reaching. Many of the cases and examples throughout this book have demonstrated some commitment to education as part of their praxis. Immigrant women whose growing English proficiency enabled many of them to develop into savvy activists (Chun, Lipsitz, and Shin 2013: 926); young people who use hip hop as an art form and philosophy to educate one another about the common challenges they face (Perry 2004); scholars/activists who envisioned race/class/gender studies through the lens of transforming colleges and universities (Dill, Zambrana, and McClaughlin 2009); and Latinidades's broad-based program that exposed participants to everything from African-influenced music and dance to how to organize against racism illustrate the scope of critical education.

Intersectionality and critical education share similar sensibilities, primarily because the same people have been involved in both projects. Many people who have been intellectual and political leaders within various social justice projects, have often emphasized critical education's part in their projects. Teachers, parents, principals, administrators, curriculum specialists, and college and high-school counsellors among others have advocated on behalf of the care and well-being of children and youth. These same people have also often been involved in advancing intersectionality. Take, for example, Marian Wright Edelman, founder and president of the US-based Children's Defense Fund. Edelman has been an activist for the rights of children and an advocate for disenfranchised people for her entire professional life. Her work illustrates how her intersectional analysis, which saw how intersections of race, class, and age differentially disadvantage children, stimulated her life's work on behalf of all children.

Critical education and intersectionality have enjoyed an intertwined relationship that has enhanced the critical inquiry and praxis of both. Both projects have much longer histories than can be presented here. Contemporary expressions of intersectionality discussed throughout this book and critical education not only emerged within the same set of social relations, they also influenced one another. Yet the changes ushered in by neoliberalism have put this synergistic relationship in jeopardy. This chapter examines contemporary challenges that confront this relationship between intersectionality and education, especially concerning issues of equity and social justice.

A critical convergence: intersectionality and education

Brazilian educator Paulo Freire's classic *Pedagogy of the Oppressed* constitutes one well-known and highly influential volume that examines how education can disenfranchise or empower (Freire 1970). While not typically categorized this way, this book can also be read as a core text for intersectionality. In the *Pedagogy of the Oppressed*, Freire rejects a class-only analysis of power relations in favor of the more robust power-laden language of the "oppressed." The oppressed of Freire's twentieth-century Brazil are similar to those oppressed today: homeless/landless people, women, poor people, black people, sexual minorities, indigenous people, undocumented immigrants, prisoners, religious minorities, disabled people, and the young. Freire's use of the terms "oppression" and "oppressed" invokes intersecting inequities of class, race, ethnicity, age, religion and citizenship. Via his choice of words, Freire links the needs of oppressed people to calls for social justice. In the context of contemporary euphemisms – including "disenfranchised," "disadvantaged," "racialized," "gendered," and similar terms that serve as replacements – Freire's language can be off-putting. Just as terms like "racial discrimination" and "racial profiling" may describe the same behavior, the terms themselves bring a different meaning. The word "oppression" may be out of favor, but the social conditions that it describes are not.

Freire also expresses a broader understanding of pedagogy than do narrow technical definitions that stress classroom management skills or how to teach subject matter. Rather, pedagogy invokes a philosophy of education that is grounded in the practice of education, in other words, education as praxis. Nancy Naples's article, "Teaching Intersectionality Intersectionally," invokes this understanding of pedagogy in her discussion of intersectionality's praxis (Naples 2009). This broader understanding of pedagogy as praxis also has ties to social justice. Pedagogy matters because engaging in specific pedagogical practices can enhance or retard social justice. Moreover, for oppressed people, different pedagogies can deepen understandings of social justice or limit them.

Freire saw the kind of pedagogies that limit understandings of social justice as governed by what he called a "banking concept of education." Banking education refers to educational practices where students master "ready-made" knowledge, the facts and ways of thinking that students need to fit into an unequal status quo. A banking approach to education can reinforce existing social inequalities, leaving some students with more opportunities than others. For example, within societies that see girls' futures solely as wives and mothers and doing the domestic labor of caring for families, it makes little sense to send girls to formal school. School funding is "wasted" on girls because they will bank skills that they will never spend.

But the process of banking education can be more pernicious than excluding people from schools. For Freire, the banking of education asks students to uncritically accept and help reproduce their assigned place in the social hierarchy. Within this logic, not only do schools teach elite white men that they are better than everyone else, schools as institutions are set up to deliver cultural capital to this group so that they can be so. Oppressed groups face an opposite reality – the tenets of banking education can teach them to uphold the very practices that produce their subordination. Freire published *The Pedagogy of the Oppressed* in 1970, well before the ascendancy of neoliberalism, yet his banking approach to education describes the same philosophical principles of neoliberalism discussed in earlier chapters. Students are encouraged to bank a certain kind of educational capital in order to procure stable jobs with fair wages and benefits when they graduate. And those who challenge the conditions of their oppression may face punishment.

Freire also presents a different pedagogy, namely, an education for critical consciousness that stands in contrast to the banking concept. This alternative pedagogy rests on a dialogical pedagogy, a way of critically analyzing the world by asking tough questions, problem solving, and critical thinking. Education for critical consciousness may be essential for oppressed people: without it, they lack important tools for analyzing their own subordination and taking action to oppose it. Developing a critical consciousness on social inequality, as well as one's own placement in it, can stimulate personal and collective empowerment. This critical consciousness supplements and elevates sociologist C. Wright Mills's notion of the sociological imagination as honed at the intersection of individual biography, history, and social structure (Mills 2000).

Significantly, while Freire grounds his analysis of critical education in the needs of oppressed people, the value of critical education is open to everyone. Everyone benefits from a better understanding of the dynamics of intersecting social inequalities, as well as the kinds of critical thinking and problem-posing skills that can remedy them. Developing a critical consciousness of how the interdependent dimensions of one's own life fit into historical and structural phenomena can be life changing. Moreover, developing a critical consciousness about how intersecting systems of power are organized within and across the structural, disciplinary, cultural, and interpersonal domains of power can result in new and powerful perspectives on social inequality.

Despite dominant rhetoric that young people, poor people, people of color, and other disenfranchised groups do not value education, the record says otherwise (Alonso, Anderson, Su, and Theoharis 2009; Lopez 2002; Perry, Steele, and Hilliard III 2003; Rios 2011). Education has long been central to political struggles, including banking education. Gaining marketable skills for survival within systems of social inequality, *and* gaining education for critical consciousness puts oppressed groups in a position to analyze and challenge the social inequalities that circumscribe their lives. Sometimes leaders within oppressed groups go to great lengths to procure the skills and knowledge of a banking education and the critical thinking skills that will enable them to criticize it. For example, black feminist educator and intellectual Anna Julia Cooper is known within US black feminism for her 1892 book *A Voice from the South* that presented an intersectional analysis (Cooper 1892). Yet Cooper also started a night school in her Washington DC living room for African-American working-class and disabled adults who could not attend public school. She invited the excluded to attend her "public" school free of charge. Cooper is known for her scholarly contributions to black feminism, yet her community education work remains less celebrated (May 2007).

Developing multiple forms of literacy constitutes one pedagogical feature of education for critical consciousness. Freire was clear that skills of basic literacy constituted the bedrock of critical consciousness – if oppressed people could not read or manage the basics of finance, they were at the mercy of privileged groups. The case of how Muhammad Yunus developed microcredit as a new way of banking for poor, rural villagers fostered their financial literacy. But gaining literacy also has a broader meaning. Skills in "reading" the social relations of one's own experiences, whether using new forms of digital media to debate the meaning of intersectionality for cyberfeminism, or using critical intersectional perspectives to analyze spreading patterns of securitization in prisons and schools or Australia's punitive immigration policies, can stimulate people who care about these issues to take action.

Engaging oppressed people in the process of knowledge production is another core pedagogical feature of education for critical consciousness. Within a dialogical concept of education, learning also entails sharing knowledge with a community of learners. For researchers working with youth, participatory action research designs, where participants are co-investigators rather than subjects within a study, can foster better questions and produce relevant knowledge (Brown and Rodriguez 2009). The identity politics of hip hop also points toward a dialogical engagement between artists and consumers that not only educates but also might empower both. Moreover, dialogical engagement can topple old ideas about what counts as knowledge and can develop new forms of knowledge creation. The new information technologies of social media, for example, and the shift on the Web from top-down distribution of knowledge to a network of broad-based knowledge creators enables new dialogs that have potentially important effects on democracy (Diamond and Plattner 2012).

Freire's focus on critical consciousness and on personal and collective empowerment points to several connections between intersectionality and critical education. First, when it comes to educational equity, Freire's pedagogical framework aligns with important philosophical distinctions between neoliberalism and participatory democracy. Neoliberalism typically rests on unstated assumptions about education and equity that are having an important influence on contemporary school policies from kindergarten through graduate education. Within the logic of neoliberalism, formal schooling should be a cost-effective social institution that delivers much-needed skills and training in a non-discriminatory fashion. Schools are not in the equity business. Contemporary debates about education and equity typically compare students using measurable criteria – grades, test scores, dropout rates, choice of subjects, time to degree, and the slippery and subjective category of the cultural values of students. Differences between students are technical problems that are amenable to diagnosis and appropriate remedies. For example, the sustained attention to the achievement "gap" between the performance of white middle-class children and everyone else preoccupies educational researchers (Banks and

Park 2010). Success occurs when the gap is narrowed. This diagnosis of the problem uncritically presumes that, beyond skills delivery, the primary purpose of schooling lies in training the youth who trail behind to catch up to the children who achieve. Working *within* neoliberal assumptions, assimilating seemingly failing youth into existing social hierarchies will eventually produce educational equity.

Participatory democracy rests on a different conceptual foundation (Hilmer 2010; Naples 2013). Within a logic of participatory democracy, schools are more than institutions where young people go to acquire technical skills and social capital that will make them attractive to employers. Schools certainly do this, but they also are venues where intersecting power relations of race, class, gender, sexuality, nationality, ethnicity, ability, and age routinely privilege some students over others. Formal schooling thus constitutes an important venue for teaching students both to fit in and criticize existing social hierarchies. Many teachers and parents see schools as places where they have to fight for the rights of children and youth not only to get an education, but also to get an education that fosters critical literacy and critical thinking skills. More importantly, schools are often important venues for social protest from young adults who are either excluded from formal education altogether or who, when mandated to have compulsory education, cast a critical eye on the schooling they receive. A critical education understands the organization of schools themselves as part of a broader education as a field of power (Bourdieu and Passeron 1977)

Historically, the struggles for a quality public education by poor people, immigrants, African Americans, women, Latinos, disabled people, and others who encountered routine and systemic discrimination within educational institutions aligned with ongoing efforts to reform US public education. In the United States, the idea that public schools prepare citizens for democracy runs deep. John Dewey, Jane Addams, William E. B. Du Bois, and other early twentieth-century American pragmatist thinkers saw education as essential for democratic citizenship (Collins 2012b). *Democracy and Education* and *The Public and Its Problems*, classic works by philosopher John Dewey, stressed the importance of public education for American democracy (Dewey 1954, 2004). For

Dewey, educating the public required communication between people so that the people could decide what problems they thought were worth pursuing and how best to move forward. Yet, since the public itself was so heterogeneous, strong democratic institutions required that people both commit to those institutions and work through their differences for the public good. An informed public had to learn how to learn from one another. In this regard, participatory democracy required dialogs across difference. In other words, people need resources and structured support for learning how to share ideas to be able to take the participatory role in their own governance that democracy is supposed to make available to them.

Many segments of the US public disagreed with this vision of participatory democracy. Prior to the new social movements of the 1950s–1980s, schools in the United States aimed to "Americanize" immigrant and ethnic minority students by assimilating them into dominant Anglo-Saxon Protestant middle-class norms and values. This version of assimilation ignored the fact that becoming American often meant upholding racism, sexism, and xenophobia by learning how to practice the discriminations that they engendered. The new social movements that were so important to black feminism, race/class/gender studies, and intersectionality were closely aligned with the concept of participatory democracy that critical education had long upheld.

Intersectionality and critical education share a similar institutional location: both projects are housed primarily in schools and thus participate in the politics of education in schools themselves. Because it helps reproduce social inequalities, formal schooling is a contested site of knowledge production. At the same time, people who attend or work in school settings also challenge these social inequalities, typically by questioning the school's curriculum and often by rejecting its rules and regulations. For example, the high-school students in *Our Schools Suck: Students Talk Back to a Segregated Nation on the Failures of Urban Education* provide a sobering analysis of how and why their schools fail them. Many have been pressured to see themselves as failures because they seemingly cannot or won't assimilate into their school's banking culture. Yet, while their high schools uphold this ideology, they provide few opportunities for students to achieve (Alonso, Anderson, Su, and Theoharis 2009).

US teenagers and young adults spend large amounts of time in middle schools, high schools, colleges, and universities. As a result, schools are important venues for youth activism. When teenagers and college students develop a critical consciousness about social inequality, their examples are often drawn from their school experiences because that's where they spend their time. The quality of the education offered to students is typically high on their list of concerns. Youth dissatisfaction with schooling, especially pressures to assimilate and conform, takes many forms. *Corridor Cultures: Mapping Student Resistance at an Urban High School* examines how high-school students use space to hone such views. Studying the tension between student-dominated hallways and teacher-dominated classrooms, students use corridors as their space that, while under teacher surveillance, is also an underground space for political speech (Dickar 2008).

Many historical examples of youth activism where education has been central to the political demands of high-school and college-age students exist, yet interpretations of the activism of young people become folded into other categories. For example, in the United States in the late 1960s and 1970s, African-American high-school and college students demanded curriculum reforms to add black studies and more African-American professors to college and university campuses (Collins 2009b). That same period included student movements by Latinos, Asian, and Native Americans that focused on educational issues, such as the creation of ethnic studies, and more inclusive and diversified curricula in higher education. These student movements were crucial in creating space on college campuses for social justice projects (Parker and Samantrai 2010). Currently, the undocumented Latino youth who spearheaded the Dream Movement aim for educational equity: the right to attend college.

Youth activism for education-related issues is also an important theme within global social protest. During South Africa's long anti-Apartheid struggle, black secondary-school students boycotted schools, some for many years, because they refused to be taught in Afrikaans. This "lost generation" rejected formal schooling that aimed to assimilate them into racial inequality (Franklin 2003). Pakistani human rights activist Malala Yousafzai's campaign in support of education for girls and women got her shot. After Malala was awarded the 2014 Nobel Peace Prize for her struggles for the right of all children to an education, she started a school for girls.

Finally, critical education's emphasis on dialogical pedagogy and intersectionality's focus on relationality speak to a similar theme, namely, navigating differences is an important part of developing a critical consciousness for both individuals and for forms of knowledge. Throughout this volume, we have cited numerous thinkers who identify negotiating differences as an important challenge facing intersectionality. Critical education's dialogical education offers a useful avenue for how intersectionality might better navigate differences. Using intersectional frameworks to rethink social inequality requires a more participatory and democratic methodology that rejects neoliberal tendencies to assess knowledge based on its "use" or "function" for one's individual project. Instead, dialogical education takes on the hard work of developing critical consciousness by talking and listening to people who have different points of view. When it comes to grappling with social inequality, this idea of dialogical education might also help think through some of the challenges that intersectionality faces with methodology. Rather than downplaying or dismissing differences, an intersectional methodology requires *negotiating* differences that exist within discrete scholarly and political traditions of race, class, gender, sexuality, ability, nationality, ethnicity, colonialism, religion, and immigration. This dialogical methodology assumes no preformatted connection between them. The goal is to make those connections within specific social contexts. Hence, intersectionality's heuristic is a starting point for building intellectual coalitions of consensus and contestation.

This dialogical approach would see conflict as an inevitable outcome of bona fide differences and strive to make them generative. In her essay "The Master's Tools Will Never Dismantle the Master's House," initially delivered at a feminist conference, Audre Lorde counsels a creative engagement with difference, transforming it into a resource:

> Advocating the mere tolerance of difference between women is the grossest reformism. It is a total denial of the creative

function of difference in our lives. Difference must be not merely tolerated, but seen as a fund of necessary polarities between which our creativity can spark like a dialectic. Only then does the necessity for interdependency become unthreatening. Only within that interdependency of different strengths, acknowledged and equal, can the power to seek new ways of being in the world generate, as well as the courage and sustenance to act where there are no charters. (Lorde 1984: 111–12)

Lorde is a poet, a visionary thinker who poses this idea of a difference-infused relationality in the abstract. But how does one actually do this beyond conversations with like-minded people? Doing intersectional work that takes difference seriously means working with people who really are different. Engaging the differences in diverse fields of study and political projects is even more challenging.

To sum up: historically, intersectionality and critical education seemingly share three similarities: both areas draw from broader philosophical traditions of participatory democracy; both work primarily in schooling and formal education as one primary institutional location for their praxis; and, for each, navigating differences is an important part of developing a critical consciousness. Yet this historical and conceptual proximity of intersectionality and critical education as intertwined projects need not mean that these projects are currently intertwined in a critical fashion, or that either one remains critical in the same way as in prior eras.

When it comes to social inequality, how is this connection between intersectionality and critical education being reframed? One way to get at this question is to trace how intersectionality has been understood and used within secondary schools and higher education. The ideas of intersectionality continue to circulate in these venues, although not always under the term "intersectionality." Instead, the term "diversity" often serves as a surrogate for intersectionality. And as the terms change, their meaning does as well. Sara Ahmed's analysis of diversity initiatives within higher education identifies why these linguistic shifts might matter:

the arrival of the term "diversity" involves the departure of other (perhaps more critical) terms, including "equality," "equal opportunities," and "social justice." A genealogy of the term "diversity" allows us to think about how the term holds institutional appeal. We might want to be cautious about the appealing nature of diversity and ask whether the ease of its incorporation by institutions is a sign of the loss of its critical edge. (Ahmed 2012: 1)

Given this linguistic substitution, paying attention to how diversity is currently understood and used within education sheds light on how intersectionality and critical education are both being reframed.

Multicultural education, diversity, and urban public schools

John Dewey and other early twentieth-century school reformers could not have foreseen how a late-twentieth century logic of neoliberalism could erase their ideas about education, participatory democracy, and public schools from public view. In the United States, neoliberalism's goals of privatizing prisons, health care, transportation, and other public institutions, scaling back the social welfare state, deregulating the labor market, and pointing to personal responsibility as the cause and cure for social problems has reshaped public education. Because schools are tasked with the job of producing workers with marketable skills, schools are frontline actors in implementing a neoliberal agenda. Yet this reshaping of formal education in the United States masks a growing reality that future workers can expect to have less permanent employment, less job security, fewer health and education benefits, and smaller pensions. Students are taught to assume the risks of the marketplace because a shrinking government will not be there to offer a safety net. The winners and losers on the playing field of FIFA football become the metaphor for playing the game of winning or losing a job.

All educational institutions have felt the effects of neoliberal reorganization, yet public schools, from elementary level through public colleges and universities, have been especially hard hit. Many current educational practices reflect neoliberalism's lack of commitment to public education: differential patterns of investment in school infrastructure leave some public schools dilapidated and overcrowded, while others with private resources that service wealthy students manage to have music teachers, football teams, state-of-the-art science and computer laboratories, and art studios; some public elementary and high schools are horribly overcrowded, sending students to school in shifts, whereas other students, one public-school district away, do not; in some states, teacher unions remain under attack, with teachers stigmatized as the cause of school problems rather than part of the solution; and the growth of part-time faculty on college campuses erodes the storied tradition of tenure as the protection of free and often unpopular speech. Practices such as the growing use of mandatory high-stakes testing for students more intensified evaluation processes for public school teachers, and tying pay to student test scores, illustrate the growth of a culture that elevates measurements above relationships. Collectively, these policies aim to install a banking model of education that can implement the core ideas of a neoliberal philosophy.

The increasing influence of neoliberalism on public education as a core democratic institution has fostered a widespread defunding of urban public schools. Privatization has been the weapon of choice for reshaping the opportunity structure of urban public education that historically provided children from poor, working-class, immigrant, and disadvantaged backgrounds access to a quality public education. The attack on the social welfare state has meant abandoning these children, often by transferring public funds and other subsidies to charter schools, boarding schools, and similar private institutions that promise to do a better job with urban youth. Policies that are designed to improve the quality of public education by introducing more competition into the educational marketplace have reshaped urban public school bureaucracies and classroom practices alike.

Many Americans believe that neoliberal policies such as these are benign, or at least they do no harm, because educational equity has been achieved. By law, all children in the United States are entitled to a free public education. Yet preexisting intersecting social inequalities assign children and youth to neighborhoods and schools that are noticeably unequal. In the United States, where children live – and the property taxes that those areas can collect – shape school policies in any given school district. Wealthy districts get better public schools whereas poor districts do not. Early in life, children are assigned to different pipelines. Some pipelines provide a smooth path manned by qualified and experienced teachers, challenging courses for college preparation, remedial help to navigate the rough spots, good counselling about college, honors programs, and contact with full-time faculty, and fellowships for graduate education. The pipeline for other children, regardless of their talent, motivation, and self-discipline, fosters less rosy outcomes – part-time jobs with no benefits, unemployment, and prison. When it comes to talent, the children start off the same. Yet different pipelines characterized by educational inequality yield markedly different results.

Children from families that are poor, of racial/ethnic groups and with undocumented immigrant status are more likely to attend urban public schools with high concentrations of students from a similar background. Regardless of social class, African-American and Latino students are more likely to attend racially homogeneous schools, a phenomenon that the Civil Rights Project at UCLA calls the resegregation of US public education.[1] The resegregation of public schooling has created urban public school districts that are overwhelmingly Latino and African American. Just as neighborhoods have tipping points where whites decide to move if too many black or Latino families move in, urban public schools have undergone a comparable erosion of support and funding when well-off, white families decide to leave. The children who remain in these underfunded schools encounter public policies that favor securitization over instruction. Ironically, primarily because middle-class and/or white families have abandoned urban public schools, children from families that are affluent, white, and hold US citizenship *also* attend racially homogeneous schools. Yet these quality suburban schools are rarely seen as segregated.

Historically, multiculturalism in the United States has been intertwined with civil rights struggles for educational equity.[2] As such, multicultural education initiatives have been part of debates about the function of US public schools, especially their responsibility for educating children from heterogene-ous backgrounds (Banks and Park 2010: 385–6). Developed in the 1970s and 1980s, the same period when race/class/and gender studies and similar critical discourses embraced a critical education model for empowerment, multicultural education was a direct descendant of school reform efforts for participatory democracy. Multicultural education initia-tives pointed to the changing demographics of youth in the United States to buttress their arguments that not only was schooling necessary, but that multicultural education needed to be an important part of public education. Yet they did not see diversity as lying primarily in the children and youth. Rather, earlier initiatives looked toward structural factors as facilitating or providing barriers to equity. Public schools were important players in bringing about structural change. In this sense, while multicultural education was sparked by the issues of, to use Freire's language, oppressed children, it aimed to assist all students by adopting the national project of school desegregation. Public schools interpreted their mandate as public institutions as one of providing fair access to opportunities for students from diverse backgrounds, as well as helping all students, including those growing up with privilege, to learn from and respect those with experiences that were very different than their own. These earlier move-ments were concerned with the growing heterogeneity of the population to be educated across differences of race, class, gender, ethnicity, linguistic communities, citizenship status, and sexuality.

The idea of multiculturalism remains. Yet the waning phi-losophy of participatory democracy in US public education, coupled with the growing influence of neoliberalism, has shifted the terms of the debate. Within education, policy makers, scholars and teachers, and government officials have increasingly moved away from the term "multiculturalism" in favor of the term "diversity." Having a commitment to "diversity" increasingly replaces multiculturalism's emphasis on reforming schools for educational equity. The changing meaning of diversity, a step along the road from intersection-ality to multiculturalism and now diversity, signals a new understanding both of the problem of educational equity and its possible solutions.

The concept of the "demographic imperative" illustrates how the rhetoric of diversity operates within resegregation. The imperative refers to the mismatch between the children who are most likely to attend public schools in the future and the teaching staff likely to be teaching them. One component of this imperative concerns the increasing percentage of youth and children from diverse racial/ethnic backgrounds and of varying immigrant status and linguistic communities within the American population. These children are much more likely to attend urban public schools, a phenomenon that will make schools themselves more "diverse." Another component focuses on teachers. Despite demographic changes in the US population overall, the teaching staff of public schools is predicted to remain overwhelmingly white and female. How will young white teachers manage the diverse children and teenagers who are likely to attend urban public schools?

This focus on the demographics of who is likely to attend public schools, as well demographic predictions about who will teach them, masks a troubling set of assumptions. In the context of racial resegregation, diversity lies in the children who bring their differences into schools settings and, by their presence, make the schools more diverse. In this sense, the word "diverse" becomes a stigmatized code word that signals that, by being "diverse," a school has "too many blacks" or "too many Latinos." In an ironic sleight of hand, the *rhetoric* of diversity inherited from multicultural education that can be celebrated as a good thing remains in use. Yet the *reality* remains that some forms of diversity remain more desirable than others. An urban district or an urban public school with too much diversity signals public institutions that are deemed to be inferior because they have too many of the wrong kind of children.

The demographic imperative – and how diversity is deployed in conjunction with it – fosters tunnel vision on broader social issues. Emphasizing the mismatch between children who are likely to attend defunded public schools and the professional staff who are likely to teach them as the reason for diversity training misdiagnoses the problem. Whatever they may be called, diversity initiatives that work with the complex identities that are important to students and that see these identities as linked to broader structural forces retain ties to multiculturalism and intersectionality. It is important to understand the multiple identifications of students who attend urban public schools and to uphold efforts at curriculum reform or teacher training that will change public schools. More humane treatment of youth and children is a good thing, as is recruiting caring, competent, and skilled school personnel. Yet diversity initiatives that aim to make teachers more culturally competent or to help students better fit into the existing system miss an opportunity to use intersectionality as an analytic tool that can enhance critical education.

Here we turn to specific policy initiatives that aim to foster diversity, namely, efforts to recruit more underrepresented youth into science. This new language of science policy and education includes multiple institutional and national initiatives tied to training more American youth for careers in the fields of science, technology, engineering, and mathematics (STEM). Many elementary and secondary schools have STEM programs, with some becoming STEM schools. Developing a workforce for STEM fields has implications for US economic growth and security. A strong diversity initiative encourages STEM to come to terms with the overlooked and underutilized talent among American youth, especially, the underrepresentation within STEM fields of two groups: girls/women; and African Americans/Latinos. How might using intersectionality as an analytic framework shed light on this initiative?

Pipelines to somewhere or nowhere?

The metaphor of "pipelines" is increasingly used to understand the causes of and cures for the underrepresentation of historically disenfranchised groups in STEM as it is in describing other social problems. When applied to education, pipelines either work well when they produce a sufficient number of the "right" kind of students or "leak" and lose talent along the way when they don't. On the surface, the logic of pipelines seems benign. In the US context, this metaphor of pipelines has been a useful tool for developing this diversity initiative within STEM. In some ways, the former national priority of ensuring equal education access for all children has been narrowed to a more targeted program of recruiting underrepresented populations into science. Attention to STEM skills and degrees, as well as the STEM fields of science, technology, engineering, and math, constitute important national priorities. Institutional and national initiatives to strengthen pipelines for girls and women, as well as for black and Latino youth, in STEM fields reflect substantial advocacy on the part of people of color to align public policy objectives with the perceived needs of disadvantaged youth.

Yet framing issues of educational equity through the either/ or logic of pipelines for girls and women and pipelines for people of color may be shortsighted. Parsing out gender, race, and class as separate entities narrows the ability of pipeline metaphors to solve the problems they encounter. Intersectionality as a form of critical inquiry points to the limited utility of trying to fix social inequality with the insufficient concept of pipelines.

Because girls of color are typically treated as a sub-category of gender pipelines, they are often not well served by this frame. This means that white girls are the core group that is underrepresented in STEM fields, and that girls of color experience "special" problems that go beyond those confronting white girls. Recruiting African-American and Latina girls and women, historically disadvantaged US populations, into science constitutes an important policy proposal for advancing the stated goals of STEM initiatives. The commitment to women and girls of color seems to be there, yet the question of how to conceptualize and remedy their absence in science raises questions of interpretive frameworks.

An intersectional analysis would replace this ranking with a view of African-American and Latina girls as having multiple identities that cannot be accommodated within either the gender pipeline or the racial/ethnic pipeline. Here intersectionality describes women of color as being at the "intersection" of women and people of color, two underrepresented groups in science education and science careers. This shift would focus increased attention on barriers to science that girls of color face, many of which are the same barriers that confront boys. Both groups meet similar barriers, but experience them differently. The language of pipelines, with its related metaphors of leaky places where pipelines lose talent, has increasingly replaced structural analyses with their language of barriers to achievement. The problem is represented as cracks in an otherwise sound pipeline in places which allow girls of color seemingly to leak out. In contrast, the structural barriers metaphor pays far more attention to the organization of formal education itself, suggesting that inadequate funding creates the barriers that block the achievement of women and girls of color. The structural barriers metaphor is likely to see remedies as lying within the structural organization of schools and in their disciplinary policies. In contrast, the leaky pipeline metaphor draws more heavily on the cultural capital that girls and women of color bring to schooling, as well as individual attributes that predispose individual girls of color to high achievement.

An intersectional analysis would also change understandings of why African-American and Latino boys are underrepresented in STEM fields. When it comes to educational equity and these boys, pipeline logic takes a different turn. Here the issue of educational achievement is linked less to questions of leakage, and more to how effectively a different pipeline works to push African-American and Latino boys out of school altogether. In this case, the pipeline metaphor can be useful up to a point.

The metaphor of a pre-kindergarten (Pre-K)-to-prison pipeline to describe dismal educational outcomes for African-American and Latino boys better fits empirical reality. The Pre-K to prison pipeline constitutes an institutional mechanism for applying policies of securitization to African-American and Latino male youth. This use of the pipeline metaphor challenges assumptions that urban public schools are places of equity and upward social mobility. This emerging framework on the Pre-K to prison pipeline refocuses attention away from the personal qualities of boys and toward institutional policies not just of schools, but of police. These studies painstakingly trace all the ways that school policies and practices discipline poor black boys, and mark them as dangerous criminals or about to become such. Tracing the connections for black boys can be heartbreaking. In elementary school, black boys encounter different disciplinary practices than other students (Arnett Ferguson 2000). Despite valuing education in the abstract, they are pushed out of high school and disproportionately drop out. Colleges offer opportunities for black boys in sports, illustrating a continuation of the pipeline for black boys who do manage to remain in school. But black boys disproportionately end up in prison, fueling the growth of the prison industry (Collins 2006). In a post-agricultural and post-industrial society, non-educated black boys are a surplus population of disposable people (Bales 1999).

Understanding the ways in which black boys are exploited and pushed through a discriminatory pipeline is important work. Yet intersectionality raises the uncomfortable issue of the framing of such work. Does the focused attention on black boys in ways that treat gender as a descriptive category of analysis inadvertently misread the problems of young African-American women who experience similar kinds of political, economic, and social control? Stated differently, gender is less often used to explain the experiences of black boys and men than to describe them. Yet gender analyses can be applied to the experiences of both black women and men. Both live in a carceral society and experience its effects.

These uses of pipeline metaphors to apply to women and girls of color and African-American and Latino boys are important in different ways. Yet this focus on gender and race also obscures a third significant way that pipeline logic is used but remains unconnected to questions of educational equity. Class is largely missing from pipeline analyses that assume educational equity. Also absent is sustained attention to the deteriorating condition of public education itself. Many people assume that the existing system is either already fair (it's amazing how many young white pre-service teachers believe that it is), or that it is so beyond reform that all one can do is fit in (help diverse populations assimilate). Pipeline metaphors rarely take these issues into account.

Overall, the changing meaning of diversity initiatives illustrates why public schools are important sites for educational equity. The interdependent domains of power (chapter 1) can shed light on multicultural education, the logic of pipelines, and other facets of formal schooling discussed here. Examining the structural domain of power shows how schooling

institutionalizes sorting mechanisms, such as admissions policies, curricular offerings, tracking, allocation of resources,
and districting policies, as well as how economic barriers to
entry, such as tuition, financial aid processes, and costs of
eligibility requirements (e.g., the cost of testing and test prep),
get solidified in school and state policies. Examining how
power works in the cultural domain shows how people both
reproduce and legitimate the ideas that uphold a given social
order, and how they critique that order and imagine alternatives to it. Inquiries into a disciplinary domain of power
reveal how rules and regulations of everyday school life –
grades, testing, zero-tolerance policies – punish already marginalized students and offer rewards to those whom the
system privileges. Each of these domains of power shapes, in
turn, how power plays out interpersonally: in interactions
among individuals and groups, including increasingly heterogeneous student populations (Collins 2009a).

Intersectionality, diversity, and higher education

On most college and university campuses in the United States,
intersectionality and diversity initiatives are strange bedfel-
lows. "Intersectionality is the intellectual core of diversity
work" (Dill 2009: 229) may have been the case when race/
class/gender studies arrived on college campuses in the 1980s,
yet is this the case today? Over the last several decades, intersectionality and campus diversity initiatives have travelled
different institutional paths. Intersectionality has emphasized
its research and teaching components, in essence, a focus on
critical inquiry. In contrast, diversity initiatives have become
much more closely aligned with administrative services.
Campus diversity initiatives now span activities as varied as
monitoring an institution's legal anti-discrimination compliance, providing diversity training for university staff (for
example, resident assistants living in college dormitories), and
providing student services. Intersectionality may have once
been the intellectual core of diversity work, and in many
places it still is. Yet the institutional changes that have taken

place on college and university campuses that pursue neoliberal agendas have altered the contours of many social justice initiatives, including the relationship between intersectionality and diversity within higher education.

Contemporary diversity initiatives vary greatly across US college campuses, in part because social inequalities in K-12 urban public schools ration college access for poor, working-class, Latino, African-American, and undocumented students, among others. Most children may have the right to a public education, yet the combination of spatial boundaries and ability to pay means that the schools that they attend are unequal. With regard to college access, most students have the right to attend college. But is this likely or even possible for students who attend K-12 schools in urban school districts? Through their recruitment mechanisms, financial aid packets, and investments in fancy student centers and upscale dormitories, colleges and universities compete for the so-called best students. Rankings of US colleges and universities in the *US News and World Report* and similar publications do not just reflect which has the best sociology program or which is the best campus for studying abroad. They also provide a snapshot of structural social inequalities in higher education. When combined, these processes of K-12 public education resegregation that relegate poor children and children of color to urban public schools and policies of recruitment that routinely overlook these populations result in a highly stratified college system with varying student populations on each college campus.

The understanding of what it means to attend college in the United States requires careful calibration of which institutions house diversity initiatives at all, as well as of the form that those initiatives might take. These differences between colleges and universities also point to different ways that intersectionality may or may not be the intellectual core of diversity work. Because the many colleges and universities within US higher education differ so much from one another, diversity initiatives vary greatly. Community colleges, elite Ivy League institutions, small liberal arts colleges, large public universities, and both regional and flagship state institutions all have varied campus environments and diversity initiatives. Many community colleges are horribly overcrowded: they service the large numbers of students who seek an affordable college education. Some students who are fortunate enough to enrol in quality community colleges, for example, Santa Monica Community College in Los Angeles or Central New Mexico Community College in Albuquerque, New Mexico, can find courses taught by master teachers who are skilled at working with students from heterogeneous backgrounds. Other students are less fortunate. For-profit colleges have become so adept both at marketing questionable degree programs and getting working-class students to take out government-backed loans to pay for them that, in 2015, the US federal government stepped in to offer assistance to students mired in debt. A small number of poor and working-class students in urban school districts may have the talent and good luck to find counsellors to help with college applications or schools that still have affirmative-action outreach programs into urban districts. More often, students most in search of a critical education are less likely to find it in colleges which themselves uncritically accept "banking" standards.

When it comes to student populations, some schools have a surplus of "diversity," whereas others have a scarcity. Reflecting understandings of diversity depicted by K-12 schools who work with heterogeneous populations, diversity initiatives, are virtually non-existent on underfunded community college campuses. Overworked and underpaid faculty, staff, and administrators are hardly in a position to offer extensive tailored services to heterogeneous student populations. These colleges already have more diversity than they can handle – recruiting students from diverse backgrounds is not the issue. In contrast, highly selective colleges and universities must work to overcome the legacy of exclusionary practices against people of color, women, ethnic and cultural minorities, and new immigrant students. These schools may appear to be more diverse and, when it comes to the visible presence of students of color and international students, they are. But elite institutions remain the preserve of students from wealthy families. Elite private institutions can afford to pay for full-service diversity initiatives.

In this universe of ranked colleges and universities, large public universities stand out as places that can both attract heterogeneous populations and, because they are seemingly public institutions, they should find ways to work with a heterogeneous public. Most large schools have diversity initiatives, organized through a chief diversity officer who oversees and coordinates a university's diversity programs. The diversity initiatives at public universities fall somewhere between those of under-resourced colleges, where funding is earmarked for more basic services, and the designer diversity initiatives of elite schools that have the resources to individualize both their instructional practices and their programs. The shifting meaning of diversity within public universities provides a window on changes in how diversity is conceptualized and managed within US colleges and universities. These shifts also shed light on the directions that intersectionality has taken or might take as the intellectual core of diversity work.

Ostensibly supported by public funding, public institutions become targeted sites for campus diversity by university employees and students, by state legislators, as well as by members of the general public. During the 1960s' social movement era, public universities were touchstones for important racial desegregation efforts, for example, James Meredith suing the University of Mississippi or the African-American students who desegregated the University of Alabama at Tuscaloosa. The University of Michigan, Ann Arbor, the University of Texas at Austin, and the public universities of the California state system have all faced legal challenges to their affirmative action policies to produce campus diversity, in part because they are *public* institutions of higher education. The steady erosion of affirmative action oversight, with its attention to structural forms of discrimination and their remedies, has effectively erased talk of oppression, intersecting oppressions, and similar structural phenomena. The absence of language to discuss social injustices, such as Freire's analysis of oppression, fosters a muteness about structural discrimination. When it comes to structural transformation, the term "diversity" may just have to suffice.

Several features of the shifting meaning of diversity within higher education are significant for intersectionality as a form of critical analysis and praxis. First, diversity initiatives have increasingly jettisoned structural analyses of social inequality in favor of individual and cultural interpretations of social problems. Within this logic, if students don't get along, the problem does not lie in their dormitories, classrooms, work-study jobs, or access to faculty. Rather, the problem lies in them: perhaps anger-management training will help or service learning that might remind them of others who are far less fortunate. If the problem is conflict among students across lines of race, gender, ethnicity, sexuality, or religion, perhaps sensitivity training will help, or at least, a diversity requirement in their curriculum.

Teaching people about diversity and how better to deal with one another is not inherently problematic. Diversity initiatives can draw upon intersectionality's scholarly attention to multiple identities to craft programs and help students manage the challenges of race, class, and ethnic desegregation. They can find a rich body of material, for example, intersectional frameworks that create spaces for individuals to express dynamic, mixed identifications, whether racial or ethnic, and non-normative or non-binary gender and sexual identities. Diversity initiatives that focus on building campus communities among heterogeneous populations of students are often highly effective, especially when their institutional mandates also reflect student interest. When done well, examining the heterogeneity of social identities and helping students deal with them humanizes the schooling process for all students.

Democratizing diversity initiatives to include additional categories of analysis makes intellectual sense, but it came at the cost of reducing hard-hitting analyses of racism, sexism, heterosexism, capitalism, and other forms of power. Adding additional categories of diversity made pragmatic sense when dealing with heterogeneous student populations. Sexual orientation, religion, ethnicity, and citizenship status bring added complexity to diversity that reflects the demands of student populations for recognition. In essence, as the heterogeneity *within* as well as *across* student populations became more apparent, diversity has stretched to become a more elastic category.

Yet the danger lies in overemphasizing individual remedies for social problems, the interpersonal domain of power, at the expense of analyzing college access and similar important practices in the structural domain. Even when anti-discrimination and affirmative action policies remain on the books, diversity initiatives can move away from this kind of oversight in favor of an institutional mandate to manage the diversity of students and employees in ways that ensure the smooth functioning of the institution. In this context, can diversity initiatives that, for whatever reason, are tasked with managing diversity continue to envision diversity work as a site of critical praxis?

Many diversity professionals try to sustain a critical praxis, but find themselves and their programs on a slippery slope that ends in watered-down understandings of diversity. As Ahmed points out, "Diversity is often used as shorthand for inclusion, as the 'happy point' of intersectionality, a point where lines meet. When intersectionality becomes a 'happy point,' the feminist of color critique is obscured. All differences matter under this view" (Ahmed 2012: 14). Social inequality and power inequalities such as those that shape K-12 public education or the rankings of colleges themselves disappear in a place where all differences matter. They also reinforce a view that the only differences that matter are those among individuals. This slippery slope of redefinition strips the term "diversity," and by implication, "intersectionality," of its analytical cachet. Earlier programs highlighted structural analyses that focused on issues of fairness and justice for the greater good, one where "feminism of color provides us with a ways [sic] of thinking through power in terms of 'intersectionality,' to think about and through the points at which power relations meet" (Ahmed 2012: 14).

A second feature of the shifting meaning of diversity that concerns how the shift to diversity seemingly made the field less critical of social inequality, intersectionality and diversity were initially closely related. Yet both may have moved away from their earlier associations with social justice. For example, earlier diversity initiatives focused on providing equal opportunities for students and on issues such as faculty diversification. Similarly, earlier statements of intersectionality were far more comfortable with terms such as oppression, equality and fairness than now.

Diversity initiatives more recently have become subject to institutional mandates. One such mandate concerns the measurable utility of diversity, especially in line with goals of colleges and universities. Diversity initiatives must find ways to contribute to the institution's bottom line. Diversity initiatives aimed at serving diverse populations increasingly found themselves recruiting those populations. Diversity initiatives became recast as useful recruitment tools that enabled colleges and universities to demonstrate their commitment to inclusion. Having a diverse student population became a draw for students seeking a multicultural experience, as well as for faculty members seeking heterogeneous classrooms.

This shift in meaning enabled institutions to redefine their diversity initiatives as student service sites for recruiting diverse students. Ironically, recruitment required flattening out the bona fide differences among students in support of a common language that travelled well within institutional circles. Take, for example, the use of the category "people of color" in the United States as a convenient umbrella term for diversity initiatives. This term aims to reduce the complexities among racial/ethnic groups. Redefining the outcomes of intersecting power relations of race and ethnicity to a simple matter of color seemed to solve the messy problem of the growing presence of racial/ethnic groups, some with contentious histories of discriminating against each other. Categorizing African-Americans, Nigerian Americans, Caribbean Americans, Latinos, Hmong, Cherokee, and South Asian immigrants of varying gender and class statuses under the umbrella "of color" reinstalled a white frame of seeing the world as white and all racial others as equivalent and interchangeable. When imposed from above, terms such as "people of color" flatten the experiences of racial/ethnic groups into a homogeneous "color" category. This naming resembles how intersectionality replaced the earlier vocabulary of race/class/gender studies in ways that may have weakened attention to the distinct forms of inequality. The terms "people of color" and "intersectionality" are less the issue than the need to ensure that initiatives are chosen and reworked from the bottom up, in the case of people of color, by people of color who engage in dialog with one another about the meaning of their experiences and how it fills out the term.

The shifting meaning of diversity within higher education is significant for intersectionality for a final reason. Another shift in vocabulary and, as a result, a shift in meaning is occurring. Institutional mandates are moving away from the language of diversity itself. The term "diversity" was already once-removed from intersectionality, a cleavage that upheld the distinction between theory and practice. Yet a more recent linguistic shift has been to encourage students and support staff not to "embrace diversity" but rather to be "culturally competent." The phrase "culturally competent" works well with neoliberal agendas in that it lends itself to criteria that can be used to develop workshops, videos, and information designed to train people to be more culturally competent. A cottage industry of consultants stands by to help campuses achieve cultural competence by providing training for a fee. Cultural competence also invokes a broader, global framework of preparing students to be global citizens. A related and more intriguing development concerns the measurement of cultural competence. If cultural skills become redefined as yet another form of intelligence, for example, "cultural intelligence," the skills of competence can be taught, learned, and evaluated using tools developed from intelligence testing.

As was the case in valuing democratizing diversity by attending to multiple identities, recognizing the significance of culture in human social interactions constitutes a worthy educational goal. Developing the "literacy" to read cultural situations, especially if they involve differences of power, can facilitate education for critical consciousness. For example, in her study *Keepin' It Real: School Success Beyond Black and White*, sociologist Prudence L. Carter identifies "cultural straddlers," the category of students in a heterogeneous student body who were most comfortable with both black and white cultures, as the group most likely to experience school success (Carter 2005). Carter's work suggests that students who can develop a skill set of working across differences, or "straddling" them, become most effective in cross-cultural settings.

Yet when it comes to the initial vision of intersectionality's practitioners, this slippery slope from race/class/gender studies to intersectionality, then intersectionality to diversity, then diversity to cultural competence may simply be too many dots to connect. Shifting from diversity to cultural competence further masks how structural inequities, especially those within education itself, contribute to social inequality. This education for critical consciousness that would equip people to solve problems is instead replaced by a training module that presents preset packets of culture that can be used as part of a curricular diversity requirement or to get continuing education credit.

Diversity professionals stand in varying relationships to these broader trends and, as a result, demonstrate varying levels of political savvy and, skill in dealing with them. On the one hand, staff, students, and faculty develop programs that draw upon intersectionality in ways that retain its social justice ethos. Ironically, they may not call their programs "intersectional." For strategic reasons, and often resembling the high-school students working the corridor cultures in urban high schools, many diversity professionals recast the social justice mandate within the narrowing interpretive frameworks of cultural competence. A range of social actors do diversity work, sometimes publicly, but often via a hidden diversity commitment that resembles the subversive opposition of K-12 school personnel. For example, the cases assembled in *Occupying the Academy* illustrate how chief diversity officers, mid-level administrators, and faculty negotiate the contemporary challenges of diversity. Written by (and not about) frontline diversity practitioners, these cases capture the perspectives of people who are actually doing diversity work, not studying how it has or should be done. Tracing the workings of diversity and the equity of actual institutional victories and frustrations provides a rare glimpse of the perspectives of people who actually do upper-level diversity work, not just research it (Clark, Fasching-Varner, and Brimhall-Vargas 2012). These narratives show how difficult diversity work is but also how committed many diversity professionals are to making it work.

Some of the most insightful work on diversity in higher education comes from people who are actively engaged in pedagogical projects that straddle the institutional mandates to separate inquiry from praxis. For example, in *Intellectual*

Empathy: Critical Thinking for Social Justice, philosopher Maureen Linker describes fifteen years of pedagogical practice at the University of Michigan-Dearborn that show how she links theory and practice with a population of African-American, Muslim, women, returning and working-class white male students. In accessible language that itself demonstrates a feel for critical pedagogy, Linker not only includes content on intersectionality, she helps her students link its main ideas to their lives (Linker 2015). Tang and Kiang's community education classroom initiatives with immigrant students show a similar sensibility (Tang 2008). In both cases, the insights of Freire's education for critical consciousness become embedded in actual pedagogical practice, putting the ideas of participatory democracy into action.

Intersectionality, critical education, and social justice

Intersectionality and critical education both initially saw social justice as central to their mission. Both projects face new challenges raised by neoliberalism, with the possibility of moving closer together or further apart. When it comes to social justice, what are some promising points of connection between these two projects? Specifically, how might intersectionality as a form of critical inquiry contribute to critical education? Conversely, how might critical education contribute to intersectionality?

First, using intersectionality as an analytic tool may provide a more expansive lens for addressing the complexities of educational equity. Aligning the copious literature on intersecting identities with real-life school settings may be especially useful for classroom teachers and school personnel. The act of making the politics of diversity visible within diversity initiatives creates possible alliances among students who look at the world not solely through the legacy explanations of families and formal school curriculum, but by seeing the interconnectedness of their heterogeneous experiences. This sensibility is built one person at a time, not with the goal of banking information, but rather as a generational sensibility that has taken up the struggle for a critical education from prior generations. The issue is to democratize this rich and growing literature of intersecting identities – not to assume that only African-American students will be interested in black history because it will help their seemingly low self-esteem, or that LGBTQ youth will be the only ones interested in queer studies. Rather, the task is to place this research on intersecting identities in broader intersectional frameworks that investigate the potential of critical education to dismantle social inequality.

Second, intersectionality's emphasis on intersecting power relations, especially as refracted through the domains of power argument of structural, disciplinary, cultural, and interpersonal domains, refocuses attention on the structural organization of schooling. Intersectionality resists neoliberal pressures to focus on individual and personal causes of social inequality, pointing out how structural factors are always at work. This revitalized focus on the connections between the personal and the political, the linchpin of identity politics, potentially facilitates new connections between traditional educational research and intersectionality. Social inequality lies neither solely in school structures nor in the cultural attributes of students, but rather in the interaction between the two. Many studies in educational research already claim some variation of intersectionality. Yet despite this recognition of intersectionality, a fair amount of the literature uses intersectionality as an analytic tool to examine the complex identities of students. For K-12 schooling, incorporating intersectionality's analytic sensibility within educational research on topics such as classroom culture, preparing culturally responsive teachers, and improving principal effectiveness with diverse populations may be a welcome improvement. Reforming these practices certainly will make schools more humane but, by itself, will not tackle the thorny issue of educational inequity.

Finally, the struggles within education suggest that if intersectionality abandons its focus on critical praxis, it compromises its own ideals. Parents, teachers, and others who work directly with youth know that if they simply ignore the political conditions in which they work, the youth that they serve will be harmed. It's hard to administer yet another standardized test, or worse yet, be forced to teach to that test, without seeing the effects that ideas honed within a banking concept of education have on youth. Critical education reminds us that praxis matters, especially for intersectionality's commitment to social justice. The ways in which diversity professionals grapple with their changing institutional context – one that has been tied to intersectionality's reputation – matters. Focusing on intersectional scholarship in a context where public schools, colleges, and universities harm the very people whom intersectionality has historically aimed to help seems shortsighted.

Yet critical education brings an important lesson to bear on social justice. Diversity initiatives have often struggled to switch gears to respond to populations who have also experienced discrimination, for example, undocumented immigrants, people living with disabilities, transgender people, and returning students. Intersectionality's scholarship on multiple, complex identities has been useful in this regard. Yet opening the diversity umbrella to encompass multiple identities raises some tough questions. Should all forms of diversity be included within diversity mandates? Does claiming a Native American ancestor make one Native American? Are some identities more important than others? Intersectionality faces a set of similar concerns. Debates about how to write intersectionality's history tap into deeper questions. What counts as intersectionality? Who will decide? Investigating intersectionality as a form of critical analysis and praxis aims to answer these questions by focusing explicitly on praxis. College students, staff, and administrators face similar questions concerning the changing meanings of diversity, albeit from the place of praxis.

Despite these shared concerns, the distinctive institutional trajectories that intersectionality and diversity initiatives take within colleges and universities result in a shrinking intellectual space to engage these questions. Dialogs about the meaning of being critical within contemporary organization of intersectionality and diversity initiatives might enhance the social justice dimensions of both endeavors.

8
Intersectionality Revisited

As a form of critical inquiry and praxis, intersectionality stands at a crossroads. In order to remain a vibrant, growing endeavor, intersectionality must cast a self-reflexive eye on its own truths and practices. Throughout this book we have maintained the distinction between intersectionality as a form of critical inquiry and of critical praxis. The creative tension joining these two dimensions constitute a self-reflexive space to understand intersectionality writ large.

On the one hand, the synergy between inquiry and praxis can be creative, catalyzing new ideas for inquiry that in turn influence praxis. This creative sensibility between knowing and doing stimulated the emergence of intersectionality and was an important dimension of its incorporation into the academy and its dispersal into policy, digital media, and scholarship.

On the other hand, this relationship between inquiry and praxis can be confrontational, one where one side aims to restrict or eliminate the other. We see these tendencies within intersectionality. Some scholars wish to extract intersectionality from praxis, leaving a purified set of ideas that can be manipulated unencumbered by the kinds of political stakes that have concerned intersectional practitioners. Conversely, activists who interpret intersectionality as being overly abstract and not worth studying, accusations made by some feminist bloggers (chapter 4), demonstrate an anti-intellectual bias that elevates praxis over serious study. We think that intersectionality is best served by sustaining a creative tension that joins inquiry and praxis as distinctive, yet interdependent, dimensions.

Thinking through this creative tension between inquiry and praxis has provided an important conceptual anchor for this book. For example, our telling the history of intersectionality's past situates it within both social movement activism and institutional incorporation in the academy. We examine the dispersal of intersectionality, as critical inquiry and praxis, across diverse human rights venues and digital space. We carry this creative tension into the identity debates that are so central to intersectional scholarship yet that also have a strong presence in praxis settings, such as the black women's movement in Brazil and the identity politics of hip hop. Our analysis of diversity in public schools and higher education examines the challenges of placing intersectionality as a field of inquiry and praxis in dialog with critical education, an area of inquiry and praxis that faces similar challenges.

This dual focus on inquiry and praxis also affects how we approach important threads that run throughout the entire book. For example, the implications of participatory democracy and neoliberalism as sets of ideas, as well as the policies and practices they engender for intersectionality, have been an important thread in this book. Democracy and neoliberalism are philosophies, social theories of power. They also have direct applicability to criminal justice, the law, and education, as well as to social movements. By focusing on these ideas, we provide a context for seeing how power influences the synergy of inquiry and praxis generally, and intersectionality specifically.

Similarly, we highlight the ideas and actions of people who made and continue to make important albeit often unrecognized contributions to intersectionality because the synergy between inquiry and praxis is often more visible in their work. Because the thinkers who have been most likely to create new ideas and praxis of intersectionality are not from elite groups, and often occupy marginalized spaces, we take special care to highlight the intellectual production of a wide array of thinkers. Standard intellectual histories routinely overlook power relations, such as those of neoliberalism and participatory democracy, as well as people who are discriminated against within intersecting power relations of race, class, gender, sexuality, disability, and nationality. Significantly, these are often the same people who are most versed in social justice praxis.

We also sought out a description of intersectionality that might encompass this dual focus on inquiry and praxis. We began this book by offering the following description of intersectionality:

> Intersectionality is a way of understanding and analyzing the complexity in the world, in people, and in human experiences. The events and conditions of social and political life and the self can seldom be understood as shaped by one factor. They are generally shaped by many factors in diverse and mutually influencing ways. When it comes to social inequality, people's lives and the organization of power in a given society are better understood as being shaped not by a single axis of social division, be it race or gender or class, but by many axes that work together and influence each other. Intersectionality as an analytic tool gives people better access to the complexity of the world and of themselves.

We used this description as a working definition to organize the volume and provide navigational tools for readers. Throughout the book, we have aimed to deepen this working definition of intersectionality in ways that encompass its heterogeneity and dynamism yet clarify its core principles. We settled on this definition because it is broad and elastic enough to encompass the diversity within intersectionality yet provides some guidance on some important boundaries around intersectionality.

The significance of this working definition goes beyond its utility in organizing this book. The definitional question is important for intersectionality because prematurely rushing to one definition, or one history or one canon, can shut down creativity and growth. We have tried to avoid these pitfalls by providing a more expansive view of intersectionality than can be found in any one location. We emphasize how intersectionality's heuristic introduces greater complexity into a host of topics, for example, global networked social movements and perceptions of the nation-state. Consensus often ends when we dig deeper into intersectionality's actual use. We have highlighted some of the debates within inter-sectionality, for example, conflicting views of the meaning of identity within intersectionality. We also discuss the challenges that intersectionality confronts to remaining critical within varying venues that increasingly adopt neoliberal frameworks, for example, its own placement within the normative standards of higher education and the changing meaning of diversity work within public schools, colleges, and universities. We avoid some of the most contentious debates that, in our assessment, sweep up intersectionality in service to other agendas, for example, arguments that "we," whoever that might be, should move "beyond" intersectionality to some sort of "post-intersectionality" landscape. These assertions remind us of similarly premature claims of post-raciality, claims that have been contradicted by ample empirical evidence.

To provide some guideposts for thinking through intersectionality, we settled on six characteristic themes: relationality, social context, power, inequality, social justice, and complexity. Just as these themes reappear, albeit in different forms, within intersectionality itself, we discuss them in different ways throughout the book. Here we revisit these themes both as a way of synthesizing some of the main ideas in the book, as well as discussing how intersectionality might cast a self-reflexive eye on its own truths and practices. Some of these themes have long been recognized and considered worthy. On others, the record is far more contested.

Relationality

The theme of *relationality* that reappears in various forms across intersectional scholarship and practice has had an important impact on both. This insight that the connections among entities that had been seen as separate and often oppositional constitute a major contribution of intersectionality to all types of projects. In chapter 1, we introduced intersectionality's basic heuristic, the seemingly simply idea that entities that are typically treated as separate may actually be interconnected. For intersectionality, this interconnectedness lies in the relationships between systems of race, class, gender, sexuality, age, ability, and citizenship status. An intersectionality framework counsels that these entities, in various combinations or in total, can all be accommodated under the umbrella of intersectionality.

We develop this idea of relationality in varying ways throughout the volume. Scholars and activists alike have found the concept useful, generating endless new questions and avenues of investigation. For example, the either/or binary thinking that has been so central to Eurocentric social thought is less relevant for intersectionality. Instead, intersectional projects look at the relationships among seemingly different phenomena. For example, interdisciplinary fields concerned with social justice are often informed by intersectional frameworks (Parker, Samantrai, and Romero 2010). Such fields strive to go beyond oppositional thinking carried out by Eurocentric binaries and attempt to forge a complex and interactive understanding of the relationships between history, social organization, and forms of consciousness, both personal and collective (Bannerji 1995: 12) – in short, *relational* thinking.

We have also been attentive to how this idea of relationality informs praxis. For example, we have criticized versions of intersectionality that reduce identity to an apolitical, individualistic category, drawing on the theme of relationality to show the complexities of collective identity politics. We also present an argument about the centrality of relationality to coalition politics, investigating how what seem to be scattered social movements may in actuality be interrelated phenomena in response to a global world order. Our case of the Afro-Brazilian women's movement in Brazil provides a sketch of how coalitions that took both similarities and differences into account were crucial to the creation and maintenance of a vibrant social movement.

We have spent less time examining intersectionality's relationship with similar discourses, such as critical race theory, feminism, ethnic studies, or the intellectual debates in which these areas participate. Although we do mention these dimensions at various places in the book, we think that intersectionality would benefit by thinking through how dialogs among forms of inquiry and expressions of critical praxis that resemble its own might unfold. Intersectionality's interconnectedness with other similar knowledge projects might draw inspiration from Freire's dialogical pedagogy or education for critical consciousness.

When engaging in global discourse, intersectionality must be wary of annexing other perspectives, such as decolonial and transnational approaches, under its wide tent umbrella. When intersectionality enters these contexts via humanitarian, developmental frameworks, and projects from the North, it can erase local resistant knowledges and praxis and silence local knowledge producers (which might also be true in northern contexts, for instance France and Germany; see Bilge 2013). There is an enormous difference between cases where disenfranchised groups *themselves* claim versions of intersectionality, for example, black women in Brazil forming an independent black feminist movement, and where some national or supranational instance imposes a top-down, watered-down diversity *qua* intersectionality agenda upon historically disenfranchised people.

We wish that we could have written a book that incorporated multiple knowledge projects and points of view from various regions of the globe and within a more expansive time period than the late twentieth and early-twenty-first centuries. We want to see more people involved in the kind of dialogical intellectual and political work that doing intersectionality entails. This openness would encourage a dialogical methodology for intersectionality that would advance a more democratic construction of knowledge itself.

The analysis of intersectionality in this book may be universally applicable, yet there is no way of knowing so without greater and different participation of scholars, activists, practitioners, policy makers, and teachers from the Global South. We have included the ideas and experiences of social actors from disenfranchised groups within the Global North as well as social actors in the Global South whenever possible, taking care to do so in ways that do not reduce their experiences to data that reinforce frameworks of the Global North. For example, our case studies of the black women's movement in Brazil and their successful project of Latinidades and the increasing visibility of the anti-sweatshop movement following the Rana Plaza collapse illustrate the significance of starting analysis in the Global South, Brazil and Bangladesh respectively. We also reject trying to fix problems of exclusion by simply adding in missing people and experiences into intersectionality as a preconceived entity. Instead, intersectionality requires a rethinking of these approaches in ways that democratize the social construction of knowledge.

Despite our best efforts, incorporating the global is not enough. Attending to global phenomena means that intersectionality must take a critical stance concerning its own social location both as a legitimated discourse within the Global North, and as a set of ideas and practices that only a small segment of educated, well-off people in the Global South can access. Because being able to read books such as this one elevates those with literacy above those who lack it, literacy articulates with individual and collective exclusion. But as we have also discussed throughout this book, people find innovative ways to access and do intellectual work, to develop multiple forms of literacy, for example, by using the media in global hip hop culture or digital activism. At maximum, intersectionality would be a much more inclusive dialogical process than is currently the case.

Social context

The theme of *social context* has many interpretations, and we use several of them in this volume. We have examined the relationship between intersectionality and the social institutions that are part of its social context whenever possible. We have highlighted the academy as an important institutional context for intersectionality: our analysis of the shifting meanings of intersectionality within social movements and incorporation into the academy contrasts the effects of these two institutional environments on intersectionality; our analysis of neoliberal state power, its discourse of securitization, and how institutional structures are shaped by these ideas is a primary theme of the volume; our comparison of varying interpretations of identity politics within the academy and hip hop also highlights the significance of the academy and mass media as two institutional sites of cultural production; our analysis of the changing contours of intersectionality and diversity within higher education highlights the significance of context. In brief, where intersectionality occurs institutionally is important for understanding its ideas.

At several points throughout this book, we have expressed our concern that the growth, acceptance, and legitimation of intersectionality within the academy and some public policy venues necessarily changes its composition and purpose, often for the better, but also for the worse. For example, we explore the politics of intersectionality's naming and incorporation into the academy as a bona fide discourse. Is intersectionality the victim of its own success? Contemporary trends that reduce intersectionality to a theory of identity also reflect the challenges of absorption. Within US higher education, the splitting of intersectionality into an academic component of scholarship and diversity initiatives of institutional service signals an attack on intersectionality's critical perspective. Via these concerns, we raised the question of who benefits from intersectionality's legitimation. The answers to this question are far from clear, and may vary from one situation to the next. It is not enough to simply bury oneself in one's own work, claiming intersectionality as a set of stimulating ideas while ignoring the conditions that make that work possible.

The tongue-in-cheek phrase "saving intersectionality from intersectionality studies" (Bilge 2013) reminds all scholars to be self-reflexive regarding our own practices in the context of intersectionality's newfound visibility and legitimation. Saving intersectionality might involve reclaiming intersectionality from people who often have little or no commitment to intersectionality's social justice ethos. This may also mean saving intersectionality from ourselves if we practice intersectionality as "business as usual", namely, as just another scholarly discourse or content specialization without implicating our work within the power relations that shape the field and academy at large. Such practices often follow prevailing canonical rules of identifying some key figures within the field whose ideas become proxy for the field itself, then moving on to use these straw-women figures as coterminous with intersectionality itself.

We also recognize the significance of how politics shapes the way in which physical and geographic space is understood and organized. Contextualizing intersectional categories that define space, for example, matters whether one is a citizen of Syria or Germany, or whether one plays soccer in South Africa or Spain. Intersectionality as a form of critical inquiry and praxis gains its meaning within specific social contexts. Placing greater emphasis on the specifics of social context of local, regional, and national geography would provide a more nuanced discussion of global processes.

Then there is the issue of historic context. The version of intersectionality that we present in this volume appears at a specific historical moment and is an intervention in that moment. While it speaks to contemporary issues, it is also simultaneously formed and transformed by them. For some scholars, the time of intersectionality as an idea came "precisely because of the plethora of authors working independently across the globe making vastly similar sets of claims" (Yuval-Davis 2011a: xii). For us, following Stuart Hall's insights: "Movements provoke their theoretical moments. And historical conjunctures insist on theories: they are real moments in the evolution of theory" (Hall 1992: 283). For current debates inflected by the growing influence of intersectionality within United Nations venues, juxtaposed with increasingly verbal critiques of intersectionality within the European academy, intersectionality seems to represent both a promise and a threat. Accordingly, we reflect upon the specificities of historical events in which intersectionality is embedded, with the aim of understanding and describing how different historical conjunctures frame different theoretical and political moments of intersectionality.

Knowing that it is impossible to give an exhaustive account of social context for every topic, we have instead provided cases where geographic place and space matter as key components of social context. Our discussion of the Rana Plaza collapse in Bangladesh showed how this event went far beyond Bangladeshi national borders. Instead, this event showed the significance of working for an employer that provides abysmal working conditions in factories in other countries. It also showed how the global anti-sweatshop movement redefined global social movement space by exposing how FIFA paraphernalia that was produced by sweatshop labor in Bangladesh was marketed and sold in Brazil. The Rana Plaza case also illustrates how social actors can develop new understandings of their institutional and geographic social context by seeing connections that were formerly obscured. Global social protest occurs both geographically in local places, as well as in cyberspace. We tried to be attentive to these connections in our discussion of hip hop and identity politics and the organization of networked global social movements.

Power relations, social inequality, and social justice

Throughout this book, we have investigated an important question – how is intersectionality situated within the power relations that it seemingly studies? *Power*, another core idea of intersectionality, is complex and contested. We have tried to situate intersectionality within contemporary power relations and analyze the significance of that positioning.

We have argued that power relations are to be analyzed both *via their intersections*, for example, of racism and sexism, as well as *across domains of power*, namely, structural, disciplinary, cultural, and interpersonal. How does intersectionality critically assess power relations of race, class, gender, sexuality, age, ethnicity, nationality, and ability? How might intersectionality better understand how intersecting power relations shape its own praxis? These questions must repeatedly be asked and answered under changing power relations themselves.

We have also criticized intersectionality when it seemed to be veering away from what we see as its core concern areas that are clearly associated with power relations. For example, because we have been especially troubled by the decreasing focus on *social inequality* within intersectionality's scholarship, we emphasize this theme. The hollowing-out of meanings of rich scholarly traditions that have long been associated with processes and systems of social inequalities – for example, capitalism, colonialism, racism, patriarchy, and nationalism

– and replacing them with shortcut terms of race, class, gender, and nation may appear to be a benign substitution, but much is lost when systems of power compete for space under some versions of intersectionality. The terms themselves may appear to be equivalent and easily substituted for one another, yet the social relations that these shorthand terms reference are far more complicated. For example, sexism, racism, and heterosexism contain the "ism" that makes them recognizable as unjust systems of power, nuance that is lost when gender, race, and sexuality become redefined as identity categories. In contrast, the term "class" performs a different kind of reduction. By reducing the complex economic relations of capitalism to class, the complexities and sophistication of Marxist social thought and other serious analyses of capitalism are minimized. The rich traditions of nationalism, both celebratory and critical, simply don't fit comfortably under the signifier of nation. So replacement terms such as "citizenship status" or "undocumented migrants" take up the slack by referencing selected populations that are penalized by nationalist ideologies and nation-state policies. They are referencing similar phenomena but are not readily reducible to one another.

This strategy of using shortcut language to make intersectionality's task of rethinking social inequality easier seemingly solves one set of problems, yet creates others. Over time, these terms no longer invoke the original meanings of racism, sexism, and capitalism, for example, but instead become recast as floating signifiers that, unmoored from specific scholarly traditions, can be assembled and reassembled far more easily than would be the case if one seriously tried to place the actual traditions in dialog with one another. This reduction of intersectionality to an assemblage of shortcut terms does appear to be more democratic in that it encompasses more categories than before. Yet the mantra of "race, class, and gender" has been so often repeated that it can become meaningless. The phrase serves as an unexamined litmus test for scholars who can claim that their work is better than race-only or class-only analyses, primarily because it references more terms of social inequality.

We have similar concerns with versions of intersectionality that may pay lip service to *social justice*, yet seem unaware of its significance. People who claim intersectionality as a field of *critical* inquiry and praxis often hold an implicit and often explicit commitment to an ethics of social justice as part of their analytical lens. For a form of inquiry that grapples with complex social inequalities, its *raison d'être* is not simply to provide more complex and comprehensive analyses of how and why social inequalities persist – critical engagement has been a strong theme within intersectionality as a field of inquiry – but also to engage questions of social justice. Social inequality and social injustice are not the same, although these ideas are often used interchangeably. The work of practitioners not only shows how social justice is critical, but also how social justice work challenges the borders between academic and activist work.

We have been careful to point out that intersectionality is not a simple substitute for social justice. Each project must be interrogated for its connections to social justice, not just assuming that because intersectional scholarship examines some facet of social inequality, it is by default furthering social justice. We raised a similar argument concerning diversity initiatives within higher education as a case where intersectionality may invoke earlier social justice traditions, yet where actual programs have been pressured to relinquish traditional emphasis on access and equity.

Intersectionality's complexity

Overall, these core ideas of relationality, social context, power, inequality, and social justice highlight intersectionality's complexity. Because each of these core ideas interact with one another, collectively they contribute to intersectionality's complexity. Thinking about social inequalities and power relations within an ethos of social justice, and doing so not in abstract generalizations but in their specific contexts, brings complexity. Attending to how intersecting power relations shape identities, social practices, institutional arrangements, and cultural representations and ideologies in ways that are contextualized and historicized introduces a level of complexity into everything. Moreover, the creative tension linking intersectionality as a form of critical inquiry and critical praxis introduces complexity into intersectional projects.

As we have argued throughout this volume, this creative tension raises important questions about which understandings of intersectionality will prevail. When we focus on intersectionality as a form of critical inquiry, we find a rich tapestry of scholarship produced by people who use intersectionality as an analytic tool in new and creative ways. Not all scholarship is like this, and not all people who claim intersectionality share this vision. But, overall, intersectionality's scholarship record thus far has been impressive. When we broaden our lens to include intersectionality as critical praxis, both its initial expression within social movements as well as its global dispersion beyond the academy, the practices and ideas of diverse people past and present, in the Global North and in the Global South, come into view.

We think that it is imperative that intersectionality remain open to the element of surprise. Our efforts to provide a useful but not final definition of intersectionality speak to the impetus to invite others into the conversation. We see the impetus toward intersectionality as more connected to the puzzles presented by the social world that we live in, rather than the concerns of established disciplinary endeavors.

Throughout this book, we have cast a self-reflexive eye not simply on intersectionality but also on our own praxis. One important point of this last chapter is to make our choices clear. Telling the story of intersectionality does a certain kind of political work in terms of authenticating and legitimizing particular schools of thought and subjects, privileging particular genealogies and national locations at the expense of others. Particular histories that chart intersectionality as a field of study in particular ways might be rightly viewed as acts of closure, be they temporary. These histories pursue in their own ways scientific recognition, authority, and legitimacy and settle intersectionality within the Euro-American scientific archive in particular ways. As such, they participate in the establishment of intersectionality as a legitimate field of knowledge, which might be at odds with the pursuit of social justice. Our history of intersectionality has emphasized praxis, a dimension of intersectionality that does not routinely appear in these legitimated histories, although a critical praxis does permeate intersectionality.

As we wrap up this book we ask: what ideas and experiences are *not* here? In what ways is our interpretation of intersectionality limited by these omissions? More importantly, how might we go about expanding the breadth of intersectionality to encompass the heterogeneity of ideas and experiences that are global without flattening their differences? Intersectionality can't engage these expansive questions if it chooses the narrow pathway of defining itself as a "feminist theory of identity," or, worse yet, if it severs its critical inquiry from its critical praxis. These questions have no straightforward answers, certainly none that can easily be resolved. Rather, they call out for more people working on them, in essence, an expansion of global conversations.

The central challenge facing intersectionality is to move into the politics of the not-yet. Thus far, intersectionality has managed to sustain intellectual and political dynamism that grows from its heterogeneity. This is immensely difficult to achieve when faced with the kinds of intellectual and political challenges that we have explored in this book. But just because something is difficult does not mean that it's not worth doing. We see intersectionality's heterogeneity not as a weakness but rather as a source of tremendous potential. Intersectionality is a tool that we can all use in moving toward a more just future.

Notes

Chapter 1   What is Intersectionality?

1   FIFA's legal troubles aside, the business of the World Cup goes far beyond the games themselves. Rather, as the scope of people who were indicted indicates, the World Cup is situated at the convergence of increasingly important global industries: sports and entertainment, global telecommunications and tourism, and the globalized World Cup paraphernalia industry. For example, the FIFA-approved official ball of the 2014 World Cup, Adidas Brazuca, at a price tag of US$160, was manufactured in The Forward Sports factory at Sialkot (Pakistan) by Pakistani women (90 percent of the workforce) who each made barely US$100 per month. After selling 13 million official World Cup match balls in 2010, Adidas made hundreds of millions of dollars. In 2014, it expected to sell more than 14 million of them.

2   In the United States, the wealthiest 1 percent captured 95 percent of post-financial crisis growth since 2009, while the remaining 90 percent became poorer.

3   In 2015, the median wealth (assets minus debts) of white households is 20 times that of black households and 18 times that of Hispanic households.

4   Black women fare worst according to a 2010 research report on wealth disparities between different racial groups in the United States. Median wealth of single black women (including household-head single mothers) in the prime of their working years (ages 36 to 49) is only US$5, compared to US$42,600 for single white women of the same age – which is 61 percent of their single white male counterparts (Chang 2010).

Chapter 2 Intersectionality as Critical Inquiry and Praxis

1 Our approach to intersectionality as a form of critical inquiry draws from French sociologist Pierre Bourdieu's notion of fields of power within schools and other social institutions (Bourdieu and Passeron 1977). Intersectionality as a form of critical inquiry takes various forms across academic disciplines, academic institutions, and national contexts. Within the United States, for example, intersectionality is differently organized, taught, and valued in elite liberal arts colleges and within community colleges. The faculty and students in these institutions have differential access to resources that shape the content and the form of their engagement with intersectionality. An expansive notion of intersectionality as a form of critical inquiry sees intersectionality as heterogeneously organized across different colleges, universities, and other sites of knowledge production.

2 Dill continues, "Finally it is a theoretical perspective that insists on examining the multi-dimensionality of human experience." We take up this theme in future chapters, but point out that race/class/gender scholars understood their work as being a theoretical perspective.

3 It is worth noting that from this letter emerged an intense Twitter campaign with the hashtag #WhyWeCantWait – referring to the 1964 book by Martin Luther King Jr that grew out of his "Letter From a Birmingham Jail" (McClain 2014).

Chapter 4 Intersectionality's Global Dispersion

1 The extent of books and PhD dissertations addressing intersectionality is also a good indicator of scholarly vitality. A 2015 literature search done with WorldCat.org database returned 451 PhD dissertations using intersectionality as a "keyword," among them 111 using it in their titles. The variety of topics is truly fascinating. We wish we had sufficient space to present this burgeoning scholarship that promises to shape intersectionality's future directions. Intersectional frameworks are deployed within the following areas: queer/trans of color theory, critical disability studies, critical native studies, queer diaspora/migration studies, critical ethnic studies, transformative justice, reproductive justice, critical prison studies, intimate partner violence, ecological disasters, human rights, juvenile delinquency, restorative and transformative justice, globalized labor markets, media representations, digital and social media, voice, agency and political resistance, critical pedagogy, social change, and identities.

The Consortium on Race, Gender and Ethnicity at the University of Maryland manages an intersectional research database that contains an extensive collection of bibliographical resources on intersectional scholarship. See also the database at Simon Frasier University in Vancouver, Canada.

2 Edited volumes or anthologies constitute the most common form of published books. Since 2000, several edited books using the term "intersectionality" as well as varying combinations of the terms "race," "class," "gender," "ethnicity," "sexuality," and "dis/ability" in their titles have been published. These volumes expand the areas of inquiry and application of intersectional frameworks by putting intersectionality in conversation with fields and topics as diverse as critical animal studies (Nocella II et al. 2014), European Union anti-discrimination law (Schiek and Lawson 2013), racism, sexism, and homophobia in video games (Embrick, Wright, and Lukacs 2012), and prison industrial complexes (Richie 2012). Undergraduate readers that introduce intersectionality to students and the lay public constitute another indicator of intersectionality's increasing dispersal (see, e.g., Andersen and Collins 2013, 9th edn, and Grzanka 2014).

3 The number of peer-reviewed scholarly journal articles using the term "intersectionality" in their titles also indicates the rapid dispersal of intersectionality within scholarship. A 2015 general database search for the term "intersectionality" in the titles of scholarly articles yields numerous hits, suggesting that the term has crossed many disciplinary boundaries. It is reasonable to assume that having the term in the title is an indication that the author not only has some affinity to the field of intersectionality, but sees value in using that term. Beyond a cursory view of their abstracts, we made no effort to analyze whether the uses of our preliminary sample of articles were critical. Instead, our concern was the simple appearance of the term.

4 Numerous special editions of journals on diverse topics have been published or are in varying stages of completion that explore various aspects of intersectionality. Between 2006 and 2015, the following journals published special issues on intersectionality:

2006: *European Journal of Women's Studies* 13(3).
2008: *Sex Roles* 59(5–6).
2009: *Race, Ethnicity and Education* 12(1); *International Feminist Journal of Politics* 11(4) (special issue on "Institutionalizing Intersectionality in Europe"); *Social and Cultural Geography* 10(8) (on "Masculinity, Intersectionality and Place").

2010: *Journal of Broadcasting and Electronic Media* 54(1); *Journal of Intercultural Studies* 31(1) (on "Women, Intersectionality, and Diasporas").

2011: *L'Homme et la Société* (in French, no. 176–7).

2012: *Social Politics* 19(4); *Gender and Society* 26(1); and *Social Science & Medicine* 74(11).

2013: *Signs* 38(4); *Du Bois Review* 10(2); and *Sex Roles* 68(11–12).

2014: *Gender in Management* 29(5) ("Exploring the intersectionality of gender and identity"); *Politique et sociétés* (in French) 33(1).

2015: *Social Identities* 21(1) ("Disability and Colonialism: (Dis)encounters and Anxious Intersectionalities"); and in French (Québec), *Nouvelles pratiques sociales* 26(2); and *Les cahiers du Cedref*.

2015–2016: the Pan-African journal *Pambazuka* has a special themed issue on the way tackling the question: "Oppressions are interlinked in Africa – Can intersectionality be a political tool to inspire social justice organising?" (73); *Work Organisation, Labour & Globalisation* 9(2) will publish a special issue on "Intersectionality, Work and Globalisation"; *New Political Science* 39(4) on "Intersectionality for the Global Age"; *Societies* has a scheduled special issue on "Intersectionality: Disentangling the Complexity of Inequality"; in French (Québec), *Recherches féministes* 28(1).

5 Considerable attention within intersectional scholarship has been devoted to thinking through what kind of concept intersectionality is. To take a small sample of the terminology that is associated with conceptualizing intersectionality itself, intersectionality scholars write about intersectionality as a perspective (Browne and Misra 2003; Steinbugler, Press, and Dias 2006), a concept (Knapp 2005), and a type of analysis (Nash 2008; Yuval-Davis 2006). Other scholars focus on intersectionality's placement in the research process, analyzing intersectionality as a methodological approach (Steinbugler, Press, and Dias 2006; Yuval-Davis 2006), an analytic perspective (Steinbugler, Press, and Dias 2006), a research paradigm (Bowleg 2008; Hancock 2007b), or a measurable variable and type of data (Bowleg 2008). Other scholars understand intersectionality not as a social theory that explains their data but rather as something we personally "experience" (Bowleg 2008). This opens the door to the many narrative works, e.g., autobiographies, autoethnographies and ethnographies, which are inspired in some

fashion by intersectionality. While this ambiguity and slippage reflects a field in formation, one criticism of intersectionality is that this imprecise terminology fosters uneven outcomes. For example, the recent literature on intersectionality, methodology, and empirical validity (see, e.g., Bowleg 2008; Hancock 2007a, 2007b) is likely a response to the critique that intersectionality scholarship lacks a precise (Nash 2008) and diverse (McCall 2005) methodological approach. Is intersectionality a social theory? Not yet. But the corpus of intersectionality's scholarship does aim to explain the social world.

6 Because there has been such a vacuum in scholarship that explicitly examines how intersectionality affects research methodology, Leslie McCall's taxonomy of intersectional categorization has received considerable attention within intersectionality scholarship (McCall 2005). Looking beyond intersectionality's mainstream, however, yields other epistemological insights. Feminist scholar Chela Sandoval contends that methodology is not politically impartial, proposing instead a "methodology of the oppressed" (Sandoval 2000). As discussed in chapter 2, activist scholarship raises new questions for intersectionality and methodology (Hale 2008).

Chapter 6 Intersectionality, Social Protest, and Neoliberalism

1 For example, in September 2012, more than 300 workers died in a fire in a garment factory in Karachi, Pakistan; in November of the same year, another 112 workers died in a factory fire in Dhaka (Bangladesh); and more recently a fire at a Manila (Philippines) slipper factory killed at least 72 workers on May 13, 2015.

2 Starting in New Caledonia and going around the world, actions took place between 12 noon and 1 pm in time zones around the world to underscore the ongoing struggles of women factory workers. Their testimonials, photographs, and videos were put online to constitute a digital archive of transnational feminist solidarities for workers in the hyper-globalized apparel industry.

Chapter 7 Intersectionality and Critical Education

1 As a research and advocacy organization, the Center evaluates trends in college access, criminal justice, immigration, K-12 education, and metropolitan and regional educational

inequalities. The Center documents and analyzes not only problems, but also projects of success. Resembling the synergy
between intersectionality's critical inquiry and praxis, the Civil
Rights Project models this same orientation in its design and
dissemination of materials (see www.civilrightsproject.ucla.edu).

2   The term "multiculturalism" has a different history in other
national contexts. For an overview of these issues, see Kivisto
2010.

References

Addams, Jane. 1994. *Twenty Years at Hull-House*. Cutchogue, NY: Buccaneer Books.

Aguilar, Delia. 2012. "From Triple Jeopardy to Intersectionality: The Feminist Perplex." *Comparative Studies of South Asia, Africa and the Middle East* 32: 415–28.

Ahmed, Sara. 2012. *On Being Included: Racism and Diversity in Institutional Life*. Durham, NC: Duke University Press.

Aidi, Hisham D. 2014. *Rebel Music: Race, Empire, and the New Muslim Youth Culture*. New York: Vintage Books.

Alarcón, Norma, Castro, Rafaela, Pérez, Emma, Pesquera, Beatriz, Riddell, Adaljiza Sosa, and Zavella, Patricia (eds). 1993. *Chicana Critical Issues: Mujeres Activas en Letras y Cambia Social*. Berkeley: Third Woman Press.

Alcoff, Linda M. 2006. *Visible Identities: Race, Gender, and the Self*. New York: Oxford University Press.

Alexander, M. Jacqui, and Mohanty, Chandra Talpade. 1997. "Introduction: Genealogies, Legacies, Movements," in M. J. Alexander and C. T. Mohanty (eds), *Feminist Genealogies, Colonial Legacies, Democratic Futures*. New York: Routledge, pp. xiii–xlii.

Alexander-Floyd, Nikol G. 2012. "Disappearing Acts: Reclaiming Intersectionality in the Social Sciences in a Post-Black Feminist Era." *Feminist Formations* 24: 1–25.

Alonso, Gaston, Anderson, Noel S., Su, Celina, and Theoharis, Jeanne. 2009. *Our Schools Suck: Students Talk Back to a Segregated Nation on the Failures of Urban Education*. New York: New York University Press.

Amar, Paul. 2011. "Turning the Gendered Policies of the Security State Inside Out?" *International Feminist Journal of Politics* 13: 299–328.

Andersen, Margaret L., and Collins, Patricia Hill (eds). 2013. *Race, Class and Gender: An Anthology*. Belmont, CA: Wadsworth.

Anthias, Floya, and Yuval-Davis, Nira. 1992. *Racialized Boundaries: Race, Nation, Gender, Colour and Class and the Anti-Racist Struggle*. New York/London: Routledge.

Anzaldúa, Gloria. 1987. *Borderlands/La Frontera*. San Francisco: Spinsters/Aunt Lute Press.

Anzaldúa, Gloria. (ed.). 1990. *Making Face, Making Soul/Haciendo Caras: Creative and Critical Perspectives by Women of Color*. San Francisco: Aunt Lute Foundation Books.

Appleby, Gabrielle. 2015. "Australia's Rigid Immigration Barrier", Op-Ed, *The New York Times*, May 7. http://www.nytimes.com/2015/05/08/opinion/australias-rigid-immigration-barrier.html?_r=0

Armbruster-Sandoval, Ralph. 2005. *Globalization and Cross-Border Labor Solidarity in the Americas: The Anti-Sweatshop Movement and the Struggle for Social Justice*. New York/London: Routledge.

Arnett Ferguson, Ann. 2000. *Bad Boys: Public Schools in the Making of Black Masculinity*. Ann Arbor: University of Michigan Press.

Arredondo, Gabriela F., Hurtado, Aida, Klahn, Norma, Nájera-Ramírez, Olga, and Zavella, Patricia (eds). 2003. *Chicana Feminisms: A Critical Reader*. Durham, NC: Duke University Press.

Asian Women United of California (AWUC) (eds). 1989. *Making Waves: An Anthology of Writing by and about Asian American Women*. Boston: Beacon Press.

Bagilhole, Barbara. 2010. "Applying the Lens of Intersectionality to UK Equal Opportunities and Diversity Policies." *Canadian Journal of Administrative Sciences* 27(3): 263–71.

Bales, Kevin. 1999. *Disposable People: New Slavery in the Global Economy*. Berkeley, CA: University of California Press.

Bambara, Toni Cade (ed.). 1970. *The Black Woman: An Anthology*. New York: Signet.

Banks, James A., and Park, Caryn. 2010. "Race, Ethnicity and Education: The Search for Explanations," in P. H. Collins and J. Solomos (eds), *The Sage Handbook of Race and Ethnic Studies*. London: Sage, pp. 383–414.

Bannerji, Himani. 1995. *Thinking Through. Essays on Feminism, Marxism and Anti-Racism*. Toronto: Women's Press.

Barvosa-Carter, Edwina. 2001. *Multiple Identity and Coalition Building: How Identity Differences Within Us Enable Radical*

Alliances Among Us, ed. J. M. Bystydzienski and S. P. Schaht. Lanham, MD: Rowman and Littlefield.

Battle, Juan, Cohen, Cathy J., Warren, Dorian, Fergerson, Gerard, and Audam, Suzette. 2002. *Say It Loud, I'm Black and I'm Proud: Black Pride Survey 2000*. New York: The Policy Institute of the National Gay and Lesbian Task Force.

Beal, Frances. 1995 [1970]. "Double Jeopardy: To Be Black and Female," in B. Guy-Sheftall (ed.), *Words of Fire: An Anthology of African-American Feminist Thought*. New York: The New Press, pp. 146–55.

Berger, Michele, and Guidroz, Kathleen (eds). 2009. *The Intersectional Approach: Transforming the Academy through Race, Class & Gender*. Chapel Hill, NC: University of North Carolina Press.

Bernstein, Elizabeth. 2010. "Militarized Humanitarianism Meets Carceral Feminism: The Politics of Sex, Rights, and Freedom in Contemporary Antitrafficking Campaigns." *Signs* 36: 45–71.

Bhandar, Brenna. 2013. "On Race, Gender, Class, and Intersectionality." *The North Star*, June 25.

Bilge, Sirma. 2012. "Developing Intersectional Solidarities: A Plea for Queer Intersectionality," in Malinda Smith and Fatima Jaffer (eds), *Beyond the Queer Alphabet: Conversations in Gender, Sexuality and Intersectionality*. Teaching Equity Matters E-book series, University of Alberta.

Bilge, Sirma. 2013. "Intersectionality Undone: Saving Intersectionality from Feminist Intersectionality Studies." *Du Bois Review* 10: 405–24.

Bilge, Sirma. 2014. "Whitening Intersectionality: Evanescence of Race in Intersectionality Scholarship," in W. D. Hund and A. Lentin (eds), *Racism and Sociology*. Berlin: Lit Verlag/Routledge, pp. 175–205.

Blackwell, Maylei. 2011. *Chicana Power! Contested Histories of Feminism in the Chicano Movement*. Austin, TX: University of Texas Press.

Blackwell, Maylei, and Naber, Nadine. 2002. "Intersectionality in an Era of Globalization: The Implications of the UN World Conference against Racism for Transnational Feminist Practices." *Meridians: Feminism, Race, Transnationalism* 2: 237–48.

Blea, Irene. 1992. *La Chicana and the Intersection of Race, Class, and Gender*. Newport, CN: Praeger.

Bogazianos, Dimitri A. 2012. *5 Grams: Crack Cocaine, Rap Music, and the War on Drugs*. New York: NYU Press.

Bourdieu, Pierre, and Passeron, Jean-Claude. 1977. *Reproduction in Education, Society, and Culture*. Beverly Hills: Sage.

Bowleg, Lisa. 2008. "When Black + Lesbian + Woman (does not equal) Black Lesbian Woman: The Methodological Challenges of

Qualitative and Quantitative Intersectionality Research." *Sex Roles* 59: 312–25.

Boylorn, Robin, and Orbe, Mark (eds). 2014. *Critical Autoethnography: Intersecting Cultural Identities in Everyday Life*. Walnut Creek: Left Coast Press.

Brown, Tara M., and Rodriguez, Louie F. 2009. "Special Edition: Youth in Participatory Action Research." *New Directions for Youth Development* 123.

Brown, Wendy. 1995. *States of Inquiry: Power and Freedom in Late Modernity*. Princeton, NJ: Princeton University Press.

Browne, Irene, and Misra, Joya. 2003. "The Intersection of Gender and Race in the Labor Market." *Annual Review of Sociology* 29: 487–513.

Bryan, Beverley, Dadzie, Stella, and Scafe, Suzanne. 1997 [1985]. *The Heart of the Race: Black Women's Lives in Britain*. London: Virago Press.

Bumiller, Kristin. 2008. *In an Abusive State: How Neoliberalism Appropriated the Feminist Movement against Sexual Violence*. Durham, NC: Duke University Press.

Burawoy, Michael. 2005. "2004 Presidential Address: For Public Sociology." *American Sociological Review* 70: 4–28.

Burchill, Julie. 2014. "Don't You Dare Tell Me to Check My Privilege" *The Spectator*, February 22.

Caldwell, Kia Lilly. 2007. *Negras in Brazil: Re-envisioning Black Women, Citizenship, and the Politics of Identity*. New Brusnwick, NJ: Rutgers University Press.

Caputo, John D. 2009. "Introduction. Postcards from Paul: Subtraction versus Grafting," in John D. Caputo and Linda M. Alcoff (eds), *Saint Paul among Philosophers*, Bloomington, IN: Indiana University Press, pp. 1–23.

Carastathis, Anna. 2013. "Identity Categories as Potential Coalitions." *Signs* 38: 941–65.

Carneiro, Sueli. 1995. "Defining Black Feminism," in A. O. Pala (ed.), *Connecting Across Cultures and Continents: Black Women Speak Out on Identity, Race and Development*. New York: United Nations Development Fund for Women, pp. 11–18.

Carneiro. Sueli. 2002. "A Batalha de Durban." *Estudos Feministas* 10(1): 209–14.

Carneiro, Sueli. 2014. *Leila Gonzalez: o feminismo negro no palco da historia [Leila Gonzalez: Black Feminism on the Stage of History]*. Brasilia: Abravideo.

Carter, Prudence L. 2005. *Keepin' It Real: School Success Beyond Black and White*. New York: Oxford University Press.

Castells, Manuel. 2015. *Networks of Outrage and Hope: Social Movements in the Internet Age*, 2nd edn. Cambridge: Polity Press.

Chakravarti, Paromita. 2014. "Living on the Edge: Mapping Homeless Women's Mobilization in Kolkata, India", in Margaret Alston (ed.), *Women, Political Struggles and Gender Equality in South Asia*. Basingstoke: Palgrave Macmillan, pp. 117–36.

Chang, Mariko. 2010. *Lifting as We Climb: Women of Color, Wealth, and America's Future*. Spring. The Insight Center for Community Economic Development.

Chow, Esther Ngan-Ling. 1987. "The Development of Feminist Consciousness among Asian American Women." *Gender and Society* 1(3): 284–99.

Chun, Jennifer Jihye, Lipsitz, George, and Shin, Young. 2013. "Intersectionality as a Social Movement Strategy: Asian Immigrant Women Advocates." *Signs* 38: 917–40.

Clark, Christine, Fasching-Varner, Kenneth J., and Brimhall-Vargas, Mark (eds). 2012. *Occupying the Academy: Just How Important is Diversity Work in Higher Education?* Lanham, MD: Rowman & Littlefield.

Clay, Andreana. 2008. "Like An Old Soul Record: Black Feminism, Queer Sexuality, and the Hip-Hop Generation." *Meridians: Feminism, Race, Transnationalism* 8: 53–73.

Clay, Andreana. 2012. *The Hip Hop Generation Fights Back: Youth, Activism and Post-Civil Rights Politics*. New York: NYU Press.

Cohen, Cathy J. 1999. *The Boundaries of Blackness: AIDS and the Breakdown of Black Politics*. Chicago: University of Chicago Press.

Cohen, Cathy J. 2010. *Democracy Remixed: Black Youth and the Future of American Politics*. New York: Oxford University Press.

Cohen, Cathy J., and Jones, Tamara. 1999. "Fighting Homophobia versus Challenging Heterosexism: 'The Failure to Transform' Revisited," in E. Brandt (ed.), *Dangerous Liaisons: Blacks, Gays, and the Struggle for Equality*. New York: The New Press, pp. 80–101.

Collins, Patricia Hill. 1998a. *Fighting Words: Black Women and the Search for Justice*. Minneapolis: University of Minnesota Press.

Collins, Patricia Hill. 1998b. "The Tie That Binds: Race, Gender and US Violence." *Ethnic and Racial Studies* 21: 918–38.

Collins, Patricia Hill. 2000. *Black Feminist Thought: Knowledge, Consciousness, and the Politics of Empowerment*. New York: Routledge.

Collins, Patricia Hill. 2006. "New Commodities, New Consumers: Selling Blackness in the Global Marketplace." *Ethnicities* 6: 297–317.

Collins, Patricia Hill. 2007. "Pushing the Boundaries or Business as Usual? Race, Class, and Gender Studies and Sociological Inquiry," in C. Calhoun (ed.), *Sociology in America: A History*. Chicago: University of Chicago Press, pp. 572–604.

Collins, Patricia Hill. 2009a. *Another Kind of Public Education: Race, Schools, the Media and Democratic Possibilities*. Boston: Beacon Press.

Collins, Patricia Hill. 2009b. "Freedom Now! 1968 as a Turning Point for Black Student Activism," in G. K. Bhambra and I. Demir (eds), *1968 in Retrospect: History, Theory, Politics*. London: Palgrave Macmillan.

Collins, Patricia Hill. 2010. "The New Politics of Community " *American Sociological Review* 75: 7–30.

Collins, Patricia Hill. 2012a. *On Intellectual Activism*. Philadelphia, PA: Temple University Press.

Collins, Patricia Hill. 2012b. "Piecing Together a Genealogical Puzzle: Intersectionality and American Pragmatism." *European Journal of Pragmatism and American Philosophy* 3.

Collins, Patricia Hill. 2015. "Intersectionality's Definitional Dilemmas." *Annual Review of Sociology* 41: 1–20.

Collins, Patricia Hill, and Chepp, Valerie. 2013. "Intersectionality," in L. Weldon (ed.), *Oxford Handbook of Gender and Politics*. New York: Oxford, pp. 31–61.

Combahee-River-Collective. 1995 [1977]. "A Black Feminist Statement," in B. Guy-Sheftall (ed.), *Words of Fire: An Anthology of African-American Feminist Thought*. New York: The New Press, pp. 232–40.

Cooper, Anna Julia. 1892. *A Voice from the South; by a Black Woman of the South*. Xenia, OH: Aldine.

Cosslett, Rhiannon Lucy. 2013. "I'm a Half-Arsed, Accidental Feminist – Like Many Other Young Women." *The Guardian*, Comment is Free. Nov. 25. http://www.theguardian.com/com mentisfree/2013/nov/25/feminism-make-space-for-half-arsed

Cosslett, Rhiannon Lucy, and Baxter, Holly. 2012. "In Defence of Caitlin Moran and Populist Feminism." *New Statesman*, October 22, http://www.newstatesman.com/lifestyle/2012/10/ defence-caitlin-moran-and-populist-feminism#comment-261774

Cotera, Marta (ed.). 1976. *Diosa y Hembra: The History and Heritage of Chicanas in the US*. Austin, TX: Information Systems Development.

Cotera, Marta (ed.). 1977. *The Chicana Feminist*. Austin, TX: Information Systems Development.

Crenshaw, Kimberlé Williams. 1989. "Demarginalizing the Intersection of Race and Sex: A Black Feminist Critique of Anti-Discrimination Doctrine, Feminist Theory, and Anti-Racist Politics." *The University of Chicago Legal Forum* 140: 139–67.

Crenshaw, Kimberlé Williams. 1991. "Mapping the Margins: Intersectionality, Identity Politics, and Violence against Women of Color." *Stanford Law Review* 43: 1241–99.

Crenshaw, Kimberlé. 2000. *Background Paper for the Expert Meeting on the Gender-Related Aspects of Race Discriminations.* Zagreb: WCAR (World Conference against Racism) Documents, 21–24 November.

Crenshaw, Kimberlé Williams, Gotanda, Neil, Peller, Gary, and Thomas, Kendall (eds). 1995. *Critical Race Theory: The Key Writings that Formed the Movement.* New York: The New Press.

Crenshaw, Kimberlé, Ocen, Priscilla, and Nanda, Jyoti. 2015. *Black Girls Matter: Pushed Out, Overpoliced and Underprotected.* The African American Policy Forum and the Columbia Law School's Center for Intersectionality and Social Policy Studies.

Cruz, Jose E. 1998. *Identity and Power: Puerto Rican Politics and the Challenge of Ethnicity.* Philadelphia: Temple University Press.

Daniels, Jessie. 1997. *White Lies: Race, Class, Gender and Sexuality in White Supremacist Discourse.* New York: Routledge.

Daniels, Jessie. 2009. "Rethinking Cyberfeminism(s): Race, Gender, and Embodiment." *Women's Studies Quarterly* 37: 101–24.

Davis, Angela Y. 1981. *Women, Race, and Class.* New York: Random House.

Davis, Kathy. 2008. "Intersectionality as a Buzzword: A Sociology of Science Perspective on What Makes a Feminist Theory Successful." *Feminist Theory* 9: 67–85.

Dewey, John. 1954. *The Public and Its Problems.* Athens, OH: Ohio University Press.

Dewey, John. 2004. *Democracy and Education.* Mineola, NY: Dover Publications.

Diamond, Larry, and Plattner, Marc F. (eds). 2012. *Liberation Technology: Social Media and the Struggle for Democracy.* Baltimore: The Johns Hopkins University Press.

Dickar, Maryann. 2008. *Corridor Cultures: Mapping Student Resistance at an Urban High School.* New York: New York University Press.

Dill, Bonnie Thornton. 1988. "Our Mothers' Grief: Racial Ethnic Women and the Maintenance of Families." *Journal of Family History* 13: 415–31.

Dill, Bonnie Thornton. 2002. "Work at the Intersections of Race, Gender, Ethnicity, and Other Dimensions of Difference in Higher

Education." *Connections: Newsletter of the Consortium on Race, Gender, and Ethnicity*: 5–7.

Dill, Bonnie Thornton. 2009. "Intersections, Identities, and Inequalities in Higher Education," in B. T. Dill and R. Zambrana (eds), *Emerging Intersections: Race, Class, and Gender in Theory, Policy, and Practice*. New Brunswick, NJ: Rutgers University Press, pp. 229–52.

Dill, Bonnie Thornton, and Zambrana, Ruth (eds). 2009. *Emerging Intersections: Race, Class, and Gender in Theory, Policy, and Practice*. New Brunswick, NJ: Rutgers University Press.

Dill, Bonnie Thornton, Zambrana, Ruth Enid, and McClaughlin, Amy. 2009. "Transforming the Campus Climate through Institutions, Collaboration, and Mentoring," in B. T. Dill and R. Zambrana (eds), *Emerging Intersections: Race, Class, and Gender in Theory, Policy, and Practice*. New Brunswick, NJ: Rutgers University Press, pp. 253–73.

Driskill, Qwo-Li, Finley, Chris, Gilley, Joseph Brian, and Morgensen, Scott Laurie (eds). 2011. *Queer Indigenous Studies: Critical Interventions in Theory, Politics, and Literature*. Phoenix: University of Arizona Press.

Dzodan, Flavia. 2011. "My Feminism will be Intersectional, or It will be Bullshit!" Tiger Beatdown, October 10. http://tigerbeatdown .com/2011/10/10/my-feminism-will-be-intersectional-or-it-will -be-bullshit/

Dzodan, Flavia. 2014. "I Can't Think of Any High Profile White UK Feminist who has 'Rejected' Intersectionality." Red Light Politics, January 1, http://www.redlightpolitics.info/post/ 71842333716/i-cant-think-of-any-high-profile-white-uk-feminist

Ehrenreich, Nancy. 2002 "Subordination and Symbiosis: Mechanisms of Mutual Support Between Subordinating Systems." *UMKC Law Review* 71(2): 251–324.

Eisentein, Zillah. 2014. "An Alert: Capital is Intersectional; Radicalizing Piketty's Inequality." *The Feminist Wire*, May 26. http://thefeministwire.com/2014/05/alert-capital-intersectional -radicalizing-pikettys-inequality/

Embrick, David G., Wright, J. Talmadge and Lukacs, Andras (eds). 2012. *Social Exclusion, Power, and Video Game: New Research in Digital Media and Technology*. Lanham, MD: Lexington Books.

Erel, Umut, Haritaworn, Jin, Rodriguez, Encarnacion Guiterrez, and Klesse, Christian (eds). 2008. "On the Depoliticisation of Intersectionality Talk: Conceptualising Multiple Oppressions in Critical Sexuality Studies," in E. Miyake and A. Kuntsman (eds), *Out of Place: Queerness and Raciality*. York: Raw Nerve Books.

Erevelles, Nirmala. 2011. *Disability and Difference in Global Contexts: Enabling a Transformative Body Politics*. New York: Palgrave Macmillan.

Evaristo, Conceição. 2007. *Ponciá Vicencio*, trans. P. Martinez-Cruz. Austin, TX: Host Publications.

Falcon, Sylvanna. 2012. "Transnational Feminism and Contextualized Intersectionality at the 2001 World Conference Against Racism." *Journal of Women's History* 24: 99–120.

Ferber, Abby L. 1998. *White Man Falling: Race, Gender, and White Supremacy*. Lanham, MD: Rowman and Littlefield.

Ferguson, Roderick A. 2004. *Aberrations in Black: Toward a Queer of Color Critique*. Minneapolis: University of Minnesota Press.

Ferguson, Roderick A. 2012. *The Reorder of Things: The University and its Pedagogies of Minority Difference*. Minneapolis, MN: University of Minnesota Press.

Fernandez, Maria, Wilding, Faith, and Wright, Michelle M. (eds). 2003. *Domain Errors! Cyberfeminist Practices*. Brooklyn, NY: Autonomedia.

Franklin, Vincent P. 2003. "Patterns of Student Activism at Historically Black Universities in the United States and South Africa, 1960–1977." *Journal of African American History* 88: 204–17.

Freeman, Michael. 2011. *Human Rights*. London: Polity.

Freire, Paulo. 1970. *The Pedagogy of the Oppressed*. New York: Herder and Herder.

Garcia, Alma M. 1997a. "The Development of Chicana Feminist Discourse," in L. A. West (ed.), *Feminist Nationalism*. New York: Routledge, pp. 247–68.

Garcia, Alma M. 1997b. "Introduction," in *Chicana Feminist Thought: The Basic Historical Writings*, vol. 1–16, ed. A. M. Garcia. New York: Routledge.

Glenn, Evelyn Nakano. 1998. "Gender, Race, and Class: Bridging the Language–Structure Divide." *Social Science History* 22: 29–38.

Glenn, Evelyn Nakano. 2002. *Unequal Freedom: How Race and Gender Shaped American Citizenship and Labor*. Cambridge, MA: Harvard University Press.

Grzanka, Patrick R. (ed.) 2014. *Intersectionality: A Foundations and Frontiers Reader*. Philadelphia, PA: Westview Press.

Hale, Charles T. 2008. "Introduction," in C. T. Hale (ed.), *Engaging Contradictions: Theory, Politics, and Methods of Activist Scholarship*. Berkeley: University of California Press, pp. 1–28.

Hall, Stuart. 1992. "What is this 'Black' in Black Popular Culture?" in G. Dent (ed.), *Black Popular Culture*. Seattle: Bay Press, pp. 21–33.

Hanchard, Michael G. 1994. *Orpheus and Power: The Movimento Negro of Rio de Janeiro and Sao Paulo, Brazil, 1945–1988.* Princeton: Princeton University Press.

Hancock, Ange-Marie. 2007a. "Intersectionality as a Normative and Empirical Paradigm." *Politics and Gender* 3: 248–55.

Hancock, Ange-Marie. 2007b. "When Multiplication Doesn't Equal Quick Addition: Examining Intersectionality as a Research Paradigm." *Perspectives on Politics* 5: 63–79.

Hankivsky, Olena. 2007. "Gender vs. Diversity Mainstreaming: A Preliminary Examination of the Role and Transformative Potential of Feminist Theory." *Canadian Journal of Political Science* 38(4): 977–1001.

Hankivsky, Olena (ed.). 2012. *An Intersectionality-Based Policy Analysis Framework.* Vancouver, BC: Institute for Intersectionality Research and Policy, Simon Fraser University.

Harris, Duchess. 1999. "All of Who I Am in the Same Place: The Combahee River Collective." *Womanist Theory and Research* 2: 9–22.

Harrison, Anthony Kwame. 2009. *Hip Hop Underground: The Integrity and Ethics of Racial Identification.* Philadelphia: Temple University Press.

Hartman, Chester, and Squires, Gregory D. (eds). 2006. *There Is No Such Thing as a Natural Disaster: Race, Class and Hurricane Katrina.* New York: Routledge.

Harvey, David. 2005. *A Brief History of Neoliberalism.* New York: Oxford University Press.

Hilmer, Jeffrey D. 2010. "The State of Participatory Democratic Theory." *New Political Science* 32: 43–63.

Hilton, Matthew. 2009. *Prosperity for All: Consumer Activism in an Era of Globalization.* Ithaca, NY: Cornell University Press.

Hong, Grace K. 2008. "The Future of Our Worlds: Black Feminism and the Politics of Knowledge in the University under Globalization." *Meridians: Feminism, Race, Transnationalism* 8: 95–115.

Howard, Sheena C. 2014. *Critical Articulations of Race, Gender, and Sexual Orientation.* London: Lexington Books.

Hutchinson, Darren Lenard. 2001. "Identity Crisis: Intersectionality, Multidimensionality, and the Development of an Adequate Theory of Subordination." *Michigan Journal of Race and Law* 6.

INCITE! n.d. Analysis. INCITE!'s Dangerous Intersections. http://incite-national.org/page/analysis

Johnson, Cedric (ed.). 2011. *The Neoliberal Deluge: Hurricane Katrina, Late Capitalism, and the Remaking of New Orleans.* Minneapolis: University of Minnesota Press.

Jones, Saeed. 2013. "Three Reasons Why Saying 'Gay Is the New Black' Isn't Helpful." Buzzfed, 31 January, http://www.buzzfed.com/saeedjones/3-reasons-why-saying-gay-is-the-new-black-is#.Sbn2qVy8a

Jónsson, Ragnar. 2013. "Is the '4th Wave' of Feminism Digital?" *Bluestockings Magazine*, August 19, http://bluestockingsmag.com/2013/08/19/is-the-4th-wave-of-feminism-digital/

Jordan, June. 1981. *Civil Wars*. Boston: Beacon Press.

Kannabiran, Kalpana. 2006. "A Cartography of Resistance: National Federation of Dalit Women," in D. Yuval, K. Kannabiran, and U. Vieten (eds), *The Situated Politics of Belonging*. London: Sage, pp. 54ff.

Kendall, Mikki. 2013. "#SolidarityIsForWhiteWomen: Women of Color's Issue with Digital Feminism." *The Guardian*. Comment is Free. August 13. http://www.theguardian.com/commentisfree/2013/aug/14/solidarityisforwhitewomen-hashtag-feminism

King, Deborah K. 1988. "Multiple Jeopardy, Multiple Consciousness: The Context of a Black Feminist Ideology." *Signs* 14: 42–72.

Kivisto, Peter. 2010. "Multiculturalism and Racial Democracy: State Policies and Social Practices," in P. H. Collins and J. Solomos (eds), *Handbook of Race and Ethnic Studies*. London: Sage, pp. 253–74.

Knapp, Gudrun-Alexi. 2005. "Race, Class, Gender: Reclaiming Baggage in Fast Travelling Theories." *European Journal of Women's Studies* 12: 249–65.

Krizsan, Andrea, Skjeie, Hege, and Squires, Judith. 2012. "Institutionalising Intersectionality: A Theoretical Framework," in A. Krizsan, H. Skjeie, and J. Squires (eds), *Institutionalizing Intersectionality: The Changing Nature of European Equality Regimes*. Basingstoke: Palgrave Macmillan, pp. 1–32.

Latina Feminist Group (ed.) 2001. *Telling to Live: Latina Feminist Testimonios*. Durham, NC: Duke University Press.

Lim, Shirley Geok-lin, and Tsutakawa, Mayumi (eds). 1989. *The Forbidden Stitch: An Asian American Women's Anthology*. Corvallis, OR: Calyx Books.

Lind, Rebecca Ann. 2010. "A Note From the Guest Editor." *Journal of Broadcasting & Electronic Media* 54: 3–5.

Lindsay, Beverley. 1979. "Minority Women in America: Black American, Native American, and Chicana Women," in E. C. Snyner (ed.), *The Study of Women: Enlarging Perspectives on Social Reality*. New York: Harper & Row, pp. 318–63.

Linker, Maureen. 2015. *Intellectual Empathy: Critical Thinking for Social Justice*. Ann Arbor, MI: University of Michigan Press.

Lockhart, Lettie, and Danis, Fran (eds). 2010. *Domestic Violence: Intersectionality and Culturally Competent Practice.* New York: Columbia University Press.

Lopez, Marta Cruells, and Garcia, Sonia Ruiz. 2014. "Political Intersectionality within the Spanish Indignados Social Movement." *Intersectionality and Social Change* 31: 3–25.

Lopez, Nancy. 2002. *Hopeful Girls, Troubled Boys: Race and Gender Disparity in Urban Education.* New York: Routledge.

Lorde, Audre. 1984. *Sister Outsider: Essays and Speeches.* Freedom, CA: Crossing Press.

Lowe, Lisa. 1991. "Heterogeneity, Hybridity, Multiplicity: Marking Asian American Differences." *Diaspora* 1: 23–44.

Manuel, Tiffany. 2006. "Envisioning the Possibilities for a Good Life: Exploring the Public Policy Implications of Intersectionality Theory." *Women, Politics and Policy* 28: 173–203.

Matua, Athena D. 2010. "Law, Critical Race Theory and Related Scholarship," in P. H. Collins and J. Solomos (eds), *Handbook of Race and Ethnic Studies.* London: Sage, pp. 275–305.

May, Vivian. 2007. *Anna Julia Cooper, Visionary Black Feminist: A Critical Introduction.* New York: Routledge.

McCall, Leslie. 2005. "The Complexity of Intersectionality." *Signs* 30: 1771–1800.

McClain, Dani. 2014. "Obama's Racial Justice Initiative – for Boys Only." *The Nation,* August 27.

McClintock, Anne. 1995. *Imperial Leather: Race, Gender, and Sexuality in the Colonial Contest.* New York: Routledge.

McCorkel, Jill A. 2013. *Breaking Women: Gender, Race, and the New Politics of Imprisonment.* New York: New York University Press.

McCulloch, Jude, and Pickering, Sharon. 2008. "The Violence of Refugee Detention," in Paul Scraton and Jude McCulloch (eds), *The Violence of Incarceration.* Advances in Criminology Vol. 5. New York: Routledge, pp. 225–42.

McWhorter, John. 2013. "Gay Really is the New Black." *New York Daily News,* January 24. http://www.nydailynews.com/opinion/gay-new-black-article-1.1246187

Mills, C. Wright. 2000. *The Sociological Imagination.* New York: Oxford.

Mitchell, Eve. 2013. "I am a Woman and a Human: A Marxist-Feminist Critique of Intersectionality Theory." *The North Star,* December 2. http://www.thenorthstar.info/?p=11425

Mirza, Heidi Safia (ed.). 1997. *Black British Feminism: A Reader.* New York: Routledge.

Monture-Angus, Patricia. 1995. *Thunder in My Soul: A Mohawk Woman Speaks.* Halifax, Nova Scotia: Fernwood.

Moraga, Cherrie, and Anzaldúa, Gloria (ed.). 2015 [1983]. *This Bridge Called My Back: Writings by Radical Women of Color*. Albany, NY: SUNY Press.

Moran, Caitlin. 2011. *How to Be a Woman*. London: Harper Perennial.

Moreno, Dorinda (ed.). 1973. *La Mujer – En Pie de Lucha*. Mexico City: Espina Del Norte Publications.

Murphy, Yvette, Hunt, Valerie, Zajicek, Anna, Norris, Adele, and Hamilton, Leah (eds). 2009. *Incorporating Intersectionality in Social Work Practice, Research, Policy, and Education*. Washington: The NASW Press.

Naples, Nancy A. 1996. "Activist Mothering: Cross-Generational Continuity in the Community Work of Women from Low-Income Urban Neighborhoods," in E. N.-L. Chow, D. Wilkinson, and M. B. Zinn (eds), *Race, Class, and Gender: Common Bonds, Different Voices*. Thousand Oaks, CA: Sage, pp. 223–45.

Naples, Nancy A. 2009. "Teaching Intersectionality Intersectionally." *International Feminist Journal of Politics* 11: 566–77.

Naples, Nancy A. 2013. "Sustaining Democracy: Localization, Globalization and Feminist Praxis." *Sociological Forum* 28: 657–81.

Nash, Jennifer C. 2008. "Rethinking Intersectionality." *Feminist Review* 89: 1–15.

Nocella, Anthony J. II, Sorenson, John, Socha, Kim, and Matsuoka, Atsuko (eds). 2014. *Critical Animal Studies: An Intersectional Social Justice Approach for Liberation*. New York: Peter Lang.

Norman, Brian. 2007. " 'We' in Redux: The Combahee River Collective's Black Feminist Statement." *Differences: A Journal of Feminist Cultural Studies* 18: 103–32.

Okolosie, Lola. 2014. "Beyond 'Talking' and 'Owning' Intersectionality." *Feminist Review* 108: 90–6.

Oliver, Melvin L. and Shapiro, Thomas M. 1995. *Black Wealth/White Wealth: A New Perspective on Racial Inequality*. New York: Routledge.

Oxfam. 2014. *Working for the Few: Political Capture and Economic Inequality*. 178 Oxfam Briefing Paper. January 20. https://www.oxfam.org/sites/www.oxfam.org/files/file_attachments/bp-working-for-few-political-capture-economic-inequality-200114-en_3.pdf

Oxfam. 2015. *Wealth: Having It All and Wanting More*. Oxfam International Research report. January 19. http://policy-practice.oxfam.org.uk/publications/wealth-having-it-all-and-wanting-more-338125

Parker, Joe, and Samantrai, Ranu. 2010. "Interdisciplinarity and Social Justice: An Introduction," in J. Parker, R. Samantrai, and M. Romero (eds), *Interdisciplinarity and Social Justice:*

Revisioning Academic Accountability. Albany, NY: State University of New York Press, pp. 1–33.

Parker, Joe, Samantrai, Ranu, and Romero, Mary (eds). 2010. *Interdisciplinarity and Social Justice: Revisioning Academic Accountability*. Albany, NY: State University of New York Press.

Pérez, Emma. 1994. "Irigaray's Female Symbolic in the Making of Chicana Lesbian *Sitios y Lenguas*," in L. Doran and R. Wiegman (eds), *The Lesbian Postmodern*. New York: Columbia University Press, pp. 104–17.

Perry, Imani. 2004. *Prophets of the Hood: Politics and Poetics in Hip Hop*. Durham: Duke University Press.

Perry, Theresa, Steele, Claude, and Hilliard III, Asa. 2003. *Young, Gifted and Black: Promoting High Achievement Among African-American Students*. Boston: Beacon Press.

Pew Research Center. 2011. "Wealth Gaps Rise to Record Highs between Whites, Blacks, Hispanics." *Social Trends*, July 26. http://www.pewsocialtrends.org/files/2011/07/SDT-Wealth-Report_7-26-11_FINAL.pdf

Pough, Gwendolyn D. 2004. *Check It While I Wreck It: Black Womanhood, Hip-Hop Culture, and the Public Sphere*. Boston: Northeastern University Press.

Richie, Beth. 2012. *Arrested Justice: Black Women, Violence, and America's Prison Nation*. New York: New York University Press.

Rifkin, Mark. 2011. When Did Indians Become Straight? Kinship, the History of Sexuality and Native Sovereignty. New York: Oxford University Press.

Rios, Victor M. 2011. *Punished: Policing the Life of Black and Latino Boys*. New York: New York University Press.

Roberts, Dorothy, and Jesudason, Sujatha. 2013. "Movement Intersectionality: The Case of Race, Gender, Disability, and Genetic Technologies." *Du Bois Review* 10: 313–28.

Rose, Tricia. 1994. *Black Noise: Rap Music and Black Culture in Contemporary America*. Hanover, NH: Wesleyan University Press.

Roth, Benita. 2004. *Separate Roads to Feminism: Black, Chicana, and White Feminist Movements in America's Second Wave*. New York: Cambridge University Press.

Sandoval, Chela. 2000. *Methodology of the Oppressed*. Minneapolis: University of Minnesota Press.

Sarma, Deepika. 2015. "Six Reasons Why Every Indian Feminist should Remember Savitribai Phule." January 5. http://theladiesfinger.com/six-reasons-every-indian-feminist-should-remember-savitribai-phule/

Schiek, Dagmar, and Lawson, Anna (eds). 2013. *European Union Non-Discrimination Law and Intersectionality: Investigating the Triangle of Racial, Gender and Disability Discrimination.* Farnham, UK: Ashgate.

Schulz, Amy J., and Mullings, Leith (eds). 2006. *Gender, Race, Class and Health: Intersectional Approaches.* San Francisco, CA: Jossey-Bass.

Sharma, Nitasha Tamar. 2010. *Hip Hop Desis: South Asian Americans, Blackness, and Global Race Consciousness.* Durham, NC: Duke University Press.

Shingler, Benjamin. 2013. "The Next Hot Sound? Powwow Step, Aboriginal Hip-Hop." *Aljazeera America.* November 28. http://america.aljazeera.com/articles/2013/11/28/the-next-hot-sou ndyouhearwillbepowwowstepaboriginalhiphop.html

Smith, Andrea. 2009. "Indigenous Feminism without Apology," in U. Minnesota (ed.), *Unsettling Ourselves: Reflections and Resources for Deconstructing Colonial Mentality.* Unsettling Minnesota, pp. 159–61.

Sokoloff, Nathalie, and Pratt, Christina (eds). 2005. *Domestic Violence at the Margins: Readings on Race, Class, Gender, and Culture.* New Brunswick: Rutgers University Press.

Spivak, Gayatri. 1996. "Subaltern Studies: Deconstructing Historiography," in D. Landry and G. Maclean (eds), *The Spivak Reader.* New York: Routledge.

Springer, Kimberly. 2005. *Living for the Revolution: Black Feminist Organizations, 1968–1980.* Durham, NC: Duke University Press.

Steinbugler, Amy C., Press, Julie E., and Dias, Janice Johnson. 2006. "Gender, Race and Affirmative Action: Operationalizing Intersectionality in Survey Research." *Gender and Society* 20: 805–25.

Stoler, Ann Laura. 1995. *Race and the Education of Desire: Foucault's History of Sexuality and the Colonial Order of Things.* Durham, NC: Duke University Press.

Tang, Shirley Suet-ling. 2008. "Community-Centered Research as Knowledge/Capacity Building in Immigrant and Refugee Communities," in C. T. Hale (ed.), *Engaging Contradictions: Theory, Politics, and Methods of Activist Scholarship.* Berkeley: University of California Press, pp. 237–64.

Taylor, Verta. 1989. "Social Movement Continuity: The Women's Movement in Abeyance." *American Sociological Review* 54: 761–75.

Terriquez, Veronica. 2015. "Intersectional Mobilization, Social Movement Spillover, and Queer Youth Leadership in the Immigrant Rights Movement." *Social Problems* 62: 343–62.

Thurman, Erica. 2014. "Because All the Women are Not White and All the Blacks are Not Men: MBK, Intersectionality, and 1000+ Of Us Who Are Brave." http://ericathurman.com/mbk-and-woc/, June 19.

Tugal, Cihan. 2013. " 'Resistance Everywhere': The Gezi Revolt in Global Perspective." *New Perspectives on Turkey* 49: 157–72.

Twine, France Winddance. 1998. *Racism in a Racial Democracy: The Maintenance of White Supremacy in Brazil.* New Brunswick: Rutgers University Press.

United Nations. 1995. *Beijing Declaration and Platform for Action Adopted by the Fourth World Conference on Women: Action for Equality, Development and Peace,* Beijing, 15 September. http://www.un.org/womenwatch/daw/beijing/platform/declar.htm

Unsettling Minnesota (UM). 2009. *Unsettling Ourselves: Reflections and Resources for Deconstructing Colonial Mentality.* A sourcebook compiled by UM collective. https://unsettlingminnesota .files.wordpress.com/2009/11/um_sourcebook_jan10_revision .pdf

Walby, Sylvia. 2007. "Complexity Theory, Systems Theory, and Multiple Intersecting Social Inequalities." *Philosophy of the Social Sciences* 37: 449–70.

Warren, Mark R. 2001. *Dry Bones Rattling: Community Building to Revitalize American Democracy.* Princeton, NJ: Princeton University Press.

Watts, Jonathan. 2014. "Anti-World Cup Protests in Brazilian Cities Mark Countdown to Kick-off." *The Guardian.* June 12. http://www.theguardian.com/football/2014/jun/12/anti-world -cup-protests-brazilian-cities-sao-paulo-rio-de-janeiro

WCAR NGO Forum. 2001. Declaration and Programme of Action. NGO Forum, World Conference Against Racism, Racial Discrimination, Xenophobia and Related Intolerance, Durban, South Africa, August 27–September 1, Section 119 (Gender) of the Declaration. Word document available at: http://academic .udayton.edu/race/06hrights/WCAR2001/NGOFORUM/

Weber, Lynn. 1998. "A Conceptual Framework for Understanding Race, Class, Gender, and Sexuality." *Psychology of Women Quarterly* 22: 13–32.

Weber, Lynn, and Fore, M. Elizabeth. 2007. "Race, Ethnicity, and Health: An Intersectional Approach," in Hernan Vera and Joe Feagin (eds), *Handbook of the Sociology of Racial and Ethnic Relations.* New York: Springer, pp. 191–218.

Weir, Allison. 2008. "Global Feminism and Transformative Identity Politics." *Hypatia* 23(4): 110–24.

"Why We Can't Wait: Women of Color Urge Inclusion in 'My Brother's Keeper.' " 2014. June 17. http://aapf.org/2014/06/woc-letter-mbk/ (retrieved on June 19, 2014).

Wiegman, Robyn. 2012. *Object Lessons.* Durham, NC: Duke University Press.

Yunus, Muhammad. 2007. "Credit for the Poor: Poverty as Distant History." *Harvard International Review* (Fall): 20–7.

Yunus, Muhammad. 2009. "Economic Security for a World in Crisis." *World Policy Journal* (Summer): 5–12.

Yunus, Muhammad. 2014–2015. "Muhammad Yunus: Global Visionary." *CUNY Forum* 2: 87–92.

Yuval-Davis, Nira. 2006. "Intersectionality and Feminist Politics." *European Journal of Women's Studies* 13: 193–210.

Yuval-Davis, Nira. 2011a. "Series Introduction: The Politics of Intersectionality," in Ange-Marie Hancock, *Solidarity Politics for Millennials: A Guide to Ending the Oppression Olympics*. New York: Palgrave-Macmillan, pp. xi–xv.

Yuval-Davis, Nira. 2011b. "Beyond the Recognition and Re-distribution Dichotomy: Intersectionality and Stratification," in H. Lutz, M. T. H. Vivar, and L. Supik (eds), *Framing Intersectionality: Debates on a Multi-Faceted Concept in Gender Studies*. Burlington, VT: Ashgate Publishing Company.

Zinn, Maxine Baca. 2010. "The Family as a Race Institution," in P. H. Collins and J. Solomos (eds), *The Sage Handbook of Race and Ethnic Studies*. London: Sage, pp. 357–82.

Zinn, Maxine Baca, Cannon, Lynn Weber, Higginbotham, Elizabeth, and Dill, Bonnie Thornton. 1986. "The Cost of Exclusionary Practices in Women's Studies." *Signs: Journal of Women and Culture in Society* 11: 290–303.

Index